Virtue Ethics

This volume provides a clear and accessible overview of central concepts, positions, and arguments in virtue ethics today. While it focuses primarily on Aristotelian virtue ethics, it also includes discussion of alternative forms of virtue ethics (sentimentalism and pluralism) and competing normative theories (consequentialism and deontology).

The first six chapters are organized around central questions in normative ethics that are of particular concern to virtue ethicists and their critics:

- What is virtue ethics?
- What makes a trait a virtue?
- Is there a link between virtue and happiness?
- What is involved in being well-motivated?
- What is practical wisdom?
- What makes an action right?

The last four chapters focus on important challenges or objections to virtue ethics:

- Can virtue ethics be applied to particular moral problems?
- Does virtue ethics ultimately rely on moral principles?
- Can it withstand the situationist critique?
- What are the prospects for an environmental virtue ethics?

Liezl van Zyl is Senior Lecturer in Philosophy at the University of Waikato, New Zealand. She works primarily in ethics, in particular virtue ethics and applied ethics.

ROUTLEDGE CONTEMPORARY INTRODUCTIONS TO PHILOSOPHY

Series editor
Paul K. Moser
Loyola University of Chicago

This innovative, well-structured series is for students who have already done an introductory course in philosophy. Each book introduces a core general subject in contemporary philosophy and offers students an accessible but substantial transition from introductory to higher-level college work in that subject. The series is accessible to non-specialists and each book clearly motivates and expounds the problems and positions introduced. An orientating chapter briefly introduces its topic and reminds readers of any crucial material they need to have retained from a typical introductory course. Considerable attention is given to explaining the central philosophical problems of a subject and the main competing solutions and arguments for those solutions. The primary aim is to educate students in the main problems, positions and arguments of contemporary philosophy rather than to convince students of a single position.

Recently Published Volumes:

Metaphysics
4th Edition
Michael J. Loux and Thomas M. Crisp

Social and Political Philosophy
2nd Edition
John Christman

Ethics
3rd Edition
Harry J. Gensler

Virtue Ethics
Liezl van Zyl

For a full list of published Routledge Handbooks in Philosophy, please visit https://www.routledge.com/Routledge-Contemporary-Introductions-to-Philosophy/book-series/SE0111

Virtue Ethics

A Contemporary Introduction

Liezl van Zyl

Routledge
Taylor & Francis Group

NEW YORK AND LONDON

First published 2019
by Routledge
711 Third Avenue, New York, NY 10017

and by Routledge
2 Park Square, Milton Park, Abingdon, Oxon OX14 4RN

Routledge is an imprint of the Taylor & Francis Group, an informa business

© 2019 Taylor & Francis

Library of Congress Cataloging in Publication Data
A catalog record for this title has been requested

ISBN: 978-0-415-83617-3 (hbk)
ISBN: 978-0-415-83616-6 (pbk)
ISBN: 978-0-203-36196-2 (ebk)

Typeset in Times New Roman
by Taylor & Francis Books

Contents

Preface

I first became interested in the virtues as a graduate student in the 1990s, while writing a thesis on end-of-life decision-making. I was puzzled to find that although terms such as compassion, mercy, and kindness featured prominently in the public discourse about the morality of euthanasia and physician-assisted suicide, debates in bioethics proceeded almost exclusively in terms of moral rules and principles. The dominant view, even among ethicists who thought the virtues were important, was that virtue ethics cannot stand on its own as a complete normative theory, and that the virtues needed to be supplemented with a set of rules or principles. Roughly, the general consensus was that it would *of course* be wonderful for medical professionals to be more compassionate and caring, but that their first priority must be to fulfill their duties to patients. Accordingly, a particular act of euthanasia could well be compassionate but *wrong* because it violates the duty not to kill an innocent person.

Since then, leading figures in the field, including Philippa Foot, Julia Annas, Rosalind Hursthouse, Christine Swanton, and Michael Slote, have shown that virtue ethics should be taken seriously as an alternative to deontology and consequentialism. Over the last two or three decades the literature on virtue ethics has grown substantially. This is most obvious in the fields of normative and applied ethics, but the interest in the virtues has also spread to other areas, such as metaethics, epistemology, philosophy of education, philosophy of psychology, and theology. The inevitable result is that newcomers encounter significant difficulty in deciding what to read and where to start. Much of the literature is inaccessible, usually because the author presupposes a familiarity with key concepts and debates.

The aim of this book is to introduce readers to central concepts and questions in contemporary virtue ethics. I focus on Aristotelian virtue ethics, given that it is by far the most popular version, but I pay a fair amount of attention to alternative versions of virtue ethics (sentimentalism and pluralism), as well as two rival normative theories (consequentialism and deontology), in particular their accounts of virtue and their objections to virtue ethics. Given limitations of space as well as expertise, I had to leave out a number of important and interesting questions and developments. Of particular note in this regard is the growing interest in Eastern philosophies in which virtue plays an important role, such as Buddhism, Confucianism, and Hinduism. Other research areas that deserve mention focus on questions about the role of virtue in moral education, the nature and possibility of moral self-cultivation, the role of virtue in political philosophy, and the merits of Aristotelian naturalism. It is my hope that the book will help prepare readers to explore these areas on their own.

Acknowledgements

I would like to thank people who gave feedback on the initial book proposal or parts of the manuscript. These include Mark Alfano, Rosalind Hursthouse, Jason Kawall, Kerry Lockhart, Nick Smith, Joe Ulatowski, and Ruth Walker, as well as a few very generous (and one or two not so generous) anonymous reviewers. Kerry Lockhart deserves a special thank you, as he gave useful feedback on each chapter (more than once) and helped prepare the final version of the manuscript. I am grateful to the Faculty of Arts and Social Sciences at the University of Waikato, New Zealand, for financial assistance, and to my editor, Andrew Beck, for his ongoing support and patience.

Plan of the Book

Chapter 1, "Virtue Ethics," introduces readers to virtue ethics as a normative theory, and distinguishes it from virtue theory, the broader field of inquiry that focuses on philosophical questions about the nature and possibility of virtue. It gives a very brief overview of relevant developments in moral philosophy, and introduces readers to the three most popular versions of virtue ethics.

Chapters 2 to 6 focus on central concepts in virtue ethics. Chapter 2, "Virtue," gives an overview of three accounts of virtue given by virtue ethicists: an Aristotelian, a sentimentalist, and a pluralistic account. It also includes discussion of two theories of virtue proposed by critics of virtue ethics: a consequentialist theory, which defines virtue in terms of good consequences, and a Kantian view, which defines it in terms of duty.

Chapter 3, "Virtue and Happiness," examines the Aristotelian account of virtue in more detail, in particular the claim that the virtues allow their possessor to live a good or happy life. We discuss two objections to this view. The first is that it amounts to a form of egoism – ultimately, what the virtuous person cares about is his own happiness. A second objection is that some virtues do not characteristically contribute to the happiness of their possessor.

Chapter 4, "Virtuous Motives," focuses on questions about motivation: Is a virtuous person motivated by good feelings or emotions (such as sympathy or care), good reasons (such as "X is right" or "It is my duty to do Y"), or both? We consider Aristotelian and Kantian views about the role of reason and emotion in motivation, and examine why consequentialists reject both these views.

Chapter 5, "Practical Wisdom," gives an overview of the Aristotelian view of the nature and role of practical wisdom. It focuses on two claims in particular: (a) practical wisdom is necessary for each and every virtue, and (b) the virtues form a unity, so that someone who has one virtue will also have all the others, at least to some degree. It also considers the reasons why some moral philosophers, including some virtue ethicists, reject either or both of these claims.

Chapter 6, "Virtue and Right Action," begins by considering whether virtue ethicists need to provide an account of right action at all, given that they can evaluate actions as virtuous or vicious. We discuss three virtue-ethical accounts of right action: an Aristotelian (qualified-agent) account, a sentimentalist (or agent-based) account, and a pluralistic (or target-centered) account.

The remaining chapters focus on important challenges or objections to virtue ethics. Chapter 7, "Applying Virtue Ethics," considers the objection that virtue ethics fails to fulfill one of the most important tasks of normative ethics, which is to help us make good decisions about how we are to act. Given its focus on character and its refusal to provide a list of action-guiding moral rules or principles, it is argued, virtue ethics cannot be applied. We consider how virtue ethics can respond to this objection, focusing specifically on the virtue rules (or v-rules) and how they differ from the rules of deontology (d-rules).

Chapter 8, "Virtue-ethical Particularism," continues the discussion of the role of moral rules or principles in moral thought and decision-making, focusing on the nature of moral knowledge. Deontologists and consequentialists support some form of moral generalism, that is, the view that there are general moral principles, and that knowledge of these principles, together with the ability to apply them to particular situations, is what allows the ideal moral agent to do what is right. By contrast, virtue ethicists support some form of moral particularism, which is the view that principles do not play a crucial role in the thought and actions of the ideal moral agent. Instead, they argue that it is practical wisdom – a kind of situation-specific know-how – that allows the ideal agent to do what is right. An important challenge for virtue ethics is to give an account of practical wisdom that doesn't reduce it to knowledge of a set of (complex and sophisticated) moral principles.

Chapter 9, "The Situationist Critique of Virtue Ethics," considers one of the most serious objections to virtue ethics, which is that the results of experiments in social psychology undermine the central claims made by virtue ethicists; in particular, the claim that virtues and vices exist and that it is possible for us to become virtuous. Situationists argue that our behavior is influenced more by situational features than by character traits. More recently, they have turned their attention to practical wisdom, arguing that our behavior is influenced by cognitive processes that we are not aware of and cannot control, which means that any attempt at self-improvement is likely to fail.

Chapter 10, "Virtue and Environment Ethics," focuses on the role of virtue in environmental ethics. Environmental ethics differs from other areas in applied virtue ethics, for it involves extending the sphere of moral consideration to animals and the environment. As such, it requires us to revisit and, in some cases, reconsider some of the central questions in normative ethics. In the case of environmental *virtue* ethics, it requires us to reconsider some of the questions explored earlier in the book: What makes a trait a(n) (environmental) virtue? Is there a link between (environmental) virtue and human happiness? Does (environmental) virtue ethics offer a better approach to practical moral problems than its rivals, deontology and consequentialism? and Can we become (environmentally) virtuous?

1   Virtue Ethics

Virtue ethics is now widely recognized, alongside consequentialism and deontology, as a major normative theory. However, the central claims of virtue ethics are frequently misunderstood. As a result, it is often rejected (or accepted) for the wrong reasons. A frequent source of misunderstanding is that the term "virtue ethicist" is sometimes used very broadly to include anyone who is interested in examining philosophical questions about the nature and role of virtues and vices (or character more generally). The problem with this usage is that a virtue ethicist might be someone who concludes, after much careful thought, that the virtues do *not* play an important role in morality. As we will see, the problem is avoided by making a distinction between *virtue theory*, which refers to the broader field of inquiry that focuses on philosophical questions about virtues and vices, and *virtue ethics*, which is a normative theory that claims that the virtues and vices play a central role in ethics. The aim of this chapter is to give an overview of virtue ethics, including the different forms it can take, and how it differs from other normative theories.

1.1 Normative Theory

To understand what virtue ethics is, it is useful to start by considering what a normative theory is. Broadly speaking, a normative theory, or what is sometimes referred to as a moral theory, is an attempt to provide a systematic and coherent account of the values, norms, ideals, and standards that we appeal to when making moral (or ethical) judgments in the course of our everyday lives. Various things can be the object of judgment, but normative theorists tend to focus on our judgments of:

a   *Actions:* We judge actions prospectively (i.e. before the fact), for instance when recommending that someone should perform a particular action or that it would be the right thing to do in the circumstances, as well as retrospectively (i.e. after the fact), when claiming that someone acted well in a given situation, or that they made the right decision. We might use "deontic" (or duty-based) language, for example by claiming that an action is wrong, impermissible, or contrary to duty, or that someone has a duty (or obligation) to do something. We might also (or instead) use "aretaic" (or character-based) language, for example by claiming that someone acted bravely, heroically, kindly, and so on, or that a particular action would be cowardly, dishonest, cruel, and so on.

b   *States of affairs:* We value certain states of affairs, such as a reduction in the rates of crime, poverty, or unemployment in a given community, and see them as goals worth striving for. On a more individual level, we value states such as being healthy, wealthy, powerful, educated, happy, and so on.

c   *Character:* We might describe someone as reliable, compassionate, and principled, or as arrogant, greedy, dishonest, materialistic, and so on.

d   *Motives and intentions:* We judge people's motives – the reasons, desires, or emotions that move them to act in particular ways – as well as their intentions – what they consciously aim or plan to do or bring about. So, for example, we might criticize someone for intending to steal from their employer (regardless of whether they actually end up doing so), and yet judge their motives (say, a desire to provide for their family) as good.

e   *Lives:* We sometimes make judgments about someone's life overall, for example when we claim, perhaps at their funeral, that they lived a good life.

It is the task of *descriptive* (or comparative) ethics to study our moral behavior and the moral judgments we actually make. By contrast, *normative* ethics is concerned with giving an account of what is involved in making *good* moral judgments. As such, it is focuses on the following sorts of question: What makes an action right or good?, Are there universal standards about how we ought to act?, Do all good states of affairs or consequences have something in common?, What makes a person good or virtuous?, What is involved in being well-motivated?, What is a good life for human beings?, etc.

A normative theory need not include an account of all five kinds of judgment, but if it omits one or more category it owes us an explanation of why it is not considered important or relevant. We might think of an account of right or good action, good states of affairs, good character, good motives and intentions, and a good life as the basic building blocks of a normative theory, where the task of the theorist is to figure out the size and shape of each block, the relationships between them, and which block is to serve as the foundation of the theory. In the course of doing so the theorist might find that what looked like a single block is actually two or more separate blocks, or that there is a gap in the theory, which means that the entire structure is unstable. In what follows, we will take a brief look at the structures of the two theories that played a dominant role during the twentieth century and continue to be popular among normative theorists and applied ethicists.

1.2 Consequentialism and Deontology

Consequentialists start with the intuition that certain states of affairs are valuable. Classical utilitarianism, which is a version of consequentialism developed by Jeremy Bentham and further refined by J. S. Mill, holds that happiness or pleasure is the only thing that is valuable in itself. All other things, such as health, wealth, employment, and so on, are considered valuable only as a means to happiness. Other consequentialists give competing accounts of what is good or valuable in itself, such as the satisfaction of desires or preferences, but what they all have in common is that an account of good states of affairs or consequences forms the foundation of their theory, lending support to their accounts of right action, good character, and good motives.

Once they have an account of good consequences in place, consequentialists tend to devote most of their attention to giving an account of right action. On the classical utilitarian view, an action is right if and only if it produces the greatest amount of happiness overall. Roughly, the idea is that if we acknowledge that happiness is good, then the right thing to do in any given situation is whatever will (or is likely to) bring about the greatest amount of happiness. Many consequentialists find this account too demanding, and have proposed alternative formulations, for example, that an action is right if and only if its consequences are good enough. But they all agree that right action can be defined in terms of good consequences.

Deontologists, by contrast, reject the claim that right action can be defined in terms of good consequences. Although they accept that certain things can be described as good or desirable, they argue that the consequences of our actions are not fully within our control, and so it is a mistake to judge actions on the basis of consequences. Morality involves choice, and we don't always choose the consequences of our actions. Further, they argue that many actions, such as telling the truth, keeping one's promises, and repaying one's debts, are right irrespective of consequences. By not acknowledging this, consequentialists are often forced to justify doing things that are intuitively wrong, such as killing and torturing innocent people, as long as doing so has good consequences.

Deontologists give what they believe to be a more plausible account of right action, which is that an action is right if and only if it is in accordance with moral duty. (The term "deontology" is derived from the Greek *deon*, which means duty or obligation.) Morality, in this view, is a matter of obeying moral rules, such as the duty to keep our promises, to benefit others, to tell the truth, not to kill or harm others, and so on. The account of right action in terms of moral duty forms the foundation of deontology, but a major concern for deontologists is to give a convincing explanation of where these duties come from (so in a sense the foundation still needs some form of support). One view is that they are obligations that arise from God's commands (a view known as "divine command theory"), but most contemporary deontologists base moral duty on reason (following Immanuel Kant) or intuition (following W. D. Ross).

For much of the twentieth century, the focus of normative ethics was on the question: What makes an action right? It was quite typical for courses in moral philosophy to introduce students to deontology and consequentialism, and then to present them with the question: Which of these theories captures the truth about morality? Consequentialists came up with a number of very serious objections to deontology, and deontologists returned fire with some serious objections to consequentialism. Some moral philosophers wondered whether both these positions were hopelessly flawed. A few toyed with the idea that morality is entirely relative or subjective, that there are no moral truths, but most people were dissuaded from embracing relativism by the thought that we want to be able to criticize people like Adolf Hitler for his horrific actions. That is, we want to be able to say that what he did was *in fact* wrong, and not merely that he acted wrongly according to the norms of our society. And so moral philosophers appeared to be faced with the choice between deontology and consequentialism. Since each side was asserting what the other denied, it was difficult to imagine a third alternative. Instead, most normative theorists tried to avoid the objections raised by their opponents by revising or refining their preferred theory.

This dynamic was echoed in debates in applied ethics, which became an increasingly popular field of inquiry in the latter decades of the twentieth century. Consider, for example, the debate about the morality of euthanasia. Deontologists tended to approach the matter by focusing on the duty not to intentionally kill an innocent person. This was seen as an absolute duty (i.e., one that does not allow for exceptions), which is grounded in the "sanctity" of human life. The basic idea was that a human being has a special moral status, which requires that their life not be taken by human (as opposed to Godly) hands. Accordingly, active euthanasia, which involves actively and intentionally ending a patient's life in order to spare them further suffering, was considered to be wrong in every case. But deontologists disagreed about whether it is ever permissible to allow a patient to die by, for instance, withholding medical treatment (e.g., not resuscitating a patient who has suffered heart failure) or withdrawing medical treatment (e.g., switching off their life support). Some argued that withholding life-preserving treatment is sometimes permissible because it doesn't constitute active killing, whereas withdrawing such treatment is wrong because it involves intentionally acting in a way that causes the patient's death. The so-called "doctrine of double effect" received a considerable amount of attention. Proponents of the doctrine argued that administering a lethal dose of morphine with the intention of ending a patient's life constitutes intentional killing (and is therefore wrong). However, administering a lethal dose with the intention of relieving suffering, even though foreseeing that this will hasten death, does not constitute intentional killing (and is therefore sometimes permissible).[1] Thus, the moral acceptability of end-of-life treatment seemed to depend on what many people regarded as mere technicalities, while an important concern – the good of the patient – was pushed to the side-lines.

Consequentialism appealed to applied ethicists who thought that the distinctions between acts and omissions, withdrawing and withholding treatment, and intending and "merely foreseeing" death were irrelevant to the morality of euthanasia. The crucial question, for them, was whether the act (or omission) in question would have good consequences.[2] This seemed to focus attention on where it should be: whether legally permitting active euthanasia would allow physicians to prevent or alleviate unnecessary suffering. However, the trouble with consequentialism, at least in its standard forms, was that it asked us to consider the consequences for everyone affected by the action or legislation, thus allowing for the justification of certain procedures on the grounds that they benefitted the patient's family and/or society as a whole. Some applied ethicists warned that consequentialist thinking would inevitably lead us down a "slippery slope," pointing out that Hitler justified his "euthanasia" program by appealing to the good of society.[3]

1.3 The Emergence of Virtue Ethics

The above sorts of objections to deontology and consequentialism motivated many normative theorists to revise and refine these theories. However, with the publication of Elizabeth Anscombe's paper, "Modern Moral philosophy" in 1958, both theories faced a far more serious objection. Anscombe argued that our moral language, in particular the concepts of moral obligation and moral duty, and of what is morally right and morally wrong, derives from the Judeo-Christian conception of ethics as a collection of universal laws, one that presupposes the existence of a divine lawgiver. In this framework, "morally right" means permitted or required by God, and "morally wrong" means not permitted by God. In due course, however, the idea that such a lawmaker existed was rejected, and yet people continued to use the concepts of moral duty and right and wrong action. The result, according to Anscombe, is that these moral concepts have become incoherent:

> It is as if the notion "criminal" were to remain when criminal law and criminal courts had been abolished and forgotten ... . The situation, if I am right, was the interesting one of the survival of a concept outside a framework of thought that made it a really intelligible one.
>
> (1958, 6)

J. L. Mackie continued this line of argument in his influential book, provocatively entitled *Ethics: Inventing Right and Wrong* and first published in 1977. He points out that normative theorists share a commitment to what has become known as "moral realism," roughly, the view that there are objective moral values and that at least some of our moral judgments can be true or false. The aim of normative ethics is to allow us to make better judgments, and consequentialists and deontologists generally take this to mean: it should help us determine, or indeed, *discover* whether a specific action is in fact right or wrong. Mackie defends a form of anti-realism known as "error theory." He argues that although we mean to make true judgments about whether an action is right or good, these judgments are all untrue, given that moral values do not exist. Mackie's claim about moral statements is similar to the claim that atheists make about statements about God. Religious people often say things like "God loves me" or "God is powerful" and assume that these statements are (or at least can be) true. Atheists don't believe in the existence of God, and so they think that the above sorts of claims about God cannot be true. In much the same way, error theorists claim that moral properties (e.g. rightness and wrongness) and entities (e.g. moral duties and values) do not exist independently of human beings, and that they are no more than conventions invented or constructed by human beings, and so it follows that we cannot discover whether a particular action is in fact right or wrong.

While arguments against moral realism persuaded some moral philosophers to give up normative theory altogether, others continued the project of refining and supporting their preferred versions of consequentialism or deontology. However, during the latter part of the twentieth century, a handful of philosophers, most notably Philippa Foot (1978b), John

McDowell (1979), Alasdair MacIntyre (1984), and Rosalind Hursthouse (1991), explored a suggestion made by Anscombe in her 1958 article, which is to reject the concepts of moral duty and morally right or wrong action, and replace them with virtue and vice terms. So instead of saying that an action is morally wrong, we can say that it is dishonest, unjust, or cowardly, and instead of saying that it is right or obligatory, we can say that it is generous, honest, or courageous (1958, 8–9). They made an appeal for a return to the ancient Greek tradition, which focused on the virtues (such as wisdom, justice, courage, and temperance) and the idea of living a good life rather than moral duty or obligation. The ancient Greek philosophers were not interested in identifying rules of right action. Instead, they considered the broader question: How can I live a good life as a human being?

One advantage of virtue and vice terms is that they are not only evaluative but also descriptive. Advising someone to do what is generous, honest, or courageous is much more informative than merely advising them to do what is right: it directs their attention to relevant features of the situation. In the case of courage, it focuses their attention on overcoming their fears for the sake of a worthy end, and in the case of generosity, it encourages them to think about the happiness of others.

Another advantage of evaluating actions as kind, honest, or courageous (or the reverse) is that we are not relying on metaphysical entities, such as a divine lawgiver or a set of moral duties. Rather, these evaluations are based in properties – character traits – that exist in the real world. We can criticize Hitler – and condemn his actions – as in fact cruel and inhumane. We don't have to appeal to a divine lawmaker or a moral duty to come to the conclusion that his actions were despicable. Similarly, we can praise our moral heroes by drawing attention to the good qualities that we see in them, and that are displayed in their actions. Consider, for example, John Major's tribute to Nelson Mandela:

> The source of his magic was the sheer moral force that clung to him as a result of all he had endured throughout his years of imprisonment – and the lack of bitterness with which he had emerged from it... . This was a man of great courage and empathy, who stood up for what he believed – and won. He had an enormous personal presence, but it was not created by power or position; it was created by the sheer force of his character, which – far from being ground down during his 27 years' imprisonment – emerged untouched, even enhanced.
>
> (2013)

Although Mandela was, by all accounts, an extraordinary human being, the character traits he possessed are ones that we recognize, at least to some extent, in the ordinary people around us: the courage shown by parents fighting for the life of their sick child, a friend's willingness to forgive her cheating spouse, the compassion shown by bystanders after a terrorist attack. Of course, it is not always clear that these responses are appropriate or truly virtuous given particular features of the situation. It could be that the parents are refusing to see that the most compassionate and, indeed, courageous thing to do would be to stop futile treatment and allow their child to die in peace. And perhaps our friend should be less forgiving and realize that her spouse is not committed to the relationship. But although particular claims about people's character and about the virtuousness (or viciousness) of their actions are often controversial, an important advantage is that we can all get involved in these debates. We are all reasonably familiar with particular virtues and vices, from reading novels and watching films, and from observing politicians, celebrities, and the ordinary people around us. In short, virtues and vices are not invented. We discover that our friend is reliable, honest, and kind.

Foot's paper, "Euthanasia" (1978a) is useful in demonstrating some of the advantages of thinking in terms of virtues and vices rather than moral duty. Foot asks us to redirect our attention from a concern with the means of procuring death and its possible usefulness to society, to the original meaning of the term: "a death understood as a good or happy event for the one who dies" (from the Greek, *euthanatos*: a good death) (1978a, 34). Seen thus, the central ethical question is: Is the act of euthanasia[4] for the sake of the one who dies? or, stated otherwise, Does it allow the patient to die a good death? Foot thinks there are two virtues that are important in this context, namely charity (or benevolence) and justice. Although it is by no means an easy task to determine when, if ever, an act of euthanasia is both charitable and just, the important thing to note is that it focuses our attention on the right questions. The virtue of charity "attaches us to the good of others" (Foot 1978a, 45), and asks us to consider whether the act of euthanasia will benefit the patient. And the virtue of justice asks us to consider what we owe the patient "in the way of non-interference and positive service" (Foot 1978a, 44).

Foot's paper on euthanasia inspired some ethicists to apply a virtue approach to other moral questions,[5] and applied virtue ethics is now a well-established area of research.[6] At the same time, many philosophers turned their attention to questions about the nature of virtue, the link between virtue and other moral concepts (such as happiness and right action), the existence of virtues, and the nature of intellectual virtue. This field of inquiry has come to be known as *virtue theory*.[7] In what follows, I give a brief outline of some topics in virtue theory before venturing a definition of virtue ethics.

1.4 Virtue Theory

1.4.1 What Is Virtue?

Virtues and vices are relatively stable dispositions to act in certain ways. People who are honest characteristically do things like tell the truth, give the correct change, pay their taxes, and so on, whereas dishonest people characteristically lie and cheat. Virtues are good character traits, and vices are bad character traits. We praise and admire people who are honest, kind, just, generous, courageous, and so on. We encourage our children to acquire the virtues, and many of us try to become more virtuous ourselves. At the same time, we blame or criticize people for being dishonest, unkind, selfish, or arrogant. These are character defects, and a common assumption is that people can and should try to correct these flaws. We tend to think of a person's character – the collection of virtues and/or vices they possess – as somehow more important, more central to their identity than other traits they might have, such as their personality traits, aspects of their physical appearance, or their talents.

People sometimes disagree about which traits are virtues. The standard list includes traits such as honesty, courage, kindness, generosity, and justice. But what about traits such as modesty, tidiness, wittiness, competitiveness, and selflessness? Should we include any of these traits in the list of virtues? To answer this question we need to consider a more fundamental question: What makes a trait a virtue? That is, do all the virtues have something in common, something that allows us (a) to distinguish them from other character traits, and (b) to explain why they are virtues and not vices (or morally neutral traits)?

An important question that arises when trying to determine what makes a trait a virtue concerns the relevance of inner states (thoughts and feelings). A virtue is a disposition to act in certain ways, and people clearly have thoughts and feelings when they act. But does it matter what these thoughts and feelings are? And does it matter which of these thoughts and feelings motivate them to act? Some argue that as long as people act in certain ways, it doesn't really matter what they think or how they feel (provided, of course, that they keep any negative thoughts and feelings to themselves). Others think that inner states do matter in some way. One view is that we admire virtuous people because "their heart is in the right place." Generous people care about other people's happiness, and honest people care about the truth, and so it might be that caring about certain things is essential for virtue. An alternative view is that virtuous people are admirable because they act for the right *reasons*, for example, because they recognize that the good of others is worth pursuing, or because they believe they have a duty to help others. A third, more demanding view is that truly virtuous people are motivated to act by the right reasons *and* the right feelings. In this view, a truly benevolent person is someone who knows they should help others and also cares about their welfare.

This leads us to a closely related question: Is a virtuous person wise or knowledgeable, and if so, what kind of knowledge do they possess? The claim that virtuous people do the right thing for the right reasons clearly suggests that they must know what the right reasons are. But how do they know this? One possibility is that they know a set of action-guiding rules or principles, which they apply to particular cases. Another possibility is that they have acquired certain intellectual skills that allow them to figure out what to do in a particular case, in much the same way that an experienced builder is able to find a creative solution to a new building problem.

Finally, it is useful to note the distinction between moral (or character) virtues and intellectual (or epistemic) virtues. Roughly, intellectual virtues are traits that allow us to attain knowledge, and include traits such as open-mindedness, curiosity, perseverance, intellectual humility, and imaginativeness. Moral virtues, by contrast, are traits that allow us to live and act well, and include traits like courage, kindness, and honesty. Virtue epistemology – the philosophical study of the nature and role of intellectual virtue and vice – was inspired by the interest in virtue concepts among moral philosophers, and has since become a well-established branch of epistemology. Given that our focus in this book is on virtue ethics as a normative theory, we will not discuss the intellectual virtues here, except for one notable exception: the virtue of practical wisdom or prudence (*phronesis*). Aristotelian virtue ethicists argue that practical wisdom is an intellectual virtue that is required for acting well.[8]

1.4.2 How Is Virtue Related to Other Moral Concepts?

Apart from questions about the nature of virtue, philosophers are interested in the link between virtue and other moral concepts. One set of questions concerns the link between virtue and happiness. It seems obvious that virtues like kindness, generosity, honesty, and fairness generally contribute to the happiness of others. Part of the reason we value these traits and reward people who have them is that they contribute to the good of society as a whole – things tend to go better when people are kind and generous, and when they can rely on each other to be honest and fair. But do the virtues also contribute to the happiness of their possessor? Some philosophers claim that the virtues are necessary for happiness, that for someone to live a good or happy life, they have to possess the virtues.

There is some intuitive support for this idea. It seems plausible that parents encourage their children to become kind, generous and just, not just for the sake of those around them but also for their own sakes. Being selfish, cruel, or dishonest can make one miserable. Further, many (perhaps most) virtuous people do appear to be happy. One of the things that surprised and impressed people when Nelson Mandela was released from prison is that he did not appear bitter or resentful at all. Instead, he seemed genuinely happy, and his happiness was not just a temporary feeling or mood but appeared to be a settled state, part of who he was as a human being. Could there be a link between his virtue – his capacity to forgive, his kindness and compassion, courage, and resilience – and his happiness? Does virtue allow one to be truly happy, or to live a meaningful or worthwhile life?

Another set of questions concerns the link between virtue and right action. It seems safe to say that virtuous people characteristically do what is right. But which of these concepts is primary: virtue or right action? That is, should we start with a theory of what makes an action right, and then go on to define virtue in terms of right action? (So, for example, if a right action is one that has good consequences, then a virtue might be a trait that typically has good consequences; or, if an action is right because it is in accordance with duty, then virtue might be a trait that involves respect for doing one's duty.) Or, alternatively, should we start with a theory of virtue, and then identify right action in terms of virtue (for example, as the kind of action that a virtuous person would perform, or an action that manifests or is motivated by virtue)?

1.4.3 Can People Become Virtuous? (or: Do the Virtues Exist?)

As noted earlier, part of the appeal of thinking in terms of virtues and vices is that we don't have to appeal to obscure metaphysical entities such as "moral duty," but rather to the character traits – dispositions that people actually possess. However, many social psychologists – or "situationists" – doubt whether people do in fact possess character traits, and argue that virtues, like moral duties, are fictional entities. The results of various experiments in social psychology show that people's behavior is influenced more by situational features, such as the number of people in the room, the presence of an authority figure, or even the smell of cookies, than by their personal beliefs, attitudes or feelings. What this suggests, according to situationists, is that people do not possess character traits. This is a controversial claim, and it has become the topic of an intense and ongoing debate, which we will explore later in this book.

1.5 Virtue Ethics

Virtue theory, then, is a field of inquiry that concerns itself with questions about the nature and existence of virtue as well as the link between virtue and other moral concepts. Virtue theory should be distinguished from virtue *ethics*, which is a normative theory rather than a field of inquiry. Virtue ethicists are concerned with many of the same questions as virtue theorists, but they are committed to a particular view about the relationship between virtue and other moral concepts, namely that virtue is a central moral concept, and that conceptions of "the good life" and of right and wrong action are secondary in the sense that they should be understood in terms of virtue.

The distinction between virtue theory and virtue ethics was first suggested by Julia Driver in 1996. Before this time, it was common to use the terms interchangeably. This didn't cause much confusion given that the majority of philosophers who were interested in questions about virtue were doing so in the course of developing or defending virtue ethics as an alternative to the two dominant normative theories: deontology and consequentialism. Indeed, one of the main objections to these two normative theories was that they ignored or neglected questions about virtue and character. While this criticism was certainly justified at the time, this is no longer the case. Kant's long-neglected doctrine of virtue, which is expounded in the second part of *The Metaphysics of Morals*, has since received a considerable amount of attention, and philosophers like Julia Driver (2001) and Thomas Hurka (2001) have developed distinctively consequentialist theories of virtue. It is now widely accepted that any normative theory should include an account of good character or virtue. For this reason, it became necessary to distinguish between the broader field of inquiry that concerns itself with questions about virtue (virtue theory) and the specific normative theory that takes virtue to be a central moral concept (virtue ethics).

If all normative theories should include an account of virtue, the question that arises is: What distinguishes virtue ethics from these other theories? One way to answer the question is to compare the structures of these theories, focusing specifically on the account of right action provided by each. As we've seen, *deontology* takes the notion of moral duty as primary. An action is right if it is in accordance with duty. It follows that a virtuous person is someone who acts from a sense of duty, and the moral knowledge they have is knowledge of a set of moral rules or principles that specify what is required by duty. Standard forms of *consequentialism*, in turn, take good consequences to be primary, and define right action in terms of (actual or expected) consequences. They hold that virtues and specific inner states, such as motives, feelings, and knowledge, only have instrumental value. By contrast, the central concept in *virtue ethics* is virtue rather than duty or good consequences. Accordingly, it evaluates actions in terms of virtue, for example, by holding that an action is right if and only if it is what a virtuous person would characteristically do in the circumstances.

While this is a fairly accurate sketch of the differences between these theories, it can also be somewhat misleading, for it suggests that the three theories are all focused on answering the question, What makes an action right? Many virtue ethicists think that the concepts of right or wrong action are relatively unimportant or uninteresting. As we've seen, philosophers like Anscombe argue that we should altogether abandon these concepts and instead evaluate actions as virtuous (kind, honest, just, etc.) or vicious (unkind, dishonest, unjust, etc.).

A significant difference between virtue ethics and its rivals concerns the role of normative theory. Deontologists and consequentialists tend to view a normative theory as useful for solving the moral quandaries or dilemmas that we encounter from time to time, such as: Should I have an abortion? Should I break a promise to help a friend? Should we separate a set of conjoined twins? and so on. And this is why their focus is on giving an account of right action. Although virtue ethics can certainly help us to find answers to these questions, it is concerned with the much broader question about living well or being a good person. As such, it is concerned with our attitudes and habits, our ways of living and perceiving things. To illustrate, consider the person who has focused all her energy on advancing her career, but one day, perhaps after reading a biography of a great philanthropist, wonders whether she should try to become more generous and less focused on advancing her own interests. She is not facing a moral quandary at all. But we can all recognize that she is facing an important ethical question, namely: How can I become a better person? And her answer might be something like: "I should make an effort to care more about others, and take time off work to do volunteer work in the community. I should buy fewer luxury items, and focus on what is really important in life." When it is claimed that virtue plays a central role in virtue ethics, then, what is meant is not merely that it evaluates particular actions in terms of virtue rather than duty or consequences. Rather, as Russell (2013a, 2) notes, "[w]hat sets virtue ethics apart is that it treats ethics as concerned with one's whole life – and not just those occasions when something with a distinctly 'moral' quality is at stake."

1.6 Varieties of Virtue Ethics

The early figures in the revival of virtue ethics were all influenced by Aristotle, and so "virtue ethics" generally meant "Aristotelian virtue ethics." However, over the last two decades, a number of normative theorists have suggested alternative forms of virtue ethics, inspired by philosophers such as Plato, David Hume, Friedrich Nietzsche, and Martin Heidegger. Our focus will be on three varieties of virtue ethics that have dominated current debates in the area.

1.6.1 Eudaimonistic Virtue Ethics

Eudaimonism (from the Greek *eudaimonia*, a good human life) is a tradition in ethics that is focused on the question: What is a good life for human beings? Ancient eudaimonists include Aristotle, Plato, and the Stoics. Aristotelian virtue ethics is the most popular version of eudaimonism among contemporary virtue ethicists, and is supported by Julia Annas (1993, 2011), Rosalind Hursthouse (1999), and Daniel Russell (2009, 2012).

Aristotelian virtue ethics is committed to a form of perfectionism, for it tries to answer the question, What is the *best* life for human beings? Accordingly, it conceives of virtues as *excellences*, and further, as *human* excellences – they are traits that make it possible for us to live well as the kind of beings we are, namely, human beings. Vices, in turn, are seen as *defects*, traits that make someone worse as a human being. To identify the virtues, we need to think about human nature, about what distinguishes us from plants and the other animals – what does it mean to function well as a human being (as opposed to a tree or a bear)? The answer given by Aristotelians is that the capacity for reason is the distinguishing feature of human beings. We are able to act from reason rather than mere instinct, feeling, or desire, and we are able to shape our emotions and desires so that they are aligned with reason. A virtuous person has practical wisdom (*phronesis*), which is an intellectual virtue that involves reasoning well about how to live and act virtuously. A good or happy life for human beings (*eudaimonia*) is a virtuous life, where the virtues are conceived as reliable dispositions to act and react well, that is, for the right reasons and with the right feelings and attitudes. Aristotelian virtue ethicists evaluate actions in terms of virtue and vice, claiming, for example, that an action is right if it is what a virtuous person would characteristically do in the situation (Hursthouse 1999).

In summary, Aristotelian virtue ethicists make five central claims, which we will explore in more detail in this book:

a   Virtue is a human excellence (Chapter 2).
b   What makes a trait a virtue is that it allows its possessor to live a good (happy or flourishing) life (Chapter 3).
c   A virtuous person is motivated by the right feelings and the right reasons (Chapter 4).

d   Practical wisdom is required for virtue (Chapter 5).
e   Actions are to be evaluated in terms of virtue and vice (Chapter 6).

1.6.2 Agent-based Virtue Ethics

Agent-based virtue ethics begins with the intuition that what makes a person good or admirable is the fact that they have good inner states. In this view, it doesn't really matter whether people actually accomplish the things they set out to accomplish, or whether their actions are in accordance with a set of moral rules. Rather, what matters is that they possess and are motivated by the right kind of beliefs, values, attitudes, and emotions. Hence virtue (or virtuous motivation) is not merely central but fundamental, in the sense that it is not defined with reference to any other moral concepts, such as good consequences, moral duty, right action, or *eudaimonia*. Virtuous inner states are seen as intuitively good or admirable, and no further explanation of what makes these states good is given.

The most popular form of agent-based virtue ethics is the sentimentalist view developed by Michael Slote (2001, 2010). Slote argues that what makes someone admirable is that they are motivated by "warm" inner states, such as compassion, care, and benevolence. Accordingly, actions are evaluated as right or good depending on whether they manifest virtuous motives. Slote accepts that well-motivated people will try to bring about good consequences, but he claims that the actual consequences of an action are irrelevant to its rightness. Similarly, he argues that although well-motivated people will try to get the facts right, knowledge or practical wisdom is not required for virtue.

The central claims of Slote's agent-based virtue ethics can be summarized as follows:

a   A virtue is an admirable trait (Chapter 2).
b   Virtue is not defined in terms of human flourishing or *eudaimonia* (Chapter 2).
c   A virtuous person is someone who acts from good or virtuous motives such as benevolence, care, and compassion it (Chapters 2 and 4).
d   Virtue does not require practical wisdom (Chapters 2 and 5).
e   Right action is defined in terms of virtuous motivation (Chapter 6).

1.6.3 Pluralistic Virtue Ethics

Eudaimonists define virtue as a trait needed for happiness, whereas agent-based virtue ethicists define it in terms of inner states. In this sense, both these approaches are monistic. By contrast, pluralistic virtue ethicists reject the view that there is a single ground of virtue. Christine Swanton (2003), the leading advocate of this view, gives a broad definition of virtue as a disposition to respond well to the demands of the world (2003, 19), but argues that what makes a trait a virtue (that is, what is involved in responding well to the demands of the world) can be any of a number of things. The virtue of compassion involves responding well to a person's suffering, and this includes having certain feelings, such as care, concern, and a desire to alleviate their suffering. By contrast, the virtue of justice does not require responding with warm feelings or fine inner states, but simply honoring or adhering to rules of justice. Swanton also rejects the view that practical wisdom is required for each and every virtue. In the case of some virtues, responding well will require knowledge or intelligence, but other virtues require creativity rather than rationality. Finally, Swanton offers a pluralistic account of what makes an action right. She argues that actions are right if they are virtuous overall, and this involves hitting the targets of the relevant virtues. So, for example, when responding to the suffering of others, an action will be right if it succeeds in hitting the targets of compassion (that is, if involves an understanding of their suffering and a concern for their welfare) and benevolence (that is, if it succeeds in alleviating their suffering).

The central claims of a pluralistic virtue ethics can be summarized as follows:

a   A virtue is a disposition to respond well to the demands of the world (Chapter 2).
b   Not all virtues characteristically contribute to the happiness of their possessor (Chapter 3).
c   Some virtues require good motivation, but others do not (Chapter 4).
d   Not all virtues require wisdom or intelligence (Chapter 5).
e   Right action is defined in terms of hitting the targets of virtue (Chapter 6).

Chapter Summary

- A normative theory is an attempt to provide a systematic and coherent account of the values, norms, ideals, and standards that we appeal to when making moral judgments of actions, states of affairs, motives and intentions, character, and lives.
- During the twentieth century, the focus of normative ethics was on right action. Deontologists give an account of right action in terms of moral

duty, whereas consequentialists argue that rightness depends on consequences.

- All normative theorists share a commitment to some form of moral realism, which is the view that there are objective moral values and that at least some of our moral judgments can be true or false. This position is challenged by anti-realists, who argue that moral values are invented or constructed by human beings, which means that moral judgments cannot be objectively true or false.

- Virtue ethics is a normative theory that claims that the virtues, understood as dispositions to act and feel in certain ways, play a central role in morality. Virtue ethicists reject the claim that we have moral duties, and in this regard they agree with anti-realists. However, they presuppose a form of moral realism because they think we can make true moral judgments in terms of virtues and vices.

- Virtue theory is a field of inquiry that focuses on philosophical questions about virtue and vice, or character more generally. Virtue theorists are not necessarily committed to virtue ethics. Some virtue theorists embrace consequentialism or deontology, whereas others remain neutral.

Notes

1 For a discussion of these distinctions see Veatch (2000, 83–100).
2 James Rachels (1975) is one of the leading proponents of this view.
3 See, for example, Ruth Macklin (1992).
4 Foot makes it clear that by an "act of euthanasia" she does not mean to exclude cases where the death is the result of an omission (passive euthanasia).
5 See, e.g., Hursthouse (1991); Solomon (1993); Pellegrino and Thomasma (1993).
6 For a good overview of the field of applied virtue ethics, see Axtell and Olson (2012).
7 For an introduction to some of the main controversies in contemporary virtue theory, see the collection *Current Controversies in Virtue Theory*, edited by Mark Alfano (2015).
8 For an interesting discussion of key debates about intellectual virtue that bear directly on virtue ethics, see Battaly (2014).

Further Reading

Alfano, Mark, editor. 2015. *Current Controversies in Virtue Theory.* New York: Routledge.

Annas, Julia. 2011. *Intelligent Virtue.* Oxford: Oxford University Press.

Anscombe, G. E. M. 1958. "Modern Moral Philosophy." *Philosophy* 33(124): 1–19. doi:10.1017/S0031819100037943

Axtell, Guy and Philip Olson. 2012. "Recent Work in Applied Virtue Ethics." *American Philosophical Quarterly* 49(3): 182–203. www.jstor.org/stable/23213479.

Besser-Jones, Lorraine and Michael Slote, editors. 2015. *The Routledge Companion to Virtue Ethics.* New York: Routledge.

Foot, Philippa. 1978b. "Virtues and Vices." In *Virtues and Vices and Other Essays in Moral Philosophy*, by Philippa Foot, 1–18. Oxford: Blackwell.

Hursthouse, Rosalind. 1991. "Virtue Theory and Abortion." *Philosophy and Public Affairs* 20(3): 223–246. www.jstor.org/stable/2265432.

Russell, Daniel C. 2013a. "Introduction: Virtue Ethics in Modern Moral Philosophy." In *The Cambridge Companion to Virtue Ethics*, edited by Daniel C. Russell, 1–6. Cambridge: Cambridge University Press.

Slote, Michael. 2001. *Morals from Motives*. New York: Oxford University Press.

Swanton, Christine. 2003. *Virtue Ethics: A Pluralistic View*. Oxford: Oxford University Press.

Van Hooft, Stan, Nafsika Athanassoulis, Jason Kawall, Justin Oakley, Nicole Saunders, and Liezl van Zyl. 2014. *The Handbook of Virtue Ethics*. Abingdon and New York: Routledge.

2 Virtue

We can say a few things about virtues and vices with a reasonable amount of certainty. Virtues are good character traits: we praise and admire people who are kind, honest, generous, or courageous, and we try to become more like them (or at least, we think we should try to become more like them). And vices are bad character traits: we criticize people who are greedy, unkind, unfair, or cruel, and we warn our children not to become like them. Virtues and vices are dispositions to act in certain ways. Honest people characteristically tell the truth and give the correct change, whereas dishonest people do not. Generous people often give freely of their time or resources to benefit others, whereas selfish people tend to do whatever they believe to be in their own best interests. We are skeptical when it is said of someone that they are "basically" (or "deep down") a kind person when in fact they hardly ever do anything to help others.

When we try to flesh out this basic description, we encounter a few difficult questions. One such question is whether virtue requires good *motivation*. If we noticed that someone reliably acts in ways that benefit others, for example by giving to charity and helping friends, do we have sufficient evidence to conclude that he has the virtue of benevolence? Does it matter what motivates him? If it turns out that his reason for helping others is to enhance his reputation in the community, do we have to conclude that he doesn't possess the virtue of benevolence after all? Further, what does it mean to be well-motivated? In the case of benevolence, does it involve acting from good or appropriate emotions (such as love or concern, or a desire to make others happy), or does it instead (or also) involve acting from certain kinds of reasons (such as "It is my duty to help" or "She needs help, and I can help her at little cost to myself")?

A second set of questions is closely related to the first: Does a virtuous person find virtuous activity *pleasant* in some way? If someone often gives to charity and does so for the right reasons (whatever these may be), does it matter if he finds it difficult or unpleasant to do so? Is he less than fully generous if he secretly feels reluctant or resentful, or if he cannot sincerely say that it is a pleasure to help out?

A third question is whether virtue requires some form of *intelligence* or *wisdom*. Most virtue theorists agree that at least some virtues require wisdom. Someone who regularly and indiscriminately blurts out whatever they believe to be the truth does not have honesty *as a virtue*. Arguably, a truly honest person knows when and how to convey the truth (and when to keep quiet), and they also make a reasonable effort to ensure that what they are saying is in fact true. Someone who supports their opinion with "facts" gained from an unreliable source is not really honest, even if they believe that what the source says is true. But it is not obvious that all the virtues require wisdom. Perhaps a virtue like kindness simply involves caring about others, and treating them with warmth and compassion.

To answer these questions, we need to consider a more fundamental question: *What makes a character trait a virtue rather than a vice or a neutral trait?* One possible answer is that the virtues typically have good consequences, whereas vices have bad consequences. Things tend to go better in societies where most people are virtuous than in societies where most are vicious. If we accept this answer, then good motives and intelligence will often accompany virtue, but will not be required for it. But if, instead, we think that what distinguishes virtue from vice is that it is a disposition to act in accordance with duty, then we would have a different view about the relevance (and nature) of good or virtuous motivation.

The aim of this chapter is to provide a brief overview of five distinctive theories of virtue. The first three – an Aristotelian, a sentimentalist, and a pluralistic theory – are examples of virtue-ethical theories of virtue. As we will see, virtue ethicists disagree with each other about the nature and role of motivation, emotion, and intelligence. But they all have one thing in common: they think virtue has a central or primary role in normative theory. That is, they deny that virtue can be defined in terms of either good consequences or moral duty. In the final two sections, we briefly discuss two theories of virtue given by supporters of rival normative theories: a consequentialist theory and a Kantian theory.

2.1 An Aristotelian Theory

Contemporary Aristotelian virtue ethicists like Rosalind Hursthouse and Julia Annas conceive of virtue as a *human excellence*. The virtues are what allow us to live a good life. To appreciate this point, we should note that the claim is not simply that the virtues are what makes a person *morally* good, that is, good in one respect, so that we might say of someone, "He is not very successful but at least he is a good person." Instead, Aristotelians are making a much stronger claim, namely, that it is a person's virtues, rather than any of his other attributes, skills, or achievements, that make him good or excellent, not just in the moral sphere but overall, *as a human being*. Aristotelianism forms part of the eudaimonistic tradition (from the Greek, *eudaimonia*, which can be translated as a good or happy human life). Eudaimonists take the starting point for ethical reflection to be: How can I live well? or: What is the best life for human beings? And their answer, in short, is: A good or happy life is a virtuous life.

Understanding this point allows us to see why Aristotelians put forward such a demanding conception of virtue. Consider the following description given by Hursthouse:

> A full Aristotelian concept of virtue is the concept of a complex character trait, that is, a disposition that is well entrenched in its possessor and, as we say, "goes all the way down." The disposition, far from being a single-track disposition to do, say, honest actions, or even honest actions for certain reasons, is multi-track involving many other actions as well: desires, emotions and emotional reactions, perceptions, attitudes, interests, and expectations. This is because your virtues (and your vices) are a matter of what sort of adult you are, and involve, most particularly, your values – what you regard as worth pursuing or preserving or doing and what you regard as not so.
>
> (2006b, 101)

In this passage (and elsewhere) Hursthouse makes a number of claims about what is required for virtue. The first is that virtue is a *reliable* disposition to act in certain ways – it is "a disposition that is well entrenched in its possessor." If someone has the virtue of honesty, then we can expect or predict that they will perform certain sorts of actions, like telling the truth and giving the correct change, and not do other things, like cheating in exams or taking other people's possessions. We are surprised and puzzled when we discover that an honest person has told a lie, and try to find some explanation for why they acted out of character: Was it a mistake, did they know that what they were saying wasn't the truth? Were they under pressure, or not feeling well that day?

The second claim is that virtue is a deep feature of the person, one that "goes all the way down." Virtue expresses itself not merely in behavior but also in *feeling* and *reasoning* in certain ways (Annas 2011, 9). We cannot judge a person's character by merely observing their behavior. We may notice that John reliably (though perhaps not invariably) takes his plate to the kitchen after dinner, but we cannot conclude from this that he is a kind or considerate person. The behavior in question could just be a good habit, ingrained in him from childhood, and done without much thought, or he could just be really afraid of his mother. To know whether John is considerate, we need to look deeper and consider his feelings and attitudes as well as his reasons for behaving in this way.

This brings us to another central claim: virtue is a disposition to act with *sound emotion*. Acting with sound emotion involves having the appropriate feeling(s) while acting. Contemporary Aristotelians support what Aristotle says in this regard, namely that the truly virtuous person finds pleasure in acting virtuously (*The Nicomachean Ethics* 1099a12). Hence, if he is truly considerate, John will happily take his plate to the kitchen, rather than doing so grudgingly. Similarly, the truly generous person enjoys giving because she cares about others' welfare, and a temperate person enjoys eating and drinking in moderation, and is not tempted to over-indulge. Annas warns that is a mistake to interpret Aristotle as claiming that virtuous activity is accompanied by pleasant *feelings*, such as joy and excitement. In situations that call for courage – wars, accidents, and emergencies – it would be inappropriate to feel any kind of enjoyment. Finding pleasure in facing dangerous situations is usually a mark of foolishness rather than courage. Instead, Annas claims that the pleasure in question is what is experienced when the virtuous activity is "unimpeded by frustration and inner conflict" (2011, 73). Consider the following example, where a police officer describes what went through his mind before he jumped off a bridge to save a man from drowning:

> I don't think I ever thought I couldn't do it; it's hard to explain. I've never felt fear like it. I was shaking and am not sure whether that was the cold or the anticipation of what I was about to do. It was only when I climbed over the rail that I actually started thinking "what am I doing?" and then I saw him go under again and for that split second everything went calm and I just jumped.
>
> (*New Zealand Herald*, August 16, 2013)

In this case, acting with sound emotion involves doing "the right thing effortlessly and with no internal opposition" (Annas 2006, 517). Or, as Hursthouse puts it, "reason and inclination/desire are in harmony in [a virtuous] person" (2006b, 104).

In the Aristotelian view, emotions are not just irrational and unpredictable responses to the world. Rather, they support a cognitive account of the emotions, which holds that the emotions can be informed and educated by reason. We can learn to respond and act with sound emotion. As Christopher Bennett explains, Aristotelians view the emotions as distinctively human ways of registering the importance of things. That is, to have an emotion is for something to strike us as *mattering* in some way (Bennett 2010, 99). The police officer's fear is a fitting response to a dangerous situation, for he cares about his own safety. To be entirely fearless in this situation would be foolish, rather than brave. What distinguishes the courageous person is that he is able to overcome this fear, and he is able to do this because he values the lives of others. He sees that attempting to save a life is a worthwhile thing to do. In the same way, an honest person appreciates the value of knowing the truth, and a benevolent person cares about the good of others. It is this sense of what matters or what is worthwhile that motivates a virtuous person to act in certain ways.[1]

An important feature of Aristotelian virtue ethics is the claim that virtue requires *intelligence* or *wisdom*. The virtuous person doesn't just happen to care about certain things; instead, she cares about the right things and has the right desires. This requires a judgment that certain things are truly good or important and therefore worth protecting or pursuing. Aristotelians refer to the intelligence that is required for virtue as practical wisdom (*phronesis*). Although many virtue theorists accept the claim that some form of knowledge or intelligence is required for at least some of the virtues, Aristotelian virtue ethicists make practical wisdom a condition for virtue. Practical wisdom, in its most general sense, is the knowledge or understanding that enables its possessor to live and act well. It is what allows her to recognize certain ends as good or worthwhile, as truly desirable. A courageous person, unlike a foolish one, knows which things are worth taking risks for. And an honest person understands that honesty makes it possible for people to trust each other, to form friendships, to learn from each other, and so on.[2]

In the Aristotelian view, then, virtue has both an emotional and an intellectual aspect: it involves feeling and reasoning in certain ways. The virtuous person is committed to certain things because she judges them to be worthwhile, and this motivates her to act in ways that protect or promote these things. We can now see why, in the Aristotelian view, being well-motivated involves acting for the right reasons and with the right emotions. A courageous person is not someone who has learnt about courage, decided that he should be brave, and then needs to find a motivation to act courageously. Instead, he is someone whose character tendencies have been formed in such a way that he acts, reasons, and reacts courageously (Annas 2011, 9–10). The courageous police officer values human life, and this is why he accepts "I can save this man's life" as a strong reason for acting.

We can now return to the claim mentioned at the beginning of this section, namely that a good or happy life for human beings is a virtuous life. Aristotelians make two closely related claims about the link between virtue and happiness. The first is that *virtuous people are (or tend to be) happy people, as the virtues benefit their possessor.* If a virtuous person has a correct grasp of what is important in life, is motivated by the right reasons, and has the appropriate emotions when she acts, we would expect things to go well for her. There are obvious ways in which the virtues are good for their possessor. People who are friendly, reliable, and honest tend to have better relationships with others, and are loved, trusted, and respected by others. Courage allows them to deal well with difficult situations, and to overcome fears standing in the way of achieving their goals. Virtues like determination and conscientiousness allow them to succeed in their pursuits. Most contemporary virtue ethicists follow Aristotle in claiming that although virtue is necessary for happiness, it is not sufficient. To be happy a virtuous person also needs what Aristotle calls "external goods," such as wealth, honor, friends, and political power. So although we can expect things to go well for virtuous people, when they don't it is a result of bad luck and not because of a tendency of the virtue itself (see Hursthouse 1999, ch. 8; Annas 2011, ch. 9.)

The second claim about virtue and happiness is that *what makes a character trait a virtue is that it allows its possessor to live well as a human being.* What allows us to identify a trait as a virtue rather than a vice (or a neutral trait) is that it is necessary for human happiness. As such, a virtue is not simply a useful trait or one that we find attractive or agreeable in some way. Rather, virtue involves functioning well as an emotional, intelligent, and social being; more specifically, it involves having a correct understanding of what is important or worthwhile in life, acting for the right reasons and with the right attitude, and having the right emotional responses. A fully virtuous person is an excellent human being, someone who lives a good or happy life.[3]

2.2 A Sentimentalist Theory

Michael Slote (2001; 2010) supports an agent-based virtue ethics as an alternative to Aristotelian virtue ethics. Slote's virtue ethics is more radical, and in a sense more pure, than other forms of virtue ethics. Virtue is a central concept in Aristotelian virtue ethics, but it is not foundational, because virtue is defined as a trait needed for happiness or *eudaimonia*. In this sense, Aristotelian virtue ethics is agent-*focused* (see Hursthouse 1999, 81–83). By contrast, Slote's virtue ethics is agent-*based* in the sense that virtue (or virtuous inner states) is foundational: actions derive their moral value entirely from character. Supporters of an agent-based virtue ethics see virtue is an admirable character trait, and what makes it admirable is that it involves having and acting from good motives. Good motivation is both necessary and sufficient for virtue, and no further explanation of what makes certain motives admirable is given (Slote 2001, 3–10).

Slote distinguishes two possible forms of agent-based virtue ethics, depending on the kind of virtues that are emphasized. The first is a "cool" form, which follows Plato in relating the morality of action to a strong and beautiful soul. The second, which is the one that Slote prefers, is a "warm" version, and follows sentimentalists like James Martineau, David Hume, and Francis Hutcheson in emphasizing virtues like compassion and benevolence (Slote 2001, 19–20).[4]

According to Slote's sentimentalism, "virtue consists in having and acting on warm motivating sentiments such as benevolence, gratitude, compassion, and love" (Frazer and Slote 2015, 197). Three aspects of this conception of virtue deserve mention. The first concerns the relevance of *consequences*. For virtue to be fundamental, Slote must deny that certain traits are virtues, at least in part, because they (often or usually) produce good effects. But can he reasonably do this? It seems very likely that the virtues do in fact produce good consequences. Surely, benevolent people bring about more good than people who are cruel or apathetic, and it seems plausible that part of the reason we value certain traits is that they typically have good consequences. Furthermore, the virtue of benevolence involves caring about and trying to promote the good of others, and so appears to presuppose an acceptance of certain states of affairs as good.

Slote deals with this issue as follows. He accepts that virtuous actions typically produce good consequences. But he argues that the good consequences are not what make a trait a virtue, that is, what gives it *moral* value. The reason for this is that consequences are subject to luck. Slote appeals to the intuition that we can only attribute praise or blame for things we can control. The consequences of our actions always depend on luck, so it follows that we cannot attribute praise or blame on the basis of consequences. Although we are (and should be) pleased when we get a good result, we shouldn't confuse our evaluation of states of affairs with our evaluation of people and their actions. Slote writes:

> [I]f we judge the actions of ourselves or others simply by their effects in the world, we end up unable to distinguish accidentally or ironically useful actions (or slips on banana peels) from actions that we actually morally admire and that are morally good and praiseworthy.
>
> (2001, 39)

Slote is not suggesting that consequences do not matter; only that they do not affect the moral value of people and their actions. We shouldn't ignore what people actually bring about when evaluating their actions, simply because consequences are often a good indicator of someone's motives and character. If someone repeatedly inflicts suffering on others, it is usually because of poor motivation rather than bad luck. Virtuous people care about others; they are concerned that their actions produce good outcomes and will therefore make an effort to succeed. Slote thinks we should restrict moral judgment to factors within the agent's control, and this requires focusing on their motives. He writes:

> [I]f someone does make every effort to find out relevant facts and is careful in acting, then ... she cannot be criticized for acting immorally, however badly things turn out.... . On the other hand, if the bad results are due to her lack of intelligence or other cognitive defects she is incapable of learning about, we can make epistemic criticisms of her performance, but these needn't be thought of as moral. (If one has cognitive defects one is capable of learning about, but one doesn't care enough to find out about them, then, once again, the genuineness of one's benevolence can be called into question.)
>
> (2001, 34)

Given the emphasis on benevolence, which concerns avoiding harm and unfairness to others, a warm agent-based view denies that there is a strong link between virtue and the agent's happiness. Since the moral life need not involve competently caring for one's self, it is possible to live a morally decent life without thereby living a happy life.

The second aspect of Slote's theory of virtue that deserves attention is his emphasis on *emotion* rather than reason in motivating virtuous action. Whereas Aristotelians claim that a virtuous person has practical wisdom, the sentimentalist tradition emphasizes moral sentiments such as care and compassion as necessary for virtue (Slote 2014, 53). According to Hume (1978), for example, we are motivated to act by desire rather than reason. A virtuous person is someone who is motivated by admirable feelings and desires. Reason is employed in the service of desire: we use rationality in order to achieve the things we desire. We can do so effectively or ineffectively, but whether or not we deserve moral praise or blame depends on the nature of our desires, whether we truly want what is good. Slote (2001, 34) appears to follow Hume in this regard, for he claims that if someone is capable of learning how to help others but fails to do so, we have reason to doubt whether she really wants to help them.

2.3 A Pluralistic Theory

Christine Swanton is the leading proponent of a pluralistic theory of virtue. She gives the following, very general definition of virtue:

> A *virtue* is a good quality of character, more specifically a disposition to respond to, or acknowledge, items within its field or fields in an excellent or good enough way.
>
> (2003, 19)

What all the virtues have in common, in Swanton's view, is that they involve responding well to the demands of the world. Upon closer examination, however, Swanton thinks there are important differences between them. Each virtue has what Swanton calls a field – those items that are the sphere of concern of the virtue. The items in a virtue's field make demands on us, and virtue is a disposition to respond well to these demands. So, for instance, temperance involves responding well to bodily pleasures, and courage involves responding well to dangerous situations (Swanton 2003, 20). One way in which her theory is pluralistic is that it recognizes many modes of moral responsiveness. We can respond well by *promoting* or bringing about something of value: the virtue of benevolence involves responding to others' needs by promoting their good. But Swanton notes that there are various other modes of moral responsiveness, such as *appreciating* the value of an artwork, nature, or the efforts of others, *respecting* an individual in virtue of her status, *creating* a work of art, and *honoring* rules of justice. Swanton draws attention to the fact that we are not only agents of change, focused on bringing about or promoting good states of affairs. Responding well often involves a more passive or less task-oriented response, such as appreciating valuable things.

The most important aspect of virtue-ethical pluralism concerns the nature of the items responded to. Swanton thinks there are at least four such features, which allows us to distinguish four fundamentally different kinds of virtue.[5] First, some traits are virtues because they involve responding well to *value*. Value-based virtues are associated with promoting, enhancing, or maintaining valuable things. Examples include courage, which involves promoting or protecting valuable things or causes, as well as some environmental virtues, which are aimed at preserving and sustaining valuable things in our environment, like beaches, forests, rock formations and so on. It is tempting to think of value-based virtues in consequentialist terms, i.e., that their value derives from their usefulness in bringing about good ends. But Swanton thinks this would be a mistake, because some value-based virtues do not involve bringing about good consequences but merely appreciating value. For example, connoisseurship is a virtue because it involves taking joy in things such as landscapes, sunsets, and art (Swanton 2003, 34–42; Swanton 2015c, 214).

Second, *flourishing-based virtues* are aimed at the good of sentient beings. Charity, benevolence, and generosity are virtues because they involve responding appropriately to the good of others. Swanton notes that the "good for" is distinct from value; there is a difference between something's being good, that is, valuable in itself, and something being good for someone in the sense of promoting or facilitating her flourishing. A benevolent person does not respond to valuable properties or the value of states of affairs, but rather, to what is good *for* sentient beings. Further, flourishing-based virtues require a very specific form of knowledge. To be able to promote someone's good, one has to have some knowledge of human beings in general but also of a particular human being. A benevolent person will aware that something can be good for one person but not for another (Swanton 2003, 47–48; Swanton 2015c, 215).

The third group of virtues involves responding well to the *status* of individuals. One can have status as an elder, a married person, a parent, a political leader, a confidant, or simply as a human being. Traits such as justice, loyalty or fidelity, obedience, (appropriate) deference, consideration, and politeness are virtues because they involve responding appropriately to status. Justice involves respecting a person because of her status as someone who has a due, whether contractual or otherwise. Fidelity involves respecting a person in virtue of her status as someone to whom a promise has been made. And politeness involves respecting a person simply because she has feelings and sensitivities (Swanton 2003, 44–47; Swanton 2015c, 214).

Finally, some virtues involve an appropriate response to relationships or *bonds*. A bond is not a property of an individual but rather an emotional tie between two or more individuals. It is something we engage in. Bond-based virtues include compassion, friendship, and parental love. They express our nature as creatures who form relationships. To illustrate how bonds are distinctive from value as a ground of virtue, Swanton uses the example of grief. Whether or not grief is an appropriate or virtuous response does not depend on the value of the person grieved for, but rather on the relationship between the person grieving and the person being grieved for (Swanton 2003, 42–43; Swanton 2015c, 215).

Given that there are fundamental differences in the modes of moral responsiveness as well as in the items responded to, Swanton thinks it is a mistake to claim that specific inner states, such as "warm" motives or practical wisdom, are a necessary condition for all the virtues. She accepts that all virtues express fine inner states, and that a virtuous person is someone who has a standing commitment to acting from virtue. But what counts as a fine or appropriate inner state depends on the virtue in question. Virtues like benevolence and care require certain kinds of feelings, but the same is not true of status-based virtues. With regards to practical wisdom, Swanton claims that although it is characteristically important, there is a significant category of virtue that requires creativity rather than wisdom (2003, ch. 7).

2.4 A Consequentialist Theory

Consequentialists tend to focus on two moral concepts: right action and good consequences. Their central claim is that rightness depends, in some way or another, on consequences. This has invited the objection that they neglect or ignore character, which is an important aspect of moral life. In recent years, philosophers like Thomas Hurka (2001) and Julia Driver (2001) have responded to this objection by providing distinctively consequentialist theories of virtue. Although they accept that virtue is important, they don't think it is a central or primary moral concept. Instead, they argue that the most plausible theory of virtue is one that defines it in terms of good consequences or states of affairs. In what follows, we will focus on Driver's theory of virtue.

Driver defines virtue as a character trait that systematically produces more good than not in the actual world (2001, 82). She notes that there is strong intuitive support for this idea:

> When we ask ourselves the question "Why is x a virtue?" we do not respond by saying things like "x displays good intentions"; rather, we point to external factors, that is, those consequences actually produced by the trait in a systematic fashion.
>
> (2001, xvii)

An obvious problem for a consequentialist theory of virtue is the phenomenon of moral luck. If virtue is an admirable trait, then we cannot judge the moral quality of a person's character solely on the basis of the actual consequences produced, given that these are not fully within their control. As we've seen, one of Slote's main reasons for preferring an agent-based theory of virtue is that it avoids the problem of moral luck. Driver shares this concern, but she thinks a consequentialist can avoid the problem without sacrificing the intuition that virtues are traits that produce good consequences. She thinks it is important that we hold people responsible for consequences and not just inner states, because this will make us more aware and cautious about the impact of our actions on others. Driver attempts to minimize the role of luck by holding that the virtues are character traits that systematically, but not infallibly, produce good effects. If an agent is the kind of person who often helps others, she deserves to be praised as a benevolent person, on the grounds that she possesses a trait that systematically produces good consequences. We don't have to withdraw our praise when we discover that her attempts to help others are not always successful. On these occasions, we might judge the act in question as wrong, given its consequences, while still praising the agent as good. Consequentialism allows us to separate judgment of character from judgment of action. An action can be wrong even though the agent is not blameworthy.

As to the role of intelligence, Driver accepts that some virtues require a form of knowledge and/or skill. What makes a trait a virtue is that it systematically produces good consequences, and intelligence is often a means to this end. In the case of benevolence, for example, one would not be able to bring about good effects in a reliable manner without possessing some form of knowledge and skill. However, Driver argues that it is a mistake to think, as Aristotelians do, that intelligence or "correct perception" is required for every virtue (2001, xiv). There are some virtues that produce good effects exactly because they involve a form of ignorance. Driver refers to these as "virtues of ignorance," and she gives as examples the virtues of modesty, blind charity, and trust. Genuine modesty, in Driver's view, requires that the agent underestimates her self-worth to some extent (2001, 16–17). Modest people make us feel at ease precisely because they are unaware of the significance of their own accomplishments.[6] Similarly, she argues that a blindly charitable person is one who fails to see all that is bad in others (Driver 2001, 28).

It follows from this that other inner states, such as good motivation or deriving pleasure from virtuous action, are not necessary for virtue either. Driver thinks that the psychological requirements placed on virtue by Aristotelians are too rigid and unrealistically demanding. She agrees that some virtues involve good motives by definition. A generous person is motivated by care or concern for others. If a person often benefits others but without caring about their welfare, we might call her beneficent but not generous. So what makes a trait an example of generosity (rather than, say, beneficence) is that it involves certain kinds of motive, but what makes generosity a virtue is not that it involves good motives but that it has good consequences. Driver points out that not all virtues involve good motivation. For example, she claims that "a person can be just, or fair in his dealings with others, without having kind thoughts toward them or without being motivated to aid them. Rather, the motive could be self-interest, the intention one of avoiding unpleasant interactions with others" (Driver 2001, 57). Another example is the virtue of sensitivity. Driver claims that a doctor may be sensitive in administering treatment to children, but be motivated by a desire to be paid well or attract more patients.

2.5 A Kantian Theory

Although it used to be common for moral philosophers to focus almost exclusively on Kant's theory of right action, a growing number of contemporary Kantians, including Marcia Baron, Barbara Herman, and Allan Wood, have turned their attention to Kant's theory of virtue. To understand the role of virtue in Kantian thought it is important to keep in mind that Kant comes to the question, What is virtue? with a theory of right action already in place. In Part I of *The Metaphysics of Morals*, Kant argues that the rightness of an action does not depend on its actual or expected consequences but on the nature of the action itself, more specifically, on whether it is in accordance with moral duty.

In Part II of *The Metaphysics of Morals*, entitled the *Doctrine of Virtue*, Kant describes virtue as a disposition to do one's duty out of respect for the moral law. It is a kind of *strength* or power:

> the moral strength of a *human being's* will in fulfilling his *duty*, a moral *constraint* through his own lawgiving reason, insofar as this constitutes itself an authority *executing* the law.
>
> (Kant 1996, 6:405)

Reason is involved in determining what is right to do, but we encounter many temptations and opposing inclinations that stand in the way of our acting in accordance with duty. A virtuous person is one who has the inner strength to resist these temptations and inclinations in order to perform her duty. Kant thinks that although our fundamental will may be good, in the sense that we may have a basic commitment to subordinate self-interest to duty, we still have a tendency to weakness of will. We therefore need to cultivate virtue, that is, to strengthen our will so that we don't give in to temptation. Thus, to be virtuous is to have a good will that is firmly resolved and fully ready to overcome the temptations of immorality. This includes, for example, helping others when one lacks the inclination to help, and refraining from suicide when one has lost the inclination to continue living.

Kant rejects a consequentialist theory of virtue for the same reason that Slote does, namely, that if we were to judge character based on consequences, then a person's moral worth would be subject to luck. In a well-known passage in the *Groundwork of the Metaphysics of Morals*, Kant writes:

> A good will is good not because of what it effects, or accomplishes, not because of its fitness to attain some intended end, but good just by its

willing, i.e. in itself; and, considered by itself, it is to be esteemed beyond compare much higher than anything that could ever be brought about by it in favour of some inclination, and indeed, if you will, the sum of all inclinations. Even if by some particular disfavour of fate, or by the scanty endowment of a stepmotherly nature, this will should entirely lack the capacity to carry through its purpose; if despite its greatest striving it should still accomplish nothing, and only the good will were to remain (not, of course, as a mere wish, but as the summoning of all means that are within our control); then, like a jewel, it would still shine by itself, as something that has its full worth in itself.

(2011, 4:394)

It is worth emphasizing that the powerlessness of the good will that Kant refers to here is not moral weakness (caving in to temptation) but causal power to bring about intended effects. Kant's point is that virtue does not depend on one's accomplishments or success in achieving the good results that one earnestly strives for. Sometimes the outcome is the best evidence we have of someone's intentions, but it doesn't follow that the consequences determine the worth of the action (Cureton and Hill 2014, 93).

Like Slote, then, Kant bases virtue in an inner state or good motivation. But whereas Slote believes that good sentiment is the appropriate moral motivation, Kant argues that feelings and innate dispositions are not the kind of things that constitute moral goodness. They are aspects of ourselves that we simply find ourselves having. I might just find myself incredibly irritated by my elderly parents' constant demands and excessive neediness, and despite my best efforts, be unable to muster up any real enthusiasm for returning their phone calls or paying them a visit, and yet end up doing just that from a sense of duty. It would be unfair to judge me on the basis of the feelings I happen to have and cannot control. Instead, I deserve admiration for my commitment to doing what is right. Our feelings or sentiments do not necessarily reflect what we choose to commit ourselves to. We cannot choose our natural dispositions and feelings, but we can choose what to do.

An important difference between Kantians and Aristotelians concerns the role and nature of practical wisdom. Practical judgment, in Kant's view, is the ability to discern what moral principles require in a particular case. It is a capacity distinct from virtue, which consists in strength of character in following moral principles. In Kant's view, a person can be virtuous or morally strong in doing what they believe to be right, but not be wise in their judgments. Conversely, they could have good practical judgment but be morally weak and therefore lacking in virtue (see Wood 2015, 310). In both cases, the agent fails to do what is right, but for very different reasons: in the first case, they are mistaken about what duty requires, whereas in the second, they lack the strength of will – or virtue – to do what duty requires. By contrast, Aristotelians think practical wisdom and good motivation are both essential for virtue. Furthermore, they have a very different view of what practical wisdom involves: it is not a matter of identifying and applying moral principles but a complex set of skills or moral sensitivity that allows them to figure out how to respond in particular situations.

A final point to note about Kant's view has to do with the link between virtue and happiness. As we've seen, Aristotelians claim that the virtues allow their possessor to live well or flourish. Kant recognizes that living virtuously is beneficial in many ways. Virtue, as a kind of strength or power, sets us free. It allows us to subject our desires and inclinations to our own free choices and not be the slave of impulse or habit. It also allows us to achieve inner peace and self-mastery through a firm commitment to moral principles. The ability to control our desires can have obvious benefits for our physical health, because we will be less likely to give in to our desires for unhealthy or unnecessary things. But more importantly, a virtuous person is rewarded by "a moral pleasure that goes beyond mere contentment with oneself … and which is celebrated in the saying that, through consciousness of this pleasure, virtue is its own reward" (Kant 1996, 6:391). Kant's point seems to be that virtue makes us worthy of others' admiration. When they recognize our worth it brings both contentment and pleasure. Kant refers to this as "sweet merit," and he contrasts it with "bitter merit," when people do not recognize our worth, in which case we experience contentment but not pleasure (1996, 6:391). Despite mentioning some of the benefits of virtue, Kant accepts a virtuous person could end up lonely, despised, and unhappy, whereas the vicious could enjoy a prosperous and happy life. But this should not affect one's commitment to morality, for to advocate a virtuous life on the grounds that it leads to happiness is to give the wrong reason for living virtuously (see Cureton and Hill 2014, 97; Wood 2015, 315).

Chapter Summary

- Aristotelian virtue ethicists like Rosalind Hursthouse and Julia Annas put forward the most demanding conception of virtue. In this view, the virtues are reliable dispositions to have the right emotions and attitudes, and to act for the right reasons. The virtues are human excellences: they are what make someone a good human being. Virtue requires fine inner states, including practical wisdom and a commitment to what is good. What makes a character trait a virtue is that it characteristically benefits its possessor by allowing her to live well or flourish as a human being.

- According to sentimentalists like Michael Slote, what makes a trait a virtue is that it involves having and acting from admirable sentiments, such as benevolence, gratitude, compassion, and love. Slote denies that practical wisdom is required for virtue. He also denies that there is a strong link between virtue and the agent's happiness or flourishing. Since the moral life need not involve competently caring for the self, it is possible to live a morally decent life without thereby flourishing. Although the virtues typically produce good consequences, the moral value of a trait does not depend on its consequences. Good moral sentiment, such as kindness and compassion, is all that is required for virtue.

- Christine Swanton defines virtue as a disposition to respond well to the demands of the world, for example, by promoting or appreciating value, honoring something, respecting someone, or creating something. She gives a pluralistic theory of what makes a trait a virtue. The grounds of virtue include the value of an object, the good (or flourishing) of a living being, the status of an individual, and the relationships between people. Different traits are virtues for different reasons. She denies that specific inner states, such as practical wisdom or warm sentiments, are required for each and every virtue. Some virtues require creativity rather than practical wisdom, and some virtues, such as those grounded in status, require respect rather than love or concern.

- Julia Driver puts forward a consequentialist theory of virtue, according to which a virtue is a character trait that systematically (but not invariably) produces good consequences in this world. She denies that practical wisdom or other inner states, such as good motivation or deriving pleasure from virtuous action, are required for every virtue. What makes a trait a virtue is the fact that it typically produces good consequences.

- Kant describes virtue as a disposition to do one's duty out of respect for the moral law. It is a kind of strength or power that allows one to resist temptation and to do what duty requires. Kant emphasizes the role of rationality in morality. In his view, practical judgment is the ability to discern what duty requires. It is a capacity distinct from virtue. A person can be virtuous or morally strong in doing what they consider to be right, but not be wise in their judgments. Kant accepts that virtuous people are often happy people, but he rejects the view that virtue can be grounded in happiness.

- In the discussion of these five accounts of virtue, we have identified a number of central questions about the nature of virtue and its link with other concepts. These questions will be examined in the chapters that follow.

a   What is the connection between virtue and happiness? Are virtuous people typically happier than vicious ones? Can we identify virtues as those traits that are necessary for human beings to live a good or happy life? (Chapter 3)

b   Are virtuous people (always or usually) well-motivated? And what is involved in being well-motivated – being moved by good sentiments, good reasons, or both? (Chapter 4)

c   Do all the virtues require practical wisdom? And what is practical wisdom? (Chapter 5)

d   Is there a link between virtue and right action? Can right action be defined in terms of virtue? (Chapter 6).

Notes

1   We will consider the role of emotion and reason in more detail in Chapter 4.
2   For further discussion, see Chapter 5.
3   We will discuss the link between virtue and happiness in Chapter 3.
4   Not all sentimentalists are virtue ethicists. For example, Hutcheson thinks that universal benevolence is a morally good motive in itself and without reference to consequences. But his account of right action is consequentialist, for he claims that a right action is one that achieves the goals sought by universal benevolence, rather than the agent's motive or her moral character (Slote 2014, 55).
5   As we will see in Chapter 3, Aristotelians agree with Swanton that there are many modes of moral responsiveness. But they disagree about what Swanton refers to as the grounds of virtue. That is, they have different responses to the question, What makes a trait a virtue? Aristotelians argue that what makes a trait a virtue is that it is needed for happiness, whereas Swanton thinks there are at least four distinctive grounds of virtue.
6   We will discuss Driver's conception of modesty and the role of practical wisdom in Chapter 5.

Further Reading

Annas, Julia. 2006. "Virtue Ethics." In *The Oxford Handbook of Ethical Theory*, edited by David Copp, 515–536. New York: Oxford University Press.

Annas, Julia. 2011. *Intelligent Virtue*. Oxford: Oxford University Press, chapter 2.

Aristotle. 2009. *The Nicomachean Ethics*. Translated by David Ross, revised by Lesley Brown. Oxford: Oxford University Press.

Bennett, Christopher. 2010. *What Is This Thing Called Ethics?* Abingdon: Routledge.

Cureton, Adam, and Thomas Hill. 2014. "Kant on Virtue and the Virtues." In *Cultivating Virtue: Perspectives from Philosophy, Theology, and Psychology*, edited by Nancy E. Snow, 87–110. Oxford: Oxford University Press.

Driver, Julia. 2001. *Uneasy Virtue*. Cambridge: Cambridge University Press, chapter 4.

Frazer, Michael L. and Michael Slote. 2015. "Sentimentalist Virtue Ethics." In *The Routledge Companion to Virtue Ethics*, edited by Lorraine Besser-Jones and Michael Slote, 197–208. New York: Routledge.

Hill, Thomas E., Jr. 2008. "Kantian Virtue and 'Virtue Ethics.'" In *Kant's Ethics of Virtue*, edited by Monika Betzler, 29–59. Berlin: Walter de Gruyter.

Hume, David. 1978. *A Treatise of Human Nature.* 2nd ed. Edited by L. A. Selby-Bigge with text revised and variant readings by P. H. Nidditch. Oxford: Oxford University Press.

Hurka, Thomas. 2001. *Virtue, Vice, and Value.* Oxford: Oxford University Press.

Hursthouse, Rosalind. 1999. *On Virtue Ethics.* Oxford: Oxford University Press.

Hursthouse, Rosalind. 2006b. "Are Virtues the Proper Starting Point for Morality?" In *Contemporary Debates in Moral Theory*, edited by James Dreier, 99–112. Malden, MA: Blackwell.

Hursthouse, Rosalind, and Glen Pettigrove. 2016. "Virtue Ethics." *The Stanford Encyclopedia of Philosophy.* https://plato.stanford.edu/archives/win2016/entries/ethics-virtue/.

Johnson, Robert N. 2008. "Was Kant a Virtue Ethicist?" In *Kant's Ethics of Virtue*, edited by Monika Betzler, 61–75. Berlin: Walter de Gruyter.

Kant, Immanuel. 1996. *The Metaphysics of Morals.* Edited and translated by Mary Gregor. Cambridge: Cambridge University Press.

Kant, Immanuel. 2011. *Groundwork of the Metaphysics of Morals.* Edited and translated by Mary Gregor and Jens Timmermann. Cambridge: Cambridge University Press.

Korsgaard, Christine. 1996. "From Duty and for the Sake of the Noble: Kant and Aristotle on Morally Good Action." In *Aristotle, Kant, and the Stoics: Rethinking Happiness and Duty*, edited by Stephen Engstrom and Jennifer Whiting, 203–236. Cambridge: Cambridge University Press.

Sherman, Nancy. 1997. *Making a Necessity of Virtue: Aristotle and Kant on Virtue.* Cambridge: Cambridge University Press.

Slote, Michael. 2001. *Morals from Motives.* New York: Oxford University Press.

Slote, Michael. 2010. *Moral Sentimentalism.* Oxford: Oxford University Press.

Slote, Michael. 2014. "Virtue Ethics and Moral Sentimentalism." In *The Handbook of Virtue Ethics*, edited by Stan van Hooft, Nafsika Athanassoulis, Jason Kawall, Justin Oakley, Nicole Saunders, and Liezl van Zyl, 53–63. Abingdon and New York: Routledge.

Stocker, Michael, and Elizabeth Hegeman. 1996. *Valuing Emotions.* Cambridge: Cambridge University Press.

Swanton, Christine. 2003. *Virtue Ethics: A Pluralistic View.* Oxford: Oxford University Press.

Swanton, Christine. 2015c. "Pluralistic Virtue Ethics." In *The Routledge Companion to Virtue Ethics*, edited by Lorraine Besser-Jones and Michael Slote, 209–222. New York: Routledge.

Wood, Allen. 2015. "Kant and Virtue Ethics." In *The Routledge Companion to Virtue Ethics*, edited by Lorraine Besser-Jones and Michael Slote, 307–320. New York: Routledge.

3 Virtue and Happiness

Consider the life of a billionaire, whom we shall call Archibald. Having inherited a fortune, Archibald is free to live life exactly as he pleases. He spends his days surrounded by beautiful people who laugh at his jokes and cater to his every desire. He enjoys activities like sailing in his luxury yacht, playing high stakes poker, collecting vintage cars, and drinking fine wine. He avoids "deep" relationships, because these can get messy, and he pays assistants, lawyers, accountants, and other professionals to take care of any unpleasant or boring business (e.g. filing tax returns, paying bills, and making hotel reservations). Some people would say he is "living the dream": he is having an immense amount of fun, while also avoiding many of the troubles that most of us have to deal with in our everyday lives: worries about money, long working days and boring commutes, relationship issues, domestic chores, and so on.

In looking at Archibald's life from an ethical perspective, the tendency among modern moral philosophers has been to focus on assessing particular actions he performs. A deontologist will focus on his treatment of other people: Does he deceive, manipulate, or exploit others, thereby using them as mere means to his own ends? A consequentialist, in turn, will be interested in the consequences of his actions: What effect does his decision to spend all his time and money indulging his own desires, rather than helping other people in need, have on the overall amount of happiness in the world? But there is a different way in which we can look at Archibald's life, which is to ask the following sorts of question: Is he really living a good life? Is the life he has chosen for himself the best one possible? Is there anything lacking in his life?

The view that ethical inquiry begins with the question, What is the best life for human beings? is known as *eudaimonism* (derived from the Greek term, *eudaimonia*, roughly, a good life for human beings). The ancient eudaimonists (most notably Aristotle, Plato, and the Stoics) consider various possible answers to this question, including: a pleasant and exciting life; a life of health and prosperity; a life of active public service and civic achievement; and a life devoted to family and friends in the pursuit of common ends. They reject all these versions of eudaimonism and instead support a position that has become known as *eudaimonistic virtue ethics*, that is, the view that the best life for human beings requires possession and exercise of the virtues. Our focus in this book will be on Aristotelian virtue ethics, as it is by far the most popular version of eudaimonism among contemporary virtue ethicists.[1] To appreciate the Aristotelian view of the nature and role of virtuous motivation, practical wisdom, and right or virtuous action, which will be explored in the following chapters, it is necessary to understand the link it makes between virtue and *eudaimonia*.

The first task in this chapter is to clarify the concept of *eudaimonia*. In the second section, we will briefly consider three possible answers to the question, What is *eudaimonia*? and note why both ancient and contemporary eudaimonists reject these answers. This will lead to a discussion of eudaimonistic virtue ethics, of the kind put forward by Rosalind Hursthouse, Julia Annas, and Daniel Russell, as well as a consideration of two important objections to eudaimonistic virtue ethics.

3.1 The Concept of *Eudaimonia*

The Greek term *eudaimonia* is usually translated as "happiness" or "flourishing," but contemporary eudaimonists are quick to point out that neither translation is entirely satisfactory. We often think of happiness as a passing mood or feeling. I can feel very happy while eating my Sloppy Joe with coleslaw, but my good mood might have passed by the time I realize it is my turn to do the dishes. This kind of happiness is entirely subjective: If I feel happy then I must be happy; it is not something I can be mistaken about. As we'll see, following Plato and Aristotle, contemporary eudaimonists believe that one can be mistaken about whether one's life is *eudaimon: eudaimonia* is not an entirely subjective state. The term "flourishing" is preferable to "happiness" in this regard. I can believe that I'm flourishing, that I'm doing well, but be mistaken. The disadvantage of "flourishing" is that plants and animals can also flourish, whereas *eudaimonia* is a good life for human beings; it is only possible for rational beings. Most eudaimonists settle on the term "happiness," but point out that they use the term in a very specific, objective sense, to refer to something like "true (or real) happiness," "the sort of happiness worth having" (Hursthouse 1999, 9–10) or "happiness in a worthwhile life" (Badhwar 2014). Robert Roberts uses an interesting thought experiment to illustrate the difference between happiness as a passing feeling, that is, an attribute of moments in a person's experience, or what he calls "positive affective time-slice happiness" (Roberts 2015, 37), and true happiness, that is, happiness as an attribute of persons. He asks us to imagine being hooked up to a happiness machine:

> This machine stimulates pleasure centers in one's brain in such a way as to give one pleasure reminiscent of a cocaine high, but so that it does no damage and the experience is always utterly "fresh": you never get tired of it. You can be in ecstasy during your whole waking day, and continue (at a lower voltage) with ecstatic dreams through the night. When you're on the machine, you can't do anything else (work, write, play the piano, interact with other humans), and further, you don't want to; you're completely satisfied. You'll have to get off the machine every now and then to eat, get some exercise, and perform necessary bodily functions, but having once experienced it, you'll always be in a big hurry to get back on it. With such a routine, and given the bodily harmlessness of the machine's action, a person who was wealthy enough not to have to work could spend seventy, eighty, ninety, or a hundred years on the machine, thus having the "happiest" possible life of any human being in history.
>
> (Roberts 2015, 38–39)

If happiness consisted only of pleasant feelings, then we would all prefer to be hooked up to the happiness machine. Even the most pleasant life, one in which the subject experiences the joys of meaningful work, good relationships, taking on risky or challenging projects, and so forth, would contain fewer pleasant moments than a life on the pleasure machine, for these activities all carry their moments of frustration and discomfort (Roberts 2015, 39). Would a wise or rational person choose to live their life on such a machine? Roberts thinks they would not, despite its superiority in terms of positive affective time-slice happiness:

> They would not regard it as a good human life, not even as assessed solely from the point of view of the one living the life. What might the wise say in favor of resisting the machine's allure? "Pleasure without meaning is empty" (they don't deny that it can be intense, and very attractive, even overwhelmingly so). "A life on the machine would be a selfish life." "It would not be a worthy life." Worthy of what? – "Worthy of a human being." These are some of the intuitions that a wise person is likely to feel, on contemplating a human life lived for the momentary pleasures of the happiness machine.
>
> (2015, 39)

In short, then, when eudaimonists ask, What is happiness? they are not using the term "happiness" to refer to pleasant feelings. Instead, they are interested in the question, What is a good or worthy life for human beings?

Julia Annas explains the concept of *eudaimonia* by asking us to consider the Greek idea of the *telos* or overall goal in life. The assumption among ancient eudaimonists is that there must be an ultimate aim for the sake of which we pursue other ends. Most of the time, we are focused on achieving specific goals, like passing an exam or training for a marathon. Ethical reflection starts when we begin to think about what our aims are, and how these fit into a good life. While undergoing the hardship and sacrifice involved in preparing for an exam, I might wonder, Why am I doing this? Is it worth the trouble? The answer might be, I need to pass this exam to become a lawyer. But this leads to a further question: Why do I want to become a lawyer? Well, it could be that I want to make a contribution to society (or earn a high salary, or whatever). But again, I could ask myself, Why do I want to contribute to society? This line of questioning will lead to ever more general answers, and will eventually end with something like, I do this in order to be happy, to live a good or worthwhile life. The final end for the sake of which we pursue all other goals, then, is what eudaimonists refer to as true happiness or *eudaimonia*. At first we might only have a very vague idea of what our "final end" is, thinking of it only as "a good life" or "a life lived well." The point of ethical reflection is to achieve a better understanding of *eudaimonia* as my ultimate goal in life (see Annas 2011, 123; Russell 2013b). Working through this process might well lead me to reassess my plans and projects. If I realize that my main reason for wanting to become a lawyer is that it is what my parents expect of me, I will do well to question whether preparing for the exam is worth the trouble.

3.2 Different Conceptions of *Eudaimonia*

Having defined the concept of *eudaimonia* as "true happiness," "a good or worthwhile human life," or "the highest human good," we encounter two further questions: What does *eudaimonia* consist of? And how can I achieve it? An accurate conception of *eudaimonia* is supposed to allow us to come up with better answers to the more specific questions that confront us in our everyday lives. Consider the following case. Theodore is a working parent who manages to juggle the demands of his career and raising his children while also finding time to do the other things he is passionate about, namely fishing, playing football, and going to the opera. One day he is offered a promotion at work, and suddenly these ends come into conflict: accepting the promotion will bring about enhanced status and a bigger salary, but also less time for family and other pursuits. And so Theodore is faced with the difficult decision: Do I accept the offer, or carry on as before? To make the right decision, Theodore needs to figure out what is important or worthwhile in life. Which of these things – status, money, a rewarding career, family, and recreational pursuits – really matter? Which of them are important in themselves, and which are good only as means to other ends? And how should he organize his life to include as many as possible of the things that do matter? In short, he needs to have a correct understanding of *eudaimonia*, and he needs to figure out how he can achieve such a life, given his particular circumstances.

One difficulty we encounter when trying to answer the questions, What is *eudaimonia*? and How can we achieve it? is to find an answer that is sufficiently general to apply to all human beings, while still being specific enough to provide answers to the questions we are faced with in everyday life. Consider the following conception of *eudaimonia*, presented by Theodore's well-meaning friend:

> True happiness is only found in family life, through the intimacy we share with those we love. Earning an income and taking care of your health are just means to this end, and anything that comes in the way of a good family life is bad.

This conception of happiness has the advantage that it is specific enough to guide Theodore in his decision-making. But its specificity is also its downfall. Family life cannot be *the* good life for human beings. Not everyone has (or wants to have) a family to devote themselves to, and we certainly don't want to say that true happiness is not available to these people. The same problem will arise, it seems, no matter what conception of happiness one advances (such as having a successful career, devoting oneself to the good of the community, etc.). It seems very unlikely that the good life will be the same for everyone. Further, one would expect the answer to the question of how someone should live to come from that person; it cannot take the form of a plan or blueprint that is imposed upon him from the outside. It therefore seems questionable whether anything useful can be said about happiness, something that would be specific enough to guide us in our decision-making, while also being general enough to apply to all human beings (see Russell 2013b).

To avoid this problem, Annas makes a distinction between *the circumstances of a life* and *the living of that life*. The *circumstances of a life* include things like one's age, gender, occupation, marital status, and wealth. Social scientists who study happiness tend to focus on these factors, finding, for example, that people who are employed (or married, educated, etc.) are happier than those who are unemployed (or unmarried, uneducated, etc.). Conceivably, combining these results could show that the happiest people are, say, females who are married and childless and in part-time employment. But this finding is not very helpful in guiding an individual's choices. One reason for this is that the factors that form the circumstances of your life are not fully under your control. As Annas notes, you can change them to some extent, but you cannot bring it about that you are a different age or were presented with different opportunities in life. Another reason is that statistics are not very useful to the individual. Even if it is the case, say, that people who have children are generally happier than people who don't, whether it is a good idea for you to have children depends on facts about you and your individual circumstances. Annas goes on to argue that we should answer the question about what happiness is by thinking about the *living of a life*. Happiness is not a matter of whether you have certain things (e.g. beauty, power, wealth) or are engaged in certain activities (e.g. parenting, recreation, travel). Instead, it is a matter of how well you deal with the circumstances of your life, whatever they might be (Annas 2011, 92–95, 128–131).

If we think about happiness in this way, the following are possible answers to the questions, What is true happiness? and How can I achieve it?

a   A happy life is a successful life, so aim for success in whatever you choose to do.
b   A happy life is a pleasant life, one devoted to the pursuit of pleasure, so find out what gives you pleasure.
c   A happy life is a life of desire-satisfaction, so aim to satisfy your desires, whatever these may be.
d   A happy life is a life of virtuous activity, so try to become virtuous.

Each of these answers can form the basis of a distinct version of eudaimonism. They all have the advantage that they are sufficiently general to allow for differences in the circumstances of people's lives, while still providing some guidance. Consider the first answer as an example. If a happy life is a successful life, then achieving it involves three (not so simple) steps. Step 1: Find something you have a talent for (whether it be golf, pottery, selling real estate, or designing wedding dresses). Step 2: Work hard at developing the skills and traits relevant to that activity. Step 3: Do whatever it takes to succeed in that particular area. So Theodore will have to decide whether he has the best chance of being successful in his career or as a parent. If it is the first, he should focus on developing his professional skills, befriending useful people, and seeking promotions, while leaving everyday parenting duties to someone else (and possibly dropping football for golf). If it is the latter, he should focus on becoming the best parent he can possible be, which will require seeing his career merely as a means to this end. He will also need to consider which of his hobbies are compatible with being a successful parent, and which ones to abandon.

Not surprisingly, eudaimonists reject the view that success can be one's ultimate aim in life. They argue that people pursue success for the sake of something else, such as recognition or admiration, wealth, or a sense of satisfaction. At best, success can be a *means* to true happiness, but it cannot be what happiness consists in. It is not uncommon for very successful people to feel dissatisfied with life, or (usually when it is too late) to come to the realization that success does not bring happiness. A successful life might not be all that *attractive*, for it requires one to neglect or sacrifice other things that are valuable in life, such as one's relationships with friends and family, and to forego activities and enjoyments that do not contribute to success in one's chosen field. And a successful life is not always *admirable*. Not all forms of success are worth pursuing. A CEO of a large tobacco company might well be very successful, but we would be hesitant to describe his life as good or truly happy.

What about Archibald's kind of life – the life devoted to the pursuit of pleasure? As we've seen, eudaimonists distinguish between happiness as a pleasant feeling and true happiness, understood as a good or worthwhile life. But one might still argue that true happiness is found in the activity of pursuing pleasure. Unlike a life spent hooked up to the happiness machine, a life devoted to pleasure or enjoyment is an active life, one that involves making decisions, taking risks, and searching for new and different kinds of pleasure. Such a life is distinctively human. While it will no doubt contain many moments of pain and discomfort (the broken leg from snowboarding, the odd hangover) it is better than life on a happiness machine because it involves choice and activity. To maximize pleasure, Archibald has had to develop various skills and strategies. He has had to learn how to enjoy the pleasures of socializing and drinking fine wine in ways that allow him to avoid the unpleasant feelings that often result from these activities. Although few of us can attain as pleasant a life as Archibald's, we might still see him as a kind of role model, and try to make our lives as pleasant as possible.

Following Plato and Aristotle, Annas argues that pleasure cannot be the ultimate aim in life:

> It's nice to have feelings of pleasure when eating a good meal, and to enjoy activities such as walking or reading, but these feelings vanish when their object does: the pleasure of eating, and the pleasure taken in walking or reading ceases when the eating, walking, or reading does. This can hardly be what matters to us when we think seriously about how to live

our lives. Pleasure is too trivial an item in life to be the most important thing in it, or the goal round which life is organized.

(Annas 2011, 132)

Annas gives give similar reasons for rejecting the claim that desire-satisfaction is our ultimate goal in life. Plato notes that people who seek happiness by fulfilling their desires are constantly trying to fill leaky jars (*Gorgias* 493d–495b). Because our desires recur as often as they are met, satisfaction is ultimately unattainable.

If we are to be happy by fulfilling our desires, and these depend on the existence of needs whose nature it is to recur as often as they are met, then trying to be happy appears to be a hopeless task: whatever we do the jar will never get filled.

(Annas 2011, 135–136)

Most eudaimonists argue in favor of the fourth position, known as eudaimonistic virtue ethics, which is the view that a life of virtuous activity is the most important thing for happiness. This position seems promising, for it gives us a fairly specific idea of how to live (e.g., be courageous, be kind, be honest, etc.) but without imposing upon us someone else's view of which activities we should engage in. For example, we all need to be courageous at times, whatever the circumstances of our lives, for we all encounter situations where we need to conquer fear (of death or injury, of being ridiculed, of losing our possessions, or whatever) in order to achieve some worthwhile goal. And we all need to be honest in order to function well in various roles, whether it be the role of a friend, parent, employer, or citizen. In Theodore's case, he will need to think about whether accepting the offer of a promotion will be consistent with living virtuously. This requires thinking about the kind of work he will be doing. Will it involve deceiving and manipulating people, or convincing them to buy things they don't need? Or will it allow him to make an important or worthwhile contribution to society? He will also have to think about how his family will be affected by the promotion. Will they have to move to a different town, away from friends and family? Will the move disrupt the children's education? Will the extra income allow Theodore to improve their quality of life in ways that really matter (or will it just allow them to buy more electronic gadgets)?

3.3 Eudaimonistic Virtue Ethics

Strictly speaking, the terms "eudaimonism" and "eudaimonistic virtue ethics" do not refer to the same thing. Eudaimonism is the more general view that the starting point for ethical reflection is the question: What is *eudaimonia*? Eudaimonistic virtue ethics is the view that *eudaimonia* is a life lived in accordance with virtue, and Aristotelians are the leading supporters of this view. It is one version of eudaimonism, but by far the most popular one, which is why the terms ("eudaimonism" and "eudaimonistic virtue ethics") are often used interchangeably. For the sake of simplicity, I will follow this usage.

The central claim made by Aristotelian eudaimonists is that a virtuous life is not only admirable but attractive or beneficial. Hursthouse formulates the claim as follows:

> A virtue is a character trait a human being needs for *eudaimonia*, to flourish or live well.
>
> (1999, 167)

But she points out that the central claim is made up of two interrelated theses, namely:

Thesis 1: Virtue benefits its possessor by allowing her to live a good life, that is, to be truly happy as a human being. Seen thus, the central claim is an answer to the question: What is good, for me, about being virtuous? or Why am I happy to be virtuous? and the emphasis is on happiness or *eudaimonia* as an attractive life.

Thesis 2: What makes a trait a virtue is that it is necessary for the happiness of human beings. Seen thus, the central claim is an answer to the question, What makes a trait a virtue rather than a vice? or Why do certain traits – the virtues – make their possessor a good human being? Here the emphasis is on happiness or *eudaimonia* as an admirable life.

In what follows, we will discuss these two theses in turn.

3.3.1 Virtue Benefits Its Possessor

The claim that virtue allows one to live a *good life*, understood as a life that is (morally) admirable or praiseworthy, seems uncontroversial. However, Hursthouse also claims, somewhat more controversially, that virtue benefits or is *good for* its possessor. Virtue allows one to live a life that is good in the sense of being attractive and desirable. An obvious difficulty with this claim is that it just doesn't seem true of all the virtues. Some virtues, such as determination and moderation or temperance, do typically benefit their possessor. Determination allows us to achieve our goals, and temperance allows us to resist being tempted by things that are bad for us. But other virtues, such as benevolence and generosity, are specifically aimed at the good of other people, and might call on the virtuous person to sacrifice her own needs or interests. All other things being equal, a generous person who gives freely of her time and resources is worse off than one who is more tight-fisted. One might want to argue that generous people typically do end up better off, despite sacrificing their short-term interests, because they are rewarded for their generosity in all sorts of ways. But if this argument succeeds, a further problem arises: Linking virtue (or morality) to the agent's happiness seems to commit Aristotelians (and indeed, all eudaimonistic virtue ethicists) to a form of egoism. Morality requires us to consider the good of others, and not to do what comes naturally to most of us, which is to pursue our own good. How, then, is it possible that the ultimate aim of virtuous activity is the agent's own happiness?

We'll set aside the egoism objection for now, and consider whether it is plausible to claim that virtue does in fact benefit its possessor. Hursthouse asks us to consider parents' reasons for teaching their children to be virtuous. Why do good parents raise their children to be kind, honest, and fair? One likely reason is that children who are selfish and disrespectful tend to make their parents – and everyone else – miserable. But Hursthouse suspects their main reason is to benefit the children themselves:

> Good parents have their children's interests at heart. They want to do what is best or good for *them*, the individual children, to enable them to live well, be happy, make a success of their lives. But, having their children's interests at heart, it does not occur to most of them to bring them up to be entirely self-interested and immoral. On the contrary, they see the natural childish impulses to self-gratification and self-indulgence as impulses that need to be modified and redirected, and their natural impulses to love and generosity and fairness as impulses that need to be developed; they see the naturally self-centred perspective of children as something that has to be enlarged – for the child's own sake.
>
> (Hursthouse 1999, 175)

Of course, this fact (if indeed it is a fact) doesn't prove that virtue is necessary for happiness, but it lends some intuitive support to the idea. If we accept that there is some kind of link between virtue and happiness, the next question is: How strong is this link? Are virtuous people always (or necessarily) happier than the non-virtuous?

The ancient Greeks disagreed about the exact nature of the link between virtue and *eudaimonia*. The predominant view, held by Plato and the Stoics, was that virtue is both necessary and sufficient for happiness: a virtuous person will be happy, regardless of any misfortune he might encounter along the way. A central aim of Plato's *Republic* is to show that possession and exercise of the cardinal virtues (namely, justice, wisdom, courage, and moderation) will allow its possessor to be happy, to live a life worthy of a human being. Aristotle, by contrast, argues that virtue is necessary for happiness, but not sufficient: we also need external goods like wealth and health in order to be happy. He has Plato's view in mind when he writes:

> Those who say that the victim on the rack or the man who falls into great misfortunes is happy if he is good are, whether they mean to or not, talking nonsense.
>
> (*The Nicomachean Ethics* 1153b19)

As much as we'd like to believe that virtuous people will always be happy, Aristotelians point out that this is simply not the case. To live a good life one needs to have a reasonable degree of wealth, health, and power. Virtuous activity (hard work, determination, a temperate life style, and so on) can help one achieve or secure these things. But one can also be deprived of these things through no fault of one's own, which means that bad luck can prevent the virtuous person from living happily. So virtue is not sufficient for happiness.

Hursthouse uses an analogy with health to demonstrate the nature of the link between virtue and happiness. Health experts commonly advise us to give up smoking, take regular exercise, and to drink and eat in moderation, on the grounds that this will allow us to be healthy. But following this advice does not guarantee that one will enjoy good health. Some people have good health *despite* ignoring their doctor's advice. But the general claim remains true, namely that a healthy life style is the most reliable means to good health. In much the same way, Hursthouse claims, living virtuously is the most reliable means to a happy life. Virtuous people can expect things to go well for them, and when they don't it is a result of bad luck rather than due to a tendency of the virtue itself:

> [T]he claim is not that possession of the virtues guarantees that one will flourish. The claim is that they are the only reliable bet – even though … I might be unlucky and, precisely because of my virtue, wind up dying early or with my life marred or ruined … . To claim that the virtues, for the most part, benefit their possessor, enabling her to flourish, is not to claim that virtue is necessary for happiness. It is to claim that no "regimen" will serve one better.
>
> (Hursthouse 1999, 172–173)

Although the health analogy is useful in helping us understand the link between virtue and happiness, it is somewhat misleading in other ways. In the case of health, it is possible to make a clear distinction between the means (e.g., a balanced diet, exercise, etc.) and the end (i.e., the state of being healthy). When someone is diagnosed with a disease, the end is good health and the means could be something like following a strict diet and exercise routine, undergoing surgery, or taking medication. In seeking out her doctor's advice, a patient is interested in learning what would be the most effective means to achieve her end. The value of the prescribed regimen depends entirely on its efficacy in bringing about the desired end. If the doctor's advice is to undergo invasive surgery, it makes sense for the patient to seek a second opinion, in the hope of finding a better or easier way to achieve the same end.

Aristotelians do not claim that virtue or virtuous activity is a means to happiness in the same way that taking medication can be a means to good health. That is, they don't think one should act virtuously so that one will (with a bit of luck) be rewarded with happiness sometime in the future. (If it were, it would make sense to ask whether there is an easier way to achieve the same end.) Rather, they believe that virtuous activity partially constitutes happiness. Living virtuously is a way of living happily. Unlike taking medication or undergoing surgery, virtuous activity is worthwhile in itself.

Another way in which the health analogy is misleading is that it suggests that there is a shared or neutral conception of happiness. People who follow a healthy lifestyle generally do not have radically different conceptions of health than those that don't. Everyone (or almost everyone) would agree that being in a state of constant physical pain does not amount to being in a state of good health. Some people *nevertheless* have an unhealthy lifestyle, not because they have a different conception of health but for all sorts of other reasons, including ignorance, lack of willpower, or lack of time, resources, or opportunity, or because they value other things (success, creativity, or wealth) more highly. Because we have a more or less neutral conception of health, it is possible to support advice on how to improve one's health by conducting empirical research. Scientists can prove, for example, that (all other things being equal) reducing sugar consumption will *as a matter of fact* bring about a reduction in the occurrence of diabetes and hence to an improvement in the health of a given group of people.

Eudaimonists don't think there is a neutral conception of happiness, one that everyone – those committed to a virtuous life as well as those who do not care one bit about being a good person – will accept. The most extreme or radical version of this view is the one held by Plato, Socrates, and the Stoics. As mentioned earlier, they believe that virtue is sufficient for happiness. That is, the *only* way in which the virtuous can be harmed is by their own wrongdoing, that is, by a loss of virtue. Most people find this view implausible, because it seems obvious that virtuous people can suffer, and have their lives ruined, by misfortunes that have nothing to do with their own choices or actions. Supporters of the sufficiency view defend it by claiming that the virtuous have a different conception of happiness, and hence of benefit and harm, than the vicious. The vicious consider loss of riches, reputation, and life as harms, but the virtuous do not, and that is why they can only be harmed by their own vicious activity. Hence, for example, Plato famously argues that a life is not worth living if the soul is ruined by wrongdoing (see *The Republic* 445b). To the virtuous, nothing that is gained by vicious action is a genuine benefit – vice is worse than death.

Aristotelians reject the view that the virtuous cannot be harmed by things such as loss of property, injury, or illness. In itself, loss of property does not constitute a harm, but if it prevents one from acting virtuously (e.g. by providing for one's children or giving to charity), then suffering it is a genuine harm. So although virtue is necessary for happiness, it is not sufficient. The virtuous are therefore vulnerable to luck (see *The Nicomachean Ethics* 1099a31–b7). Richard Kraut explains the Aristotelian view as follows:

> If one's ultimate end should simply be virtuous activity, then why should it make any difference to one's happiness whether one has or lacks these other types of good? Aristotle's reply is that one's virtuous activity will be to some extent diminished or defective, if one lacks an adequate supply of other goods (1153b17–19). Someone who is friendless, childless, powerless, weak, and ugly will simply not be able to find many opportunities for virtuous activity over a long period of time, and what little he can accomplish will not be of great merit. To some extent, then, living well requires good fortune; happenstance can rob even the most excellent human beings of happiness. Nonetheless, Aristotle insists, the highest good, virtuous activity, is not something that comes to us by chance. Although we must be fortunate enough to have parents and fellow citizens who help us become virtuous, we ourselves share much of the responsibility for acquiring and exercising the virtues.
>
> (Kraut 2016, section 2)

Although Aristotelians think there is some overlap between the virtuous and the immoralist's conceptions of happiness, benefit, and harm, they agree with Plato and the Stoics that there is no neutral conception. Hursthouse asks us to consider the lives of those who are wealthy and powerful and appear to be perfectly happy, but who lie, cheat, and tread on others. For the immoralist, this kind of life may be desirable, but to the virtuous, it is just not the kind of life they strive for or find attractive

(Hursthouse 1999, 177). Similarly, in the case of Archibald, our billionaire pleasure-seeker, a virtuous person might accept that there are aspects of his life that are attractive (not having to worry about money or the long commute to work), but also point out that Archibald is missing out on many of the things that make life worth living: meaningful work, enduring friendships, creative pursuits. Of course, Archibald himself is unlikely to agree with this – after all, his opportunities are almost unlimited, and this is the life he has chosen for himself.

One implication of this is that, unlike in the case of good health, we cannot turn to empirical science in order to *prove* that virtue benefits its possessor. The eudaimonist thesis (that virtue benefits its possessor) is not a straightforwardly empirical claim. Hursthouse writes:

> There is no possibility of "justifying morality from the outside" by appealing to anything "non-moral," or by finding a neutral point of view that the fairly virtuous and the wicked can share. We may say ... that the greedy and dishonest are not *eudaimon*, not truly happy, that they are missing out on "joy and warmth," but when we do, we are not making a merely empirical remark, based on the observation that all of them go round with long faces saying, "Oh, woe is me." We are, in part, saying, "That's not the sort of life *I* count as *eudaimon*, because it does not involve the exercise of the virtues."
>
> (1999, 179)

Consider, again, Hursthouse's observation that good parents raise their children to be virtuous. In an attempt to falsify this claim, someone might point out that there are many loving parents who want their children to be happy, but who don't encourage them to be benevolent and honest. Instead, they might teach them the skills needed for attaining fame and fortune: how to avoid paying taxes, how to manipulate influential people, how to attract media attention, and so on. Should we, in light of this, reject the claim that good parents raise their children to be virtuous, and hence that virtue does not contribute to happiness? Aristotelians would respond as follows: These people are not really good parents. They value wealth and fame over virtue, and what they want for their children is not what we consider to be true happiness. In a sense, then, Aristotelians believe that a virtuous life just is an attractive life. It follows that they cannot use the claim that the virtues benefit their possessor to convince immoralists to change their ways and to adopt a life of virtue instead. Such an attempt is likely to fail: the immoralist will not find a virtuous life attractive. He just doesn't see things like friendship, honesty, and the good of others, as valuable in themselves.

3.3.2 Virtues and the Happiness of Human Beings

When asked to produce a list of traits they consider to be virtues, most people will include honesty, courage, kindness, justice, and fairness. But there is likely to be some variation. Should we include traits like competitiveness, tidiness, and wittiness in our list of virtues? Some critics of virtue ethics object that whether a given trait is considered a virtue is entirely relative to the group or culture one belongs to. For example, it could be the case that good teachers and nurses need to be kind and compassionate, but that these same traits are vices in professional athletes or businesspeople, who need to be ambitious, competitive, and ruthless in order to succeed. Further, people might agree that a particular trait is a virtue, but have different conceptions of what that virtue involves. In the case of courage, they might disagree about whether a person who risks his life to make a funny video can be called courageous.

To resolve these kinds of disagreement, we need to have an account of what makes a trait a virtue. Hursthouse's central claim, namely that "[a] virtue is a character trait a human being needs for *eudaimonia*, to flourish or live well" (1999, 167) is a response to this question. In her view, the virtues should be identified as those traits that make their possessor good *as a human being*. Virtues are human excellences; they involve functioning well as a human being. This position is known as *ethical naturalism*, roughly, the view that ethics can be based on a conception of human nature (see Foot 2001; Hursthouse 1999, Part II).

To illustrate this view, consider the virtue of honesty. It seems safe to say that honesty doesn't play an important role in the lives of animals. For humans, however, it is crucially important. Honesty makes it possible for people to trust each other, and hence, to make plans for the future, to form intimate relationships, to acquire knowledge, and so on. A society in which most people are dishonest will be a very difficult one to live in, for it will require everything to be locked away, everyone to be searched, and no-one to be taken at their word (Hursthouse 1999, 168–169). Given facts about human nature, in particular our being rational, social, and emotional beings, honesty is a trait that human beings need in order to live well.

It is for this reason that Aristotelians deny that wittiness and tidiness are virtues. They can be useful traits, and it can be pleasant to have witty or tidy people around. But they are not required for living well as a human being in the same way that honesty, courage, and kindness are. Tidy people prefer things to be neat and organized, and they might even say things like, "I cannot bear to live in a messy house." But most tidy people will readily accept that it is a matter of personal preference – some people feel more comfortable in a more ordered environment, whereas others prefer a bit of clutter. Annas notes, in this regard, that wittiness and tidiness do not involve a commitment to the good; they are not *"deep* feature[s]" of a person (2011, 102).

Reflecting on the role of honesty in human society also allows us to answer the more specific question, namely, What is the virtue of honesty? Honesty cannot simply be a matter of always telling the truth, for the simple reason that compulsive truth-telling is not the kind of trait that allows us to achieve important aims. Instead, the virtue of honesty is a more complex disposition, requiring a sense of when and why it is appropriate to tell the truth, and of why knowing the truth is important.

Thinking about what is required for living a good human life lends support to the Aristotelian conception of virtue outlined in Chapter 2. Virtue, as a human excellence, involves:

a   having the right feelings, emotions, and attitudes;
b   acting for the right reasons; and
c   doing what is right.

We will consider these three aspects of virtue in the following three chapters. At this stage a few brief comments on each will have to suffice. Consider, first, the emotional aspect. If a virtue is a trait needed to live well, then it cannot involve suppressing our true feelings and desires for the sake of doing what is right. Someone who goes through life constantly having to deny, suppress, or ignore his true feelings and desires, will forever be unfulfilled and dissatisfied. By contrast, a virtuous person is wholehearted in what he does. His attitudes and emotions reveal his *commitment* to what is good. Hence, an honest person is someone who:

> disapproves of, dislikes, deplores dishonesty, is not amused by certain tales of chicanery, despises or pities those who succeed through deception rather than thinking they have been clever, is unsurprised, or pleased (as appropriate) when honesty triumphs, is shocked or distressed when those near and dear to her do what is dishonest and so on.
>
> (Hursthouse and Pettigrove 2016, Section 1.1)

Regarding the second, intellectual, aspect of virtue, Aristotelians argue that virtue involves acting for the right reasons and hence requires practical wisdom. In this view, the person who risks his life to make a funny video does not display courage as a virtue. Rather, he is being foolish, and such foolishness typically stands in the way of happiness. True courage involves fighting for things that are worthwhile, and requires an understanding of what things in life are worth taking risks for, as well as the practical skill needed to succeed in achieving these ends. In the same way, honesty cannot simply involve a habit of always telling the truth, or obeying a moral rule that says, "Always tell the truth." A truly honest person exercises good judgment; she understands when and why it is important to tell the truth.

Finally, for a trait to be a human excellence, it must include a disposition to act well or do what is right. Merely having good feelings or motives and knowing what is right or good is not sufficient for virtue. One also has to act virtuously.

3.4 Objections to Eudaimonistic Virtue Ethics

3.4.1 The Egoism Objection

Perhaps the most frequent objection to eudaimonism is that it is a form of egoism. One version of this objection can be formulated as follows:

a   The virtuous person is an egoist because she is motivated to act virtuously by a concern for her own happiness.

Eudaimonists claim that virtue benefits its possessor by allowing her to live a happy life. If this is the case, then it seems that what motivates a virtuous person to act on any particular occasion is the thought that this will make her happy. Further, as noted in Chapter 2, Aristotelian eudaimonists claim that a virtuous person finds pleasure in acting virtuously. Generous people enjoy giving, temperate people enjoy eating and drinking in moderation, and honest people are pleased when honesty triumphs. Annas (2011, 73) argues that the pleasure in question is not joy or excitement but instead a kind of contentment or lack of inner conflict. But even if we accept this, the worry remains that virtuous activity produces (or is accompanied by) an inner state that is good for the agent. Isn't this a form of egoism?

Aristotelians respond to this version of the objection by pointing out that what motivates the virtuous person to act virtuously on any particular occasion is not the thought that the action will benefit her. Generous people enjoy giving, and generosity does benefit its possessor, but what motivates the generous person (and indeed, what makes her generous) is the fact that she cares about the welfare of others. There are times when the virtuous person's concern for the welfare of others will motivate her to sacrifice her own interests. Similarly, virtues like courage and loyalty can motivate someone to take considerable risks to her own safety. She will be comfortable with doing so, but this does not amount to being motivated by self-interest.

The claim that the virtues are needed for happiness should therefore not be understood as the claim that *particular virtuous actions* (a) are motivated by personal gain, (b) actually promote the agent's good, or (c) are aimed at promoting the agent's good. Instead, the claim is that *possession and exercise of the virtues* benefit their possessor by allowing her to live a good human life.

If we accept this response, the first formulation of the egoist objection gives way to what Anne Baril (2013, 515) calls "the sophisticated egoism objection":

b   Eudaimonistic virtue ethics is a form of egoism because the virtuous person's ultimate reason for acquiring the virtues is that she believes it will ensure or promote her own good.

We can accept that a virtuous person is not motivated to act virtuously on any particular occasion by a concern for her own good, but still be worried that her commitment to virtue is ultimately based on a concern for her own happiness or *eudaimonia*. That is, her first-order motivations may not be egotistical, but her second-order motivations – her reasons for acquiring and sustaining virtue – are based on her own good (Baril 2013, 514). Thomas Hurka (2001) argues that eudaimonism is inescapably egoistic. It takes the starting point for ethical reflection to be, What is a good life for a human being? and then answers the question as follows: The good life for a human being – their final end or ultimate aim – is their own happiness. Even if we make it clear that a happy life is not a pleasant or successful life, the problem remains that my final end, the ultimate justification for why I should acquire and exercise the virtues, is my happiness, not yours.

In response to this objection, Annas draws attention to the kind of good that *eudaimonia* is. She writes:

> [H]appiness is precisely not a state; it consists in activity, because it is dynamic rather than static... . [M]y happiness is my living happily, and what life can I live other than mine? ... I can aid you to live your life by improving your circumstances, but it must always be up to you to live your life in those circumstance.
>
> (2011, 156)

The point, then, is that a person's happiness is a kind of good that can only be realized or achieved by that person herself. Eudaimonism might well be a form of egoism but not one that is objectionable. The reason we think that egoism is objectionable is not so much that the egoist is concerned with his own good, but rather the fact that he is prepared to advance his own good at others' expense. But one's own happiness or *eudaimonia* is not the kind of good that one can achieve at the expense of others. If anything, by being kind, considerate, generous, honest, and so on, the virtuous person can help make it possible for others to live well. As we've seen, people need external goods in order to be happy, and the virtuous person will make an effort to help others attain or maintain these goods. Whether they succeed in living well, however, can only be up to them.[2]

3.4.2 The Moral Saint Objection

The second objection to eudaimonistic virtue ethics comes from pluralists like Christine Swanton. Swanton accepts the claim that virtue is necessary for happiness. In her view, virtue involves responding well to the demands of the world, and it is only to be expected that someone who succeeds in responding well to these demands will tend to be happy. However, Swanton rejects the claim that what *makes* a trait a virtue is that it characteristically benefits its possessor. Not all virtues contribute to the agent's happiness, and even in cases where they do make such a contribution, it is not necessarily this fact that makes the trait a virtue.

Consider the virtue of benevolence, where this is broadly defined as the virtue of caring for others and promoting their good. It seems reasonable to claim that benevolent people are generally happy, precisely because of their benevolence. They tend to have good relationships with others, they are generally well-liked and respected, and other people are usually happy to help them out when needed. But is it this fact – that benevolence characteristically contributes to the agent's happiness – that makes it a virtue? Swanton doesn't think so. She asks us to consider a moral saint, someone whose life is shaped by a commitment to improving the welfare of others:

> A woman works ceaselessly saving lives and relieving suffering in the jungle. She suffers repeatedly from bouts of malaria and dysentery, and is most of the time in great discomfort even when not ill. She is always exhausted. Though she is standardly strong-willed, she sometimes falters in her humanitarian purposes, questioning her calling. Her suffering is not mitigated by a religious or quasi-religious joy, often experienced by saints, and which makes the latter happy ... . Having seriously undermined her health, she succumbs to a virus, and dies prematurely of complications.
>
> (Swanton 2003, 82)

Swanton claims that although the moral saint is clearly virtuous (admirable and praiseworthy), she cannot possibly be described as happy.[3] Does this show that it is a mistake to define virtue as a trait needed for happiness?

One response on behalf of Aristotelianism is to insist that the moral saint *is* happy. Her life contains a sort of personal satisfaction; it is meaningful because it is devoted to projects that are worthwhile. Swanton rejects this response on the grounds that there is a difference between a meaningful life, one the agent finds worthwhile, and a life that is attractive and thereby personally satisfying. Although Swanton doesn't want to reduce happiness to a life of pleasure, she thinks that a happy life must contain some pleasure; it must be *attractive* to the one whose life it is (2003, 84–87). Indeed, Aristotelians themselves accept that pleasure, while not an ultimate end, is part of a happy life (see Annas 2011, 131).

Another possible response would be to argue that although benevolence characteristically contributes to the happiness of its possessor, the moral saint is one of those exceptional cases where, tragically, this does not happen. So the example only supports the Aristotelian view that virtue is not sufficient for happiness, and that in addition to virtue, one also needs certain external goods to be happy. But this response also seems flawed, because the saint's unhappiness is not tragically bad luck. Instead, it is entirely predictable that such a deep commitment to the good of others would come at the cost of the agent's own happiness. It is predictable precisely because she is committed to, and therefore focused on, securing the good of others and not her own.

It therefore seems that the only response available to the eudaimonist is that saintly benevolence is not a virtue, given that it makes it difficult or even impossible for its possessor to live a happy life, not only sometimes but characteristically. As odd as this sounds, the moral saint is not truly or fully virtuous. This does not commit the eudaimonist to the view that benevolence is never a virtue. Instead, their view would be that there are different forms of benevolence. Saintly benevolence, which involves a selfless commitment to promoting the good of others, is not a virtue, but other forms of benevolence could well be virtues (if they characteristically contribute to the agent's happiness).

Against this, Swanton argues that saintly benevolence is an admirable character trait and hence a virtue. She claims that "some virtues contribute to aspects of a human's goodness other than her personal flourishing ... . [and that] some virtues are inimical to personal flourishing while making that contribution" (Swanton 2003, 80). In her view, benevolence is a virtue if it involves responding to the needs of others in a good enough way. Saintly benevolence is even more admirable because it involves responding to the needs of others in an excellent way.

Chapter Summary

- *Eudaimonism* is the view that ethical inquiry begins with the question: What is a good life for human beings? or: What is *eudaimonia*?
- *Eudaimonistic virtue ethics* is the view that *eudaimonia* is a life lived in accordance with virtue.
- Aristotelian virtue ethics is the most popular version of eudaimonistic virtue ethics. Hursthouse is one of the leading proponents of this view. She defines virtue as "a character trait a human being needs for *eudaimonia*, to flourish or live well" (1999, 167). She makes two important claims: 1. Virtue benefits its possessor by allowing her to live a good life, that is, to be truly happy as a human being. 2. What makes a trait a virtue is that it is necessary for the happiness of human beings.
- A frequent objection to eudaimonistic virtue ethics is that it is a form of egoism, because the virtuous person's ultimate reason for acquiring and exercising the virtues is that she believes it will ensure or promote her own good.
- Another objection to eudaimonistic virtue ethics is the moral saint objection, which holds that some traits are virtues even though they do not contribute to the happiness of their possessor. Swanton claims that although the moral saint is clearly virtuous, her life cannot be described as truly happy, because a happy life must be both admirable and attractive.

As we've seen in Chapter 2, there are two important questions about the nature of virtue. The first is whether virtue requires good motivation, and the second is whether it requires practical wisdom. If eudaimonism is correct, that is, if virtues are traits that are necessary for true happiness, then whether good motivation and practical wisdom are required for virtue will depend on whether they are needed for happiness. We will consider the role of motivation and practical wisdom in Chapters 4 and 5 respectively.

Notes

1 It is worth noting, however, that not all virtue ethicists are eudaimonists. Although they don't dispute the fact that virtuous people tend to be happy, both Michael Slote (2001) and Christine Swanton (2003) reject the view that virtue can be defined in terms of *eudaimonia*.

2 Consider the analogy to writing an exam. We don't criticize a person as selfish or self-centered if they focus on doing their best when taking an exam. The obvious reason is that, under strict exam conditions, they don't have the option of helping others do well in their exams. The best they can do is focus on doing as well as they can. In the days or weeks leading up to the exam

they can help others by organizing a study group, explaining the material to them, and so on. But when it comes to writing the exam, each student can only be responsible for their own performance.

3 Lisa Tessman (2005, 107–132) similarly argues that some virtues are "burdened," that is, they are disjoined from the happiness or well-being of their possessor. Conditions of oppression call on people to acquire traits like courage, loyalty, and fierceness, needed for resisting injustice. Freedom fighters are praised and admired for their courage and their loyalty to the struggle, but these same traits often make it impossible for them to flourish.

Further Reading

Annas, Julia. 2008. "Virtue Ethics and the Charge of Egoism." In *Morality and Self-Interest*, edited by Paul Bloomfield, 205–221. New York: Oxford University Press.

Annas, Julia. 2011. *Intelligent Virtue*. Oxford: Oxford University Press, chapters 8 and 9.

Badhwar, Neera K. 2014. *Well-Being: Happiness in a Worthwhile Life*. Oxford: Oxford University Press.

Baril, Anne. 2013. "The Role of Welfare in Eudaimonism." *The Southern Journal of Philosophy* 51(4): 511–535. doi:10.1111/sjp.12042

Besser-Jones, Lorraine. 2014. *Eudaimonic Ethics: The Philosophy and Psychology of Living Well*. New York: Routledge.

Foot, Philippa. 2001. *Natural Goodness*. Oxford: Oxford University Press.

Hurka, Thomas. 2001. *Virtue, Vice, and Value*. Oxford: Oxford University Press.

Hursthouse, Rosalind. 1999. *On Virtue Ethics*. Oxford: Oxford University Press, chapter 8.

Hursthouse, Rosalind, and Glen Pettigrove. 2016. "Virtue Ethics." *The Stanford Encyclopedia of Philosophy*. https://plato.stanford.edu/archives/win2016/entries/ethics-virtue/.

LeBar, Mark. 2013. *The Value of Living Well*. Oxford: Oxford University Press.

Roberts, Robert C. 2015. "How Virtue Contributes to Flourishing." In *Current Controversies in Virtue Theory*, edited by Mark Alfano, 36–49. New York: Routledge

Russell, Daniel C. 2012. *Happiness for Humans*. Oxford: Oxford University Press.

Russell, Daniel C. 2013b. "Virtue Ethics, Happiness, and the Good Life." In *The Cambridge Companion to Virtue Ethics*, edited by Daniel C. Russell, 7–28. Cambridge: Cambridge University Press.

Swanton, Christine. 2003. *Virtue Ethics: A Pluralistic View*. Oxford: Oxford University Press, chapter 4.

Tessman, Lisa. 2005. *Burdened Virtues: Virtue Ethics for Liberatory Struggles*. Oxford: Oxford University Press.

4   Virtuous Motives

Most virtue theorists agree that being well-motivated is important for virtue. But there are different views about what is involved in being well-motivated. According to sentimentalists like Michael Slote, being well-motivated involves having and acting from good or "warm" sentiments such as sympathy, benevolence, love, and compassion. What makes someone virtuous or admirable is that they are genuinely good-hearted. Bad people, by contrast, are motivated by emotions such as jealousy, hatred, greed, and spite. Consider the example of Nelson Mandela, who was greatly admired for the warmth and kindness he displayed, and the fact that he did not appear angry or bitter after having spent 27years in prison. Upon his release, he spoke about the generosity of his jailers, urged people to forgive and forget, and showed immense kindness and compassion, not only to the victims of apartheid but also to its perpetrators. According to a sentimentalist, Mandela's good-heartedness is what made him a truly virtuous person.

Interestingly, and quite controversially, Richard Stengel, Mandela's biographer, has a different view of how Mandela truly felt. Stengel claims that Mandela was in fact "deeply pained about what had happened to him." Having been deprived of the opportunity to be a good husband, father, and lawyer he felt anger and resentment. He did not respect his jailers or the government leaders with whom he had entered negotiations. But he knew that he had to keep these feelings hidden if he wanted to attain his goals: "He understood that expressing his anger would diminish his power, while hiding it increased it" (Stengel 2010, 98). Assuming that this is true, does it follow that Mandela was not as good-hearted and hence as well-motivated as he appeared to be? Sentimentalists would have to say yes.

Against this, Kantians would argue that Mandela's true feelings do not affect his admirability at all. In their view, being well-motivated involves acting for the right reason, and the right reason is always the fact that the action is required by duty. The agent's feelings, desires, and inclinations can make it easier or harder for him to act from duty, but they are irrelevant from the point of view of morality. Stengel (2010, 103) claims that Mandela was "a man of principle." What motivated him, every step of the way, was a firm belief that he had a duty to fight for justice, freedom, and equality. In the Kantian view, this kind of commitment to doing what is right is what constitutes virtuous motivation.

Aristotelian virtue ethicists argue that reason and emotion both play a crucial role in evaluations of an agent's admirability. They agree with Kantians that a virtuous person is motivated by the right reasons, and in Mandela's case, the right reasons certainly had something to do with his commitment to justice, equality, and freedom. But they claim that a virtuous person acts from sound emotion as well as right reason; he has the right desires, feelings, and attitudes. He loves the right things, and this, in part, is what allows him to live well or be truly happy. It is important to note that the right feelings are not always warm or loving feelings. In the Aristotelian view, Mandela's anger and resentment are entirely appropriate emotional responses to injustice and oppression, and do not detract from his virtue. Stengel's account of Mandela points to another important aspect of Mandela's character that was crucial in allowing him to live and act well: his wisdom. Although his anger was appropriate, he knew that to express it publicly would come in the way of his efforts to bring about peace and reconciliation.

Consequentialists like Julia Driver reject the sentimentalist, Kantian, and Aristotelian views and argue that the thoughts and feelings that motivate people to act only have instrumental value. What made Mandela virtuous was that he possessed traits, such as courage, modesty, self-control, discipline, wit, and charm, that reliably produce good consequences.

Our focus in this chapter will be on the debate between Aristotelians and Kantians about the role of reason and emotion in virtuous motivation. In the course of doing so, we will consider their reasons for rejecting the sentimentalist view, and conclude with a discussion of a consequentialist view of the moral relevance of motivation.

4.1 Aristotle and Kant on Pleasure and Self-Control

According to Aristotle, the desires of a virtuous person are in harmony with his reason: he doesn't have to struggle against contrary inclinations or feelings. When he has decided what to do, he does it gladly, and feels satisfied having done it (see *The Nicomachean Ethics* 1120a 24–31). The pleasure in question is not a feeling of joy or excitement. Rather, it is best described as an inner harmony, where the activity is "unimpeded by frustration and inner conflict" (Annas 2011, 73). Aristotle contrasts the virtuous person with one who is merely continent or self-controlled (*enkratês*). The continent person typically knows what he should do, but is often tempted by his emotions and appetites to do otherwise. Despite this, he usually manages to resist temptation and to do the right thing. Aristotle thinks the continent person is more admirable than someone who is incontinent or weak-willed (*akratês*). An incontinent person is someone who typically knows what to do, but usually fails to resist the temptation to do wrong. The worst kind of person is the one who doesn't even know what is right and therefore has no desire to do what is right. Such a person is evil or vicious. He doesn't recognize the value of kindness, justice, or temperance, and is instead driven by desires for wealth, power, and luxury. Table 4.1 below represents the differences between these four kinds of people, ranked in order of admirability.

Our focus in this section is on the distinction between the virtuous and the continent person, as it highlights the role of emotion in Aristotle's thought. It is also a controversial distinction. We might ask: If both agents characteristically succeed in doing the right thing and doing it for the right reason, does it really matter whether they have the right emotions when they act? Is Aristotle's virtuous person truly more admirable than the continent one?

Aristotle's view of the role of emotion in moral motivation is often contrasted with Kant's view, namely that acting from feelings such as sympathy can actually *detract* from an action's moral worth. In a well-known passage in the *Groundwork of the Metaphysics of Morals*, Kant describes two philanthropists, the sympathetic philanthropist and the sorrowful one. Both of them do what is right, but their feelings and motives differ. The sympathetic philanthropist is motivated by warm feelings. He finds "an inner gratification in spreading joy around [him]" and delights in the happiness of others. The sorrowful philanthropist does not sympathize with others because his mind is "beclouded by his own grief" and hence occupied with his own needs. Nevertheless, he tears himself out of this "deadly insensibility" and benefits others because he believes he has a duty to do so (Kant 2011, 4:398).

Table 4.1

	Right reason	*Right emotion*	*Right action*
Virtuous	✓	✓	✓
Continent	✓	X	✓
Incontinent	✓	X	X
Evil/vicious	X	X	X

Kant claims that the action of the sympathetic philanthropist has no moral worth. Although he does the right thing, that is, he acts *in accordance with duty*, he doesn't do the right thing for the right reasons – he doesn't act *from duty*. He is therefore less admirable than the sorrowful philanthropist, who performs a right action from a sense of duty rather than from feelings of sympathy. Kant's main reason in support of this view is that we cannot rely on emotions such as sympathy and honor to steer us towards acting well. We cannot control our emotions, and so it is merely a matter of luck when they motivate us to do the right thing. The sympathetic man doesn't make a deliberate choice to help others. He just does what he happens to feel like doing. Barbara Herman illustrates this point by using the example of a man who sees someone struggling with a heavy burden at the back door of an art museum. He is moved by sympathy to help the person, not realizing that they are, in fact, an art thief:

> In acting from immediate inclination, the agent is not concerned with whether his action is morally correct or required. That is why he acts no differently, and, in a sense, no better, when he saves a drowning child than when he helps the art thief. Of course we are happier to see the child saved, and indeed, might well prefer to live in a community of sympathetic persons to most others, but the issue remains. The man of sympathetic temper, while concerned with others, is indifferent to morality.
>
> (Herman 1981, 365)

The problem, according to Kant, is not merely that emotions are not sufficiently strong or stable to serve as a reliable guide to action. Even if a person's sympathy is strong enough to ensure that he tries to help others whenever there is an opportunity to do so, it would still generate morally right actions only by accident rather than by choice.

A second, related reason in support of Kant's view is that the sympathetic man finds it easy to help others – he simply does what he feels like doing, and so does not manifest strength of character or a commitment to morality when he does what is right. By contrast, the sorrowful philanthropist finds it hard to do the right thing, but he nevertheless chooses to do so, and this suggests that he is more admirable than the sympathetic philanthropist.

Some interpreters conclude that Aristotle and Kant hold opposite views about the role of emotion in moral motivation: whereas Aristotle thinks the self-controlled agent is less admirable than the one who gladly does the right thing, Kant thinks an agent who is motivated solely by his belief that it is the right thing to do is more admirable than the one who acts from sympathy or inclination. If we accept Kant's reasons in support of his view, then it presents a challenge to Aristotelian virtue ethics, for it seems that the continent person is more admirable than someone who does the right thing with pleasure.

4.2 An Aristotelian View of Reason and Inclination

In response to the above challenge, Rosalind Hursthouse argues that it is a mistake to interpret Kant and Aristotle as holding opposite views about the role of inclination. She thinks Aristotle would agree with Kant's assessment of the relative moral worth of the sympathetic and sorrowful philanthropists. She begins by considering Kant's sympathetic philanthropist, the one with the "good-natured temperament," and argues that Aristotle would not consider him to be truly virtuous. Aristotle agrees that the emotions, as natural inclinations, are unreliable as sources of acting well. Feelings of love or sympathy can lead us astray. They can motivate us to help people who don't need our help, or to offer the wrong kind of help. There is no reason to think our natural inclinations will occur at the right times, towards the right people, and to the appropriate degree (Hursthouse 1999, 101–102).

Hursthouse thinks that Kant's criticism of the sympathetic philanthropist is not directed at Aristotle but rather at the sentimentalist view put forward by David Hume. According to Hume, human beings are motivated by desire or passion and not by reason. A good person is someone who is motivated by good desires or passions, like benevolence, love, and sympathy, rather than by evil ones, like hatred, envy, and jealousy. Kant rejects this view of motivation and instead claims that we are motivated by both reason and desire, and that being well-motivated involves acting from reason rather than desire. Hursthouse notes that Aristotelians agree with Kant on both these points. Aristotle claims that a virtuous person does the right thing with pleasure, but it is a mistake to interpret him as saying that a virtuous person acts from inclination or passion. Indeed, Aristotle would not consider the sympathetic philanthropist to be admirable at all:

> [I]n Aristotelian terms, we could say that the happy [i.e., sympathetic] philanthropists, supposing them to have "Humean" benevolence ... , do not *act* in the strict sense of the term at all. They live ... by inclination, like an animal or a child; their "doings" issue from passion or emotion ... not "choice".... . It is *actions* proper, which issue from reason, that are to be assessed as virtuous (or vicious), but their "doings" are not actions, and thereby cannot be said to be, and to be esteemed as, virtuous ones.
>
> (Hursthouse 1999, 103)

In short, Kant's sympathetic philanthropist and Aristotle's virtuous agent are not the same person; the sympathetic philanthropist, who is driven by emotion rather than reason to do the right thing, does not appear on Aristotle's list (Table 4.1). This can be made more obvious by comparing Aristotle's list with a similar representation of Kant's philanthropists (Table 4.2).

Hursthouse next turns her attention to the sorrowful philanthropist, the one who finds it hard to help others. On the face of it, he appears to be identical to Aristotle's continent agent: he performs the right action for the right reason, but doesn't feel the right emotion. Yet Kant thinks he is admirable, whereas Aristotle doesn't. Again, Hursthouse questions this interpretation, and argues that Aristotle will not necessarily consider the sorrowful philanthropist to be merely continent as opposed to fully virtuous. To determine whether he is admirable, we need to know *why* he finds it hard to do the right thing on this particular occasion.

Citing Philippa Foot, Hursthouse (1999, 94) draws our attention to an apparent contradiction in our everyday thoughts about people who find it hard to do what is right:

> [W]e both are and are not inclined to think that the harder a man finds it to act virtuously the more virtue he shows if he does act well. For on the one hand great virtue is needed where it is particularly hard to act virtuously; yet on the other it could be argued that difficulty in acting virtuously shows that the agent is imperfect in virtue: according to Aristotle, to take pleasure in virtuous action is the mark of true virtue, with the self-mastery of the one who finds virtue difficult only a second best. How then is this conflict to be decided?
>
> (Foot, 1978b, 10)

Foot argues that Aristotle's claim, namely that *virtuous conduct gives pleasure to the lover of virtue* (*Nicomachean Ethics* 1099a12), needs careful qualification. In some cases, it is true that the harder it is for a person to do what is right, the less virtue he shows if he acts well. The person who reluctantly helps his friend because he would rather stay home and watch

Table 4.2

	Right reason	*Right emotion*	*Right action*	*Moral worth*
Sympathetic philanthropist	X	✓	✓	X
Sorrowful philanthropist	✓	X	✓	✓

movies is less admirable than someone who does so with pleasure. In other cases, however, it seems that the harder it is for a person to do what is right, the *more* virtue he shows if he acts well. A desperately poor person who finds it hard to restore a wallet full of cash to its owner is more admirable than the rich person who finds it easy to do the same thing. Foot thinks the key to resolving these conflicting intuitions is to consider what makes it hard for someone to do what is right. In the first case, what makes it hard for the man to help his friend pertains to character: he is selfish and lazy. If he succeeds in doing the right thing, he manifests continence rather than virtue, and hence is less admirable than the person who finds it easy to help his friend. By contrast, what makes it hard for the poor person to restore the wallet is not some character flaw or weakness, but rather the circumstances in which he finds himself (see Foot 1978b, 10–14; Hursthouse 1999, 94–99).

We can now see why Aristotle would not necessarily describe Kant's sorrowful philanthropist as merely continent: what makes it hard for him to do the right thing is that he has been severely tested by his circumstances – his mind, as Kant says, is "beclouded by his own grief." The fact that he nevertheless manages to do what is right tells us something about his character, namely that he is committed to doing what is right. So even though he doesn't feel the right emotion on this occasion, there is a good explanation for this, one that does not detract from his moral worth. Aristotle would therefore agree with Kant that the sorrowful philanthropist is more admirable than the sympathetic one (Hursthouse 1999, 99–107).

4.3 The Role of Emotion in Motivation

The most important point to take from Hursthouse's discussion so far is that Kant and Aristotle agree about two things:

a   The emotions, conceived merely as natural inclinations, are unreliable guides to acting well.
b   A virtuous person acts from reason rather than merely from inclination or passion.

However, Hursthouse goes on to discuss an important point of disagreement between Aristotle and Kant – and between Aristotelians and Kantians – regarding the role of emotion in motivation. Kant thinks that acting for the right reason is all that is required, whereas Aristotle thinks that reason and emotion both have a role in moral motivation.

Consider, first, Kant's position. Following his discussion of the sympathetic and sorrowful philanthropists, Kant introduces a third philanthropist, one who is by nature "cold and indifferent to the sufferings of others" but benefits them because he believes he has a duty to do so (Kant 2011, 4:398). It seems reasonable to claim that the cold philanthropist is admirable *in some way*. He helps others, despite being cold and indifferent to their sufferings, and despite finding it hard. He acts from a strong commitment to duty and therefore possesses what Kant calls "a good will." However, most people (including, as we'll see, many Kantians) reject the stronger claim that Kant makes, namely that the cold philanthropist is *morally superior* to any other kind of agent. Aristotelians consider the cold philanthropist to be, at best, continent, because he doesn't have the right emotions and attitudes. The problem is not merely that he fails to act from sound emotion on this particular occasion, as might be the case with the sorrowful philanthropist. Rather, there seems to be something seriously wrong with his character. Kant notes that "nature had as such placed little sympathy in the heart of this ... man" (2011, 4:398), thereby suggesting that it is not really his fault, but Aristotelians will want to say that he *should not* be so cold and indifferent. He should make an effort to care about others, that is, he should try to cultivate the virtues of benevolence and sympathy.

This raises the question of whether it is possible for the cold philanthropist to choose to react more sympathetically towards others. Kant thinks it isn't. In his view, the emotions belong to the animal, non-rational side of human nature, and so it is not possible to control one's emotional reactions. We are lucky if our emotions happen to prompt us to act in accordance with duty or reason. But we cannot rely on our emotions for they are likely to lead us astray. Reason is the only reliable source of moral action. As Nafsika Athanassoulis explains:

> Kant deeply mistrusts our inclinations; he views humans as likely to be blinded by self-deceit because of inclinations that mislead us and distort the demands of morality. For example, because we are (naturally) full of self-conceit we misjudge ourselves to be morally better than we are; because we are (naturally) full of jealousy we misjudge others to be morally worse than they are. Humans have a propensity to evil, so we must constantly guard against the motive of self-love and we must always view our natural inclinations with mistrust. The source of moral worth, therefore, can never be inclinations as they are both likely to mislead us and be fickle, unreliable and not under our control.
>
> (2013, 138–139)

According to Kant, then, there is no such thing as the *right* emotion. Consider, again, the sympathetic philanthropist. On Kant's view, he happens to feel an emotion, which happens to motivate him to act in accordance with duty. On this particular occasion he is lucky that his feelings make it easy for him to do what is right, but we can now see that it is a mistake to describe sympathy as the *right* emotion. We should therefore replace Table 4.2 with Table 4.3 (see below).

For Kant, the presence or absence of a particular emotion is irrelevant to the moral worth of the action or the agent. Whether or not a right action has moral worth depends entirely on whether it is motivated by the right reason.

Aristotelians, by contrast, believe that the emotions form part of our rational nature, and that it is possible to have the *right* emotion. Fear is in part constituted by an evaluative belief or judgment that something is dangerous, and this belief can be true or false. Sadness, in turn, is an emotional response that requires a belief that one has suffered some loss. A person who, following a devastating earthquake, is more upset about the damage to her property than she is about her neighbor's serious injury manifests a flawed grasp of what constitutes harm, and hence of what matters in life. In the Aristotelian view, a truly caring person is not someone who happens to have a tendency to be overwhelmed by strong feelings of sympathy for others, but rather someone who appreciates that other people's happiness matters, that it is a goal worth pursuing.

In short, then, Aristotelians think the emotions are morally significant. Part of what makes a person virtuous is the fact that he characteristically feels the *right* emotions "on the *right* occasions, towards the *right* people or objects, [and] for the *right* reasons" (Hursthouse 1999, 108). Someone who has, and is moved to act by, the appropriate emotion is more admirable than the person who acts from a sense of duty alone. Kant's cold philanthropist, who characteristically responds to the suffering of others with the wrong emotion – indifference – must hold evaluative beliefs that are false. He might believe that others deserve to suffer, or that their happiness doesn't really matter. Interestingly, Kant himself supplies a possible

Table 4.3

	Right reason	Emotion	Right action	Moral worth
Sympathetic philanthropist	X	Sympathy	✓	X
Sorrowful philanthropist	✓	Sorrow	✓	✓

reason for this indifference, namely that "he himself is equipped with the peculiar gift of patience and enduring strength towards his own [suffering], and presupposes, or even requires the same in every other" (2011, 4:398). Aristotelians would claim that what Kant describes here is an error in judgment: the cold philanthropist doesn't understand that others are vulnerable in ways that he is not. Unlike the sorrowful philanthropist, who is temporarily overcome by his own sorrows and therefore finds it hard to focus on the good of others on this occasion, the cold philanthropist has the wrong attitude towards the suffering of others.

It is worth noting that many contemporary Kantians also reject the claim that the cold philanthropist is morally superior to any other sort of agent, and accept that the emotions are morally significant in some way. Allen Wood (2008) points out that Kant, particularly in his later work, allows room for rational desires that accompany reason. For example, in *The Metaphysics of Morals* (Kant 1996, 6:399–403, 456–457), Kant claims that human beings have *moral* feelings, which include things like self-respect, love of their neighbor, guilt, and shame. He also notes that the motive of duty gives rise to reverence: a special feeling of respect for the moral law. While Kant doesn't think these feelings can have moral worth in themselves, he claims that they can make us more receptive to the demands of duty. We experience a kind of pleasure when we succeed in acting from duty, and displeasure – guilt, shame, or embarrassment – when we fail to do so. Kant even goes so far as to argue that we have a duty to cultivate love, sympathy, and other inclinations that make it easier to carry out our duties. This suggests that he revised his earlier views and came to accept that we have some control over these feelings. The view Kant presents in his later work is much closer to Aristotle's view, namely that a virtuous person has the right feelings at the right times, and that there will be a harmony between his reason and his emotions (see Herman 1981; Louden 1986; Anderson 2008; Wood 2008). However, an important difference remains: In the Aristotelian view, the appropriate emotions and desires can help us see what we ought to do. By contrast, Kant thinks it is reason alone that guides us to right action and produces in us a feeling of joy and reverence for the moral law. As Athanassoulis puts it, "for Kant, rational desires are a by-product of the work done by reason alone" (2013, 145).

4.4 The Commitment to Morality

To really appreciate the difference between Kant and Aristotle – and between Kantians and Aristotelians – we need to look beyond the reasons and emotions that motivate the agent to act on any particular occasion and consider the kind of person he is. Kant and Aristotle agree that the ideal moral agent is deeply *committed* to the good. He has chosen to live a good life, and being virtuous has become part of his identity. This is why we can rely on him to do what is right, not only sometimes, but characteristically. But Kant and Aristotle have very different views about the kind of commitment that is involved in living a good life.

The Kantian agent is motivated by duty, that is, he has respect for and a commitment to the moral law. To understand what is involved in being motivated by duty, it is useful to consider the rules or laws of a club such as the Boy Scouts. Club rules create duties. If we do something because it is our duty as a boy scout, our motivation is respect for the rules that make it our duty. These duties only apply to us as members of the club, and so we can rationally opt out and lay aside our membership. Moral laws are similar in that they give rise to duties, and a person who acts from duty is motivated by respect for these laws. But unlike the rules of a club, moral laws are thought to prescribe what any rational agent must do. They are universally valid – one cannot rationally opt out of doing one's moral duty. According to Kant, when we do something because it is our moral duty, we are motivated by the thought that as rational beings we must act only as this fundamental law of reason prescribes (Johnson and Cureton 2017, section 3). The Kantian agent is committed to morality in the sense that he accepts and obeys the commands of morality. He acknowledges the binding force of morality, both as a command (a set of prescriptions or imperatives) and as a constraint (a set of prohibitions).

We can now see why Kantians cannot allow emotions to play a central role in morality. The Kantian agent has a *rational* commitment to doing what duty demands, which implies that he must be prepared to set aside his emotions and desires in order to do what duty requires. While having the right feelings can make it easier for him to do his duty, it is not a mark of virtue and hence irrelevant to his moral worth.

A frequent objection to Kant's view of moral motivation is that there are many contexts in which acting from a sense of duty is not admirable. Michael Stocker (1976, 462) uses the example of Smith who goes to visit his friend Jones in hospital. When Jones expresses her gratitude to Smith, he responds – sincerely – that there is no need to thank him since he was only doing his duty. Stocker notes that Jones is likely to be disappointed by this response, and that she would much prefer to be visited by a friend who cares about her. Stocker's point, then, is that the focus on duty is not compatible with the motives required for goods such as love and friendship. The best reason for visiting a friend in hospital is something like, "She's my friend" or, "She needs company," and not, "It is my duty."

As we have seen, Aristotle's virtuous person acts for the right reasons and with the right attitude and emotions. But this does not merely involve acting for the right reasons and with the right emotions on a particular occasion. Rather, the virtuous person acts *from virtue*, or, as Aristotle puts it, "from a firm and unchangeable character" (*The Nicomachean Ethics* 1105a35a). The claim that someone acted from virtue is not merely a claim about her reasons and feelings on a particular occasion, but also a claim about her character, the sort of person she is – about what she values or finds important or worthwhile. As such, it is also a claim about the future, about the kinds of actions we can expect her to perform (Hursthouse 1999, 123). Like Kant's ideal agent, Aristotle's virtuous person is deeply committed to morality. However, her commitment does not take the form of respect for a set of commands or imperatives. Instead, Aristotle's virtuous person is committed and attracted to goodness, that is, to goals or ends that she finds worthwhile. As Julia Annas explains:

> The brave person's action reveals that he is committed to something valuable that is centrally important to him. He tries to save others from danger even when this puts at risk his own safety, perhaps his life. He is putting forward efforts to achieve an aim with value for his life as a whole: it is important for him to be brave in this kind of situation. The coward's actions, on the other hand, indicate that he fails to have this kind of aim.
>
> (2011, 102)

The fact that the virtuous person is not only committed but *attracted* to goodness explains why he typically finds it easy to do what is right, and why he is not tempted by contrary inclinations. He correctly perceives that certain things are more worthwhile or important than others. A generous person realizes that sharing her good fortune with others is a better (more attractive) way to spend time than enjoying life's luxuries all by oneself, and so she is pleased when she has an opportunity to do so. The continent person, by contrast, is still attracted to the wrong things; he is not (yet) committed to goodness.

We are now in a position to fully appreciate what Aristotelian virtue ethicists mean when they say that virtue is a "deep feature" of a person (Annas 2011, 9, 102, 105), one "that goes 'all the way down'" (Hursthouse 1999, 123, 160). A virtuous person chooses goodness because it is good, that is, she has an understanding and appreciation of what is good, worthwhile, or important, and is attracted to it for this reason. Her commitment to goodness therefore manifests itself in her behavior and in her feelings, attitudes, reactions, and desires.

This conception of virtue makes it clear why Aristotelians believe that children cannot act from virtue. Aristotle's claim, namely that children are not capable of acting virtuously,[1] strikes many people as odd. If virtue requires acting for the right reason(s) and with the right emotion(s), then it follows that many children qualify as acting virtuously at least some of the time. Consider, for example, a child who appears genuinely concerned about others and helps them for the right reasons (e.g., "They were hurt" as opposed to, "I wanted to impress my mother"). What more is required for virtue? In the Aristotelian view, most children cannot yet have virtue because they are not committed to goodness. They do not yet have a conception or understanding of what is good, and so cannot truly act from virtue. As Hursthouse notes, "They may have personalities, they may have natural virtues, but they do not yet have character traits; their characters are forming but not yet formed and settled" (1999, 145).

Whether morality is best conceived as a commitment to duty, as Kantians believe, or, instead, as a commitment to the good, as Aristotelians believe, will depend on whether universal moral rules and duties actually exist. If they do exist (and if it is possible to identify them), then it seems plausible to claim that a virtuous person is someone who acts from a sense of duty. If they don't, then it seems more plausible to view the virtuous person as someone who is committed to the good. We will set this issue aside for now, and return to it in Chapter 8. In what follows, we will consider a consequentialist view of the role of motivation in morality, one that raises important questions for Aristotelian virtue ethics.

4.5 A Consequentialist View of Motivation

Consequentialists are committed to the view that virtue is somehow connected to good consequences, but this connection can take various forms. Driver (2001, xiv–xv) makes a useful distinction between *evaluational externalism*, which is the view that the moral quality of a person's action or character depends on external factors (such as their consequences or effects), and *evaluational internalism*, which is the view that the moral quality of a person's action or character is determined by factors internal to the person's agency (such as their motives, feelings, or expectations). Consequentialists can support either an externalist or an internalist theory of right action. Objective consequentialism is a version of evaluational externalism, for it ties the rightness of an action to its actual consequences. Subjective consequentialism is a version of evaluational internalism, for it ties rightness to intended or expected consequences. Our focus in this section will be on a consequentialist account of virtue, and here again, consequentialists can support either an externalist or an internalist view.

Consider, first, a straightforward externalist view of virtue, namely that someone is virtuous whenever they succeed in bringing about good consequences. Hence, they are benevolent whenever they benefit others, and cruel, selfish, or unkind whenever they harm others. An obvious shortcoming of this view is that it is vulnerable to the problem of moral luck. The consequences of our actions are not entirely within our control. Someone who accidentally brings about a good result doesn't deserve praise or admiration, and someone who brings about a bad result through no fault of their own doesn't deserve blame or condemnation. The problem can be mitigated, to some extent, by attributing praise and blame based on whether someone *typically* succeeds in bringing about good results. In this view, we should praise someone for their benevolence if they often make an effort to help others and usually succeed, and ignore or excuse the occasional exception. However, the problem of moral luck remains, because it is possible for someone to devote their entire life to promoting a worthy goal (such as developing a cure for a disease) and yet to fail through absolutely no fault of their own. To view such a person as blameworthy or as lacking in virtue seems deeply counterintuitive. As Annas points out, we admire people like Mahatma Gandhi and Nelson Mandela for their courage and their commitment to the good, and our admiration is not contingent upon whether they actually succeed in bringing about good consequences (2011, 109).

Some consequentialists try to avoid the problem of moral luck by opting for evaluational internalism. In this view, an agent is admirable or praiseworthy whenever she is *motivated* by a sincere desire to bring about good consequences. Whether she succeeds can affect whether her action is right, but not whether she herself is good or praiseworthy. Although it avoids the charge of moral luck, such an account is vulnerable to another objection from Stocker. It is similar to the one we discussed earlier on, but this time the objection is that a desire to bring about good consequences is not always the best kind of motive. To illustrate, Stocker (1976, 462) puts forward another version of the Smith and Jones case. Smith visits Jones in hospital, and mentions to Jones that he was motivated by a desire to bring about good consequences (which he thought he could achieve by visiting Jones in hospital). Stocker thinks Jones would be disappointed by this response, and that she would have preferred to be visited by her friend because he cares about *her*, and not merely about bringing about good consequences. Hence, (this version of) consequentialism fails to account for the important role that emotion and personal relationships play in moral life. According to Stocker, we are often motivated, and appropriately so, by an attachment to particular people and projects. To expect people to be motivated by an impartial desire to bring about the greatest good is to alienate them from their personal relationships and commitments.[2]

It appears, then, that consequentialists encounter serious problems, regardless of whether they take an externalist or an internalist route.

Driver thinks both these problems can be avoided. She supports a form of evaluational externalism, for it connects virtue with actual consequences in the real world. In her view, a virtue is a character trait that reliably – though not invariably – produces good results (Driver 2001, 82). But she thinks it avoids the problem of moral luck, given that it assigns praise and blame based on the agent's character rather than the consequences of her actions. A fire fighter who risks his life to save someone can be praised for his courage, even if, through sheer bad luck, the rescue is unsuccessful. And a person who has devoted her entire life to a worthy cause but fails to do much good can still be praised and admired for her benevolence. *Whether a person has the virtue of courage or benevolence depends on facts about her,* which may include facts about her psychological states (emotions, reasons, attitudes, and motives) and behavior. In this regard, Driver's conception of virtue accounts for the intuition that a person's inner states sometimes matter for virtue. And she avoids Stocker's objection by accepting that not all the virtues involve a desire to bring about good consequences. However, she argues that *what makes a trait like courage or benevolence a virtue is the fact that it systematically produces good consequences in this world.* We admire and praise people who are honest, generous, or courageous because these traits typically produce good consequences, and we criticize and blame people who are dishonest, miserly, or cowardly because these traits typically produce bad consequences.

As we've seen, Aristotelian virtue ethicists argue that certain psychological states are necessary for virtue. A virtuous person's commitment to goodness shapes her attitudes, reasons, and emotions, and this is why we find her not only admirable but inspiring. An interesting question is whether a consequentialist must deny this claim. Driver's view seems to be that we do admire people who are committed to good ends, but that our admiration is only appropriate when and because such a commitment reliably produces good consequences. In other words, a commitment to goodness (together with other psychological states) can have instrumental value. Driver also accepts that particular psychological states may be necessary for particular virtues. She notes, for example, that generosity *by definition* "requires a concern for the well-being of others" (Driver 2015, 324). But what makes generosity a virtue is that it typically has good consequences, and not that it involves good motivation or a commitment to the good of others.[3] To support this view, Driver uses the following thought experiment:

> Suppose that it turned out that the long-term effects of a trait that we currently take to be a virtue – let's say "generosity" – turned out to

be disastrous. Perhaps there are lots of short-term good effects, but the long-term effects of behaving generously undermine character, lead to weakness, etc.

(2015, 324)

Would we still consider generosity a virtue if this were the case? If good motivation is inherently valuable, it seems, we would have to say that generosity is an admirable character trait, regardless of whether it typically produces good long-term effects. Driver finds this view implausible. She thinks it likely that we will change our minds about generosity. We will no longer praise people for acting generously. We will discourage such actions and will try to change people's attitudes by making them aware of the disastrous consequences of generosity. Once we become aware of its long-term consequences, we will see that generosity was never a virtue (Driver 2015, 324).

Another way to support this position is to note that what we commonly refer to as "generosity" is actually a collection of distinct traits. All forms of generosity involve an active concern for the well-being of others, but this can take many different forms. Consider, for example, the form of generosity that is manifested in each of the following agents:

> Ann, who likes to lavish her friends and family with expensive gifts because she thinks it will make them happy;
> Ben, who is concerned about the welfare of future generations, and often makes large anonymous donations to research institutions that aim to find ways of combatting global warming;
> Charles, whose concern for the good of others motivates him to spend much of his free time doing volunteer work in his community.

It seems appropriate to describe all three these agents as generous, given their motivations and the kinds of action that they characteristically perform. But it is unclear whether all of them have generosity *as a virtue*. Aristotelians think it depends on their inner states (their thoughts, reasons, attitudes, and emotions), and whether these allow the agent to live a good or happy life. By contrast, Driver thinks it depends on whether the particular form of generosity reliably produces good results. It could well be the case that Ann's type of generosity typically causes other people to feel uncomfortable, or that Charles's kind of generosity tends to reduce employment opportunities in the long run. In short, according to the consequentialist, the kind of generosity we should admire and encourage (and call a virtue) is whichever kind reliably produces good consequences in this world.

Chapter Summary

- According to sentimentalists like Slote, being well-motivated involves acting from "warm" desires and emotions like sympathy, compassion, and love. A caring person will use reason in order to achieve her goals, but reason itself does not motivate us to act.
- Kantians claim that being well-motivated involves acting from reason and not from desire or inclination. The ideal moral agent is committed to morality in the sense that he accepts and obeys the demands of duty.
- Aristotelian virtue ethicists argue that reason and emotion both play crucial roles in morality. The fully virtuous agent acts for the right reasons and with the right emotions, and is committed and attracted to what is good.
- Consequentialists define virtue in terms of good consequences. According to Driver, what makes a trait a virtue is the fact that it reliably produces good consequences. While good motivation often has instrumental value, it is not required for virtue.

In the following chapter, we will examine the Aristotelian claim that virtue requires practical wisdom. Practical wisdom is an intellectual virtue, and it has various functions. It allows the virtuous agent to act from the right reasons (that is, it allows her to see what ought to be done in a particular situation and also why it ought to be done). Further, practical wisdom makes it possible for the virtuous agent to have a correct understanding of what matters in life, and thereby to have the right emotions. It also involves a kind of know-how or skill, which is needed for successful virtuous action. Our focus in Chapter 5 will be on the debates between Aristotelian virtue ethicists, consequentialists, pluralists, and sentimentalists. We will return to the debate between Aristotelians and Kantians in Chapters 7 and 8.

Notes

1 See *The Nicomachean Ethics* Book I, ch. 9; Book X, ch. 8.
2 Bernard Williams develops this objection in *Utilitarianism: For and Against* (1973).
3 As we will see in Chapter 5, Driver thinks there are traits that have good consequences (and hence can be described as virtues) even though they do not involve a commitment to the good.

Further Reading

Anderson, Elizabeth. 2008. "Emotions in Kant's Later Moral Philosophy: Honour and the Phenomenology of Moral Value." In *Kant's Ethics of Virtue*, edited by Monika Betzler, 123–145. Berlin: Walter de Gruyter.

Annas, Julia. 2011. *Intelligent Virtue.* Oxford: Oxford University Press, chapters 5 and 7.

Athanassoulis, Nafsika. 2013. *Virtue Ethics.* London: Bloomsbury, chapters 3 and 8.

Driver, Julia. 2001. *Uneasy Virtue.* Cambridge: Cambridge University Press.

Driver, Julia. 2016. "Minimal Virtue." *The Monist* 99(2): 97–111. doi:10.1093/monist/onv032

Foot, Philippa. 1978b. "Virtues and Vices." In *Virtues and Vices and Other Essays in Moral Philosophy*, by Philippa Foot, 1–18. Oxford: Blackwell.

Herman, Barbara. 1981. "On the Value of Acting from the Motive of Duty." *The Philosophical Review* 90(3): 359–382. doi:10.2307/2184978

Hursthouse, Rosalind. 1999. *On Virtue Ethics.* Oxford: Oxford University Press, chapters 4 to 7.

Hursthouse, Rosalind and Glen Pettigrove. 2016. "Virtue Ethics." *The Stanford Encyclopedia of Philosophy.* https://plato.stanford.edu/archives/win2016/entries/ethics-virtue/.

Johnson, Robert and Adam Cureton. 2017. "Kant's Moral Philosophy." *The Stanford Encyclopedia of Philosophy.* https://plato.stanford.edu/archives/spr2017/entries/kant-moral/.

Louden, Robert B. 1986. "Kant's Virtue Ethics." *Philosophy* 61(238): 473–489. doi:10.1017/S0031819100061246

Stocker, Michael. 1976. "The Schizophrenia of Modern Ethical Theories." *The Journal of Philosophy* 73(14): 453–466. doi:10.2307/2025782

Wood, Allen W. 2008. *Kantian Ethics.* Cambridge: Cambridge University Press.

5 Practical Wisdom

The claim that practical wisdom is required for virtue forms a central tenet of Aristotelian virtue ethics (Hursthouse 1999; Russell 2009; Annas 2011). Virtue is not merely a useful, agreeable, or admirable trait but a human excellence, and this means that it must involve the exercise of reason. Aristotle argues that the ability to reason is distinctively human: it is what separates us from the other animals. Whereas animals act impulsively and instinctively, human beings are able to reason about whether a particular action or emotion is good or appropriate in a given situation. Of course, this doesn't mean that they always reason well. People often go wrong because of mistaken assumptions and faulty reasoning. They might think, for example, that it would be generous to give a poor relative an expensive gift, when in fact it will make the relative feel awkward about not being able to reciprocate. Practical wisdom, according to Aristotle, is an acquired disposition that involves reasoning well about such matters. It is what allows someone to make intelligent judgments about which actions and emotional responses are appropriate in any particular situation.

This chapter begins with a brief overview of the Aristotelian view of the nature and role of practical wisdom in the life of a virtuous person. The claim that ethical thought and decision-making involves reasoning is relatively uncontroversial. As we've seen in the previous chapter, Kantians claim that the ideal moral agent acts from reason. Even sentimentalists, who define virtue in terms of emotions like love and benevolence, accept that a truly virtuous person will be careful to discover the relevant facts so that their benevolence will be truly useful (see Slote 2001, 18). But Aristotelians make three very strong and distinctive claims about the nature and role of practical wisdom. The first is that practical wisdom is necessary for virtue. That is, one cannot have any of the individual virtues without having practical wisdom. The second is known as the "unity of virtue" thesis, and follows from the first: if practical wisdom is required for each individual virtue, then a person who has one virtue will also have the others (at least to some degree). The third claim is that a fully virtuous person, one who has practical wisdom, does not rely on moral rules or principles but instead exercises judgment in discerning the morally relevant features of particular situations. Our focus in this chapter will be on the first two claims, as these are closely related. We will return to the third claim in Chapters 7 and 8.

5.1 What Is Practical Wisdom? An Aristotelian View

According to Aristotle, practical wisdom (*phronesis*) is an intellectual virtue that makes it possible for a virtuous person to act well. He distinguishes practical wisdom, which has to do with action, from theoretical wisdom (*sophia*), which is the intellectual virtue required for discovering universal truths (e.g. in science and mathematics). He also distinguishes it from technical skill (*technē*), which is an intellectual virtue required for producing things (e.g. tables and chairs) or states (e.g. health and wealth).[1]

It is surprisingly difficult to give a precise definition of practical wisdom. Part of the reason for this is that it is not a single form of intelligence, but rather a collection of different forms of knowledge and skill. A useful starting point is to consider the Aristotelian view of moral motivation. As we've seen in Chapter 4, a virtuous person is motivated to do what is right for the right reasons and has the right attitude and feelings when she acts. This suggests that a virtuous person knows: (a) which action is right in the situation, and (b) the reason(s) why it is right. She must also know (c) which feelings and attitudes are appropriate in the situation, and (d) the reason(s) why these feelings and attitudes are appropriate.

To illustrate, consider the example of Victor, who is a fully virtuous person. Victor has been looking forward to watching a movie all week. On his way to the theater he runs into an old friend, who appears upset. When he asks what troubles her, she says that she's just been the victim of a robbery – a man on a motorcycle took off with her handbag, which had "all her things" in it. And so he does the right thing, which is to abandon his plans to watch the movie in order to help her, without feeling in the least resentful or annoyed. Instead, he is grateful that he happened to run into her at just the right time. At a minimum, what allows Victor to act well in this situation is that he knows (a) that he should help his friend rather than continue on his way, and (b) that he should help her because she needs help (and not because he owes her a favor, wants to impress her, or whatever). He also knows (c) that sympathy and concern are appropriate feelings in this situation (and that annoyance and resentment are not), and (d) why these feelings are appropriate.

Of course, these are things that any minimally decent or well-meaning person knows, and while it may allow him to avoid wrongdoing, it is not what allows him to succeed in acting well. To see what else is needed for virtuous action, Aristotelians encourage us to think about what an experienced virtuous person has that a good-natured but inexperienced person lacks. Consider how a good-natured but inexperienced person, let's call him Adam, might behave in Victor's situation. Clearly, Adam will try to be helpful, because his heart is in the right place. But he is less likely to be successful. A frequent reason for this is that he doesn't quite know what would count as being helpful in the situation. Adam might offer emotional support, but not realize that what his friend really (or also) needs is protection from other threats to her personal security, such as identity theft and credit card fraud. The general aim of helping his friend needs to be made specific, that is, Adam has to figure out what would help *this* person in *these* circumstances. Another, more mundane reason why Adam might fail is that he doesn't know *how to* bring about the desired ends. For example, he might see that his friend is upset and needs emotional support, but not know how to provide it. Or he might just not have the necessary practical skills, such as knowing how to locate the nearest police station or how to cancel credit cards, to be of much help. So we can add two further things to our list of what a virtuous person knows: (e) what counts as being beneficial (i.e., which ends are desirable or good for someone) and (f) how to bring about the desired ends (i.e., how to execute virtuous plans). The latter form of knowledge is what Aristotle refers to as "cleverness" (*deinotēs*). It is a kind of technical expertise that is necessary for virtuous action, but because it is entirely mundane and non-moral Aristotelians tend to see it as a separate intellectual virtue rather than as part of practical wisdom.[2] The former kind of knowledge, an understanding or correct conception of what is beneficial or advantageous, is a crucial part of practical wisdom.

This account of practical knowledge is not yet complete, for it still needs an explanation of how Victor knows that helping his friend is the right thing to do, and how he knows that concern and kindness are appropriate emotions in the situation. In seeking this explanation, we are looking for what distinguishes a virtuous person from someone who is vicious. A vicious (selfish, unsympathetic, unkind) person in Victor's situation might realize that his friend needs help, and know how to help her, but simply think to himself, "I already have plans, and I shouldn't have to sacrifice my interests to help someone else." So what does the virtuous person know that the vicious one doesn't?

In response to this question, deontologists argue that a virtuous person knows that he has a duty to help a friend in need if he can do so at little cost to himself, or, stated otherwise, he knows that by helping her he is obeying (or acting in accordance with) a moral command or imperative. By contrast, Aristotelian virtue ethicists argue that a virtuous person correctly perceives that certain things are more worthwhile than others. Victor will see that the welfare and safety of his friend is a goal worth pursuing, far more worthy than the pursuit of pleasure. And so he will not consider the fact that he was looking forward to watching a movie as a morally relevant feature of the situation, or as a reason against helping his friend.

It is important to be clear about what Aristotelians mean when they claim that certain things are more worthwhile than others. It is not merely a matter of comparing two goods, in this case his friend's welfare and the pleasure he will get from watching a movie, and correctly concluding that the former is more valuable than the latter (which is what a consequentialist might do). The virtuous person also sees that helping his friend is a more worthwhile pursuit, a better thing for him to do, than watching a movie. To illustrate this point, consider the example of Connor, who finds himself in the same situation as Victor. Connor can see that his friend needs emotional support and practical help, and he knows how to provide these. But he has a movie to go to, and so he phones a friend who lives nearby, and who he knows has nothing planned for the evening and will be happy to give exactly the kind of help and support that is needed. And, indeed, Franny comes straight over and does just that, while Connor goes off to enjoy his movie.

Arguably, from a consequentialist perspective, Connor does the right thing, and what allows him to do so is that he has a correct conception of what is good for his friend (that is, he knows what would make her happy in the long term), and he knows how to achieve the desired end. He also realizes that he will be made happy by the decision, as he gets to enjoy his movie, thereby maximizing the amount of happiness in the circumstances. From an Aristotelian perspective, however, Connor does not act well. He doesn't understand that helping a friend is a much better way to spend an evening than watching a movie. He doesn't grasp that being kind and generous is a good way to be, that it is part of what constitutes a good life. In short, then, what allows a virtuous person like Victor to act well is that he has knowledge of (g) what is good or worthwhile. And it is this knowledge that allows him to see what is right and why it is right, and that guides his appetites and emotions – he wants to help his friend, and given his changed circumstances, he no longer sees watching a movie as a desirable or attractive thing to do on that particular evening.

In summary, practical wisdom is an intellectual virtue that involves an understanding of what is good or worthwhile in life. It allows an agent to see what ought to be done in particular situations and to understand the reasons why it ought to be done. This requires the ability to deliberate well, that is, to see which features of the situation are relevant and count as reasons in favor or against certain actions, and to know what would count as beneficial or harmful in particular situations. His understanding of what is good or worthwhile also directs his feelings and attitudes, such that these are in harmony with reason. In addition, he has a set of technical skills required for successfully executing virtuous plans.[3]

Aristotelians emphasize three further points about practical wisdom. The first is that it is very different from theoretical wisdom. Theoretical wisdom is a set of intellectual virtues needed for acquiring knowledge of scientific and mathematical truths. This includes knowledge of universal laws or principles (e.g., the law of gravity), as well as particular truths that can be deduced from these laws (e.g., the fact that this object will fall to the ground when dropped). Some moral philosophers think that moral knowledge is very similar to scientific knowledge: a moral expert is someone who has knowledge of moral laws or principles (e.g. "Making false promises is always wrong"), which allows him to deduce the truth of particular moral claims (e.g., "Making a false promise to Abdullah is wrong"). Aristotelians reject this view and claim that the virtuous person is someone who has certain intellectual capacities or skills rather than knowledge of laws or principles. In order to act well one has to have a correct understanding of what is good or bad, what is beneficial or harmful, and this is not the kind of knowledge that can be captured in a set of rules.[4]

The second point follows from the first, namely that practical wisdom can only be gained through experience. An understanding of what is beneficial, worthwhile, and good is not something one can get from reading a textbook or going to lectures (Hursthouse 1991, 231). In the Aristotelian view, people begin the process of acquiring virtue by imitating the behavior of virtuous people. They might regularly or habitually do things such as telling the truth and apportioning things equally, and, if they are lucky, succeed in doing the right thing most of the time. But they will struggle in unusual situations, for example, when telling the truth will damage someone's reputation. To reliably do what is right, they have to understand why honesty typically calls for telling the truth, such that they are able to identify situations in which these reasons do not apply. And this kind of knowledge only comes with practice and experience. Once they have gained practical wisdom, they have progressed from merely imitating honest or just people to actually being honest or just in a reliable and self-directing way.

The third point is that practical wisdom is similar to technical skills. Julia Annas gives a helpful discussion of virtue as analogous to skill in her book, *Intelligent Virtue* (2011). A puzzling thing, which seems to contradict the Aristotelian account of practical wisdom, is that virtuous action does not always or even typically involve conscious thought. When asked about their reasons for doing a heroic thing, like risking their life to save someone from a burning building or helping victims of a terrorist attack, people often say that they acted instinctively, that it was immediately obvious what to do, or that they didn't give it any thought. This makes it look like virtuous action does not always require deliberation, and that Aristotelians are guilty of having an overly "intellectualist" conception of virtue (Annas 2011, 28).

Annas's solution to this puzzle is to note how virtue is analogous to practical skill. The development and exercise of virtue involves practical reasoning of a kind we also find in the development and exercise of a practical skill, such as playing the piano. In both cases, we learn from other people, our role models or teachers. But it is not just a matter of copying the teacher or following her instructions. Learning to play the piano involves coming to understand what our teacher is doing and why she is doing it. That is, we need to learn the skill for ourselves, so that we can follow her instructions in ways that are intelligently selective. And this obviously requires conscious thought. However, once we've mastered the skill, we don't have to consciously think about it. A good pianist does not think about how to play a particular phrase but does so spontaneously. As Annas explains, "[t]he expert pianist plays in a way not dependent on conscious input, but the result is not mindless routine but rather playing infused with and expressing the pianist's thoughts about the piece" (2011, 13–14).

Annas argues that the same is true about learning virtue: it is not just a matter of imitating our role models but coming to understand their reasoning, and this will often require conscious thought. But once we have acquired a virtue, we don't have to think about these reasons. It becomes immediately obvious that we should act in certain ways. This does not mean it is a matter of mindless routine or habitual action. Instead, it is an active and intelligently engaged form of practical mastery. Although the virtuous person is guided by intelligence, he doesn't have to think through each step of the action all over again.[5]

We are now in a position to consider the two central claims that Aristotelians make about practical wisdom.

5.1.1 The Virtues Require Practical Wisdom

The first claim is that practical wisdom is required for each and every virtue. This does not mean that the virtuous person must be all-knowing. Clearly, in most situations, there will be things that even the most virtuous person cannot be aware of. Consider, for example, the all-too-familiar situation of having to resolve a dispute between two children. One child accuses the other of hurting him on purpose, whereas the second vehemently denies this. Having not been a witness to the interaction, it is impossible for the parent to know the truth. And yet, if she is wise, the parent will find a way to resolve the dispute and restore the peace. The important point to note, however, is that although Aristotelians accept that a certain degree of ignorance is consistent with virtue, they deny that it is ever required for virtue. In the above case, the parent's ignorance of the facts does not form any part of what makes her virtuous. Instead, in describing her virtue an Aristotelian will make reference to the things that she does know: how to deal with small children, how to tell when they're lying, how to be fair, and so on.

Aristotelians give three closely related reasons in favor of the claim that practical wisdom is required for virtue. The first has to do with their view of virtue as a human excellence, that is, with their commitment to perfectionism. Moral thought and decision-making necessarily involves practical reasoning (or what Aristotle refers to as "deliberation"), and this can be done well or poorly. Practical wisdom is an intellectual virtue that allows us to reason well about how to act. While having good intentions and motivations is admirable, it is not sufficient for excellence (see Russell 2009, 32).

The second reason has to do with moral responsibility and praiseworthiness. According to Aristotle, an action can only be praiseworthy if it is the result of deliberation and choice. People who accidentally do the right thing, or do so for the wrong reasons, do not deserve moral praise. Even people who habitually do things like give the correct change or help people in need are not praiseworthy unless they do the right thing for the right reasons, that is, if they have knowledge of and are committed to what is good. But if their behavior is just a matter of good habit, then they don't really deserve our praise or esteem. They might well be pleasant to have around, for the same reasons that it is (sometimes) pleasant to have attractive or talented people around, but they are not virtuous.

The third reason is that practical wisdom is necessary for right action. According to Aristotle, traits that do not include practical wisdom cannot be relied upon (*The Nicomachean Ethics* 1144b8–12). Although a well-meaning adolescent will sometimes get it right, she will often make mistakes. Whether or not she tries to help people in need will depend on whether she is moved by their plight, and so she might end up being kind to small children but not to the elderly or the mentally ill, to some children but not to others, and in some situations but not in others. By contrast, someone who has the virtue of kindness will consistently act kindly when it is appropriate to do so, and this requires "seeing things as they are." He will notice, for example, that the elderly and the mentally ill are vulnerable in ways that are similar to those of young children, but also that what would amount to kindness will be different in different situations. In short, virtue is a reliable disposition to act well, and it is practical wisdom that makes this reliability possible.

5.1.2 The Virtues Form a Unity

Aristotle defends a strong version of the unity of virtue thesis, namely that if a good person has practical wisdom, then she will possess all the virtues. His reasoning in defense of this thesis goes roughly as follows: Practical wisdom is necessary for all the (character) virtues. One cannot be courageous, kind, generous, honest, just and so on, without having practical wisdom as an intellectual virtue. Practical wisdom is the same for each virtue for they all require a broad or general conception of the ends of action, that is, about what is good or worthwhile for human beings. It follows from this that someone who has practical wisdom will have all the virtues (see *The Nicomachean Ethics* 1144b29–1145a2).

The unity of virtue thesis is very controversial, given that it appears to conflict with what we know from empirical observation. It might well be the case that people who are kind are also generous, compassionate, and forgiving, for these virtues all involve a commitment to the good of others. However, there seems to be no connection between kindness and courage, or between justice and temperance. We all know people who are kind but cowardly – always ready to help others but not strong enough to stand up to a bully, or fair but intemperate – like the person who often overindulges in sweets yet is always careful to divide them up evenly (so that everyone can overindulge equally). This calls into question whether the virtues are unified.

Although the unity of virtue thesis is often dismissed as one of the most implausible aspects of ancient virtue ethics, quite a few contemporary Aristotelians defend a strong version of the thesis (see Russell 2009; Annas 2011; Toner 2014). Others defend a limited (or weak) unity of virtue thesis, which holds that someone who possesses one virtue will have all the others to some degree (see Badhwar 1996; Watson 1984). In what follows, we consider some of the arguments in favor of the strong version.

Following Aristotle, defenders of the unity of virtue thesis point out that people who appear to have one virtue but not another, don't have "proper virtue" at all. What they have, instead, is "natural virtue," that is, they are naturally disposed to have certain feelings and to be moved to behave in certain ways. Some children are by nature kind and sympathetic and often try to do nice things for other people. Others are by nature brave or fearless and disposed to risk-taking. There is no reason to expect that someone who is naturally kind will also be naturally courageous. That is, there is no unity of natural virtue (see *The Nicomachean Ethics* VI.13). However, natural virtue differs in an important respect from virtue proper in that it does not involve deliberation and choice. This is why sympathetic and brave children often make a mess of things, harming the people they are trying to help, or risking their lives for worthless goals. To have virtue proper, a person should be able to give reasons for what he does. Someone progresses from having natural kindness to proper kindness when they come to understand that the good of others is worth promoting. But that same understanding also underlies the virtue of courage: a truly courageous person will see that standing up to a bully to protect a friend is worth the risk, whereas risking your life to retrieve a kite is not. The virtues all involve making judgments about what is good, beneficial, or worthwhile, and so it follows that someone who has a good understanding of these concepts, that is, who has practical wisdom, will be able to make good judgments across the board (see Hursthouse 1999, 153–157; Annas 2011, 85–86).

A closely related argument in favor of the unity of virtue thesis is the "due concern view" (Watson 1984; Russell 2009; Toner 2014). Many, if not most of the situations we encounter in our day-to-day lives call for more than one virtue, and sometimes the demands of different virtues conflict. For a trait to be an excellence of character, it cannot be narrowly focused on its own field. In exercising one virtue, one has to be aware of how the demands of that virtue are affected by the demands of other virtues. Someone who thinks he should tell the truth but neglects to consider the harm it might cause does not have honesty as a virtue. To have a particular virtue, one has to be aware of, and responsive to, the demands of other virtues. As Toner puts it, virtue "must show *due* concern for items in that field, and that involves also being cognizant of and responsive to what might be due to items in the fields of other virtues" (2014, 209).

Annas supports the idea that the virtues are interconnected by drawing attention to the moral development of children, and the fact that we don't teach the virtues one by one. She uses the example of generosity. We cannot teach a child to be generous by simply encouraging her to give things away, for she needs to have some conception of ownership as well as fairness and justice. The child has to learn that she has a right to keep or hold on to her own possessions, but that it would be kind or generous to share them with others. She also has to learn that she cannot be generous with someone else's possessions. Further, true generosity requires benevolence – giving away things that are not needed or wanted by others is not generous; she has to actually care about the good of others and think about how to promote it. Annas thinks this shows that some virtues "cluster" – children don't learn each virtue in isolation. Life itself is not "compartmentalized," and so we cannot learn to deal with the complexities of life by acquiring different virtues, each with their own form of practical wisdom. Moral decision-making is not a matter of identifying the claims of various virtues and then trying to compare and assess these claims in an effort to work out an overall right decision on the grounds of some higher value or principle. Instead, Annas argues, "the practical intelligence involved is one which integrates and unifies all the relevant aspects of the situation from the start, rather than developing on separate tracks and then trying to tie the results together" (2011, 87). For example, a compassionate person might need courage to stand up to a bully on someone else's behalf, and so if he lacks courage, his compassion will also be less than perfect.

Another way to support the unity of virtue thesis is to point out that a virtue can be manifested in various ways. It is fairly easy to recognize the courage of a soldier or firefighter. But courage is not only manifested in situations where physical safety is at risk. We also need courage to overcome fear of failure, humiliation, or pain. So we shouldn't be too quick to conclude that someone lacks courage on the grounds that she hid in the closet (rather than do something courageous) when a knife-wielding intruder broke into her house. To be able to act courageously in this kind of situation one needs to have some relevant experience, knowledge, and skill, and lacking these, hiding in the closet might well be the best thing to do. But the same person can display remarkable courage in the way she deals with other forms of hardship, such as battling mental illness, or taking care of a difficult patient. We develop the virtues in ways that allow us to deal well with the circumstances of our lives, and these differ from one person to another, and so we shouldn't expect the virtues to manifest in the same way in different individuals (see Annas 2011, 93–95).

In the remainder of this chapter, we will consider three objections to the Aristotelian view of practical wisdom. The first is an objection by Julia Driver, who uses the example of modesty to dispute the claim that practical wisdom is required for each and every virtue. The second is an objection by Christine Swanton, who disputes the claim that the virtues form a unity. The final objection, by Michael Slote, is aimed at both theses.

5.2 Consequentialism and the Virtue of Modesty

Julia Driver presents an interesting challenge for the Aristotelian view that practical wisdom is necessary for virtue. As we've seen in Chapters 2 and 4,

Driver defines virtue as a trait that systematically produces good consequences in this world (2001, 82). She accepts that there are some virtues
that have good consequences because they involve knowledge and skill. As
she puts it, correct perception of morally relevant facts often helps virtue
along (2001, 1). A truly benevolent person must know what is good for
others and must have the skills to bring about this good. Driver also
accepts that many virtuous people do in fact have knowledge, and that this
knowledge often allows them to act virtuously. However, the fact that
virtue often requires a form of intelligence should not lead us to the conclusion that it always does so. Driver thinks there is a class of virtue that
requires its possessor to be ignorant of a morally relevant feature of the
situation. She calls these the "virtues of ignorance," and they include
modesty (a disposition to underestimate one's self-worth), blind charity (a
disposition not to see defects in others), trust (a disposition to believe in
others' innocence despite evidence to the contrary), the disposition to
"forgive and forget," and impulsive courage (a disposition that involves a
failure to perceive danger to oneself). To support her view that practical
wisdom is not required for each and every virtue, Driver only needs to give
one convincing example of a virtue of ignorance. If she can do this, she
will be a step closer to convincing us that what makes a trait a virtue is
that it systematically produces good consequences.

5.2.1 Driver's Account of Modesty

It seems plausible to claim that modesty is a genuine virtue: we admire
people like Nelson Mandela, Edmund Hillary, and Malala Yousafzai not
only for their courage, generosity, and greatness of spirit, but also for their
modesty. Modest people characteristically behave in certain ways: they
don't brag, they avoid drawing attention to themselves and their achievements, and they don't participate in ranking exercises. As a result, they're
less likely to provoke competitive and envious responses in others. But
what motivates a modest person? And are they unaware of the value of
their achievements, or do they just pretend to be?

According to Driver, modesty is a virtue of ignorance: a modest person
is someone who underestimates his self-worth; he thinks he is less deserving
and less worthy than he actually is, and this causes him to behave in ways
that other people (though not he himself) can describe as modest. When
he talks about his own accomplishments, he understates the truth, but he
does so unknowingly. Driver calls this the "underestimation" account of
modesty. She distinguishes it from the "understatement" account, which
holds that a modest person knows the truth about his own accomplishments and self-worth, but understates it for some reason (he might want to

avoid boasting, for instance). Driver rejects this account, for she thinks such a person manifests false modesty: "If a person understates her self-worth and others had reason to believe that she knows herself to be better than she says she is, they would tend to call this *false* modesty on her part" (2001, 18).

Driver thinks modesty serves as a counter-example to the Aristotelian claim that virtue requires knowledge. A modest person is ignorant of relevant facts, that is, facts about his self-worth. He doesn't know that he is acting modestly, and he doesn't act modestly for the right reasons. Simply put, he doesn't see things as they are. Nevertheless, modesty is widely regarded as a virtue, and Driver thinks the best explanation for this is that it systematically produces good consequences in the world. In particular, she claims that the modest person "seems less likely to provoke an envious response in others" (Driver 2001, 27). Modest behavior has this effect precisely because the individual appears to be ignorant of their self-worth. Given that the good effects are relatively minor, Driver accepts that modesty is only a minor virtue.[6] A modest person is unaware that he is acting modestly, and so, by implication, is not motivated by a desire to be modest. Instead, Driver claims that what motivates a modest person could be any of a number of things, such as a desire to tell the truth or a concern not to appear vain. She thinks a modest person can even be motivated by a desire to present himself well, and mistakenly think that he is overstating his self-worth when in fact he is understating it.

5.2.2 An Aristotelian View of Modesty

One way to assess the claim that modesty requires ignorance is to ask how, in Driver's view, one acquires modesty. Driver claims that the modest person underestimates his self-worth because he just doesn't feel the need to spend a lot of time ranking and estimating his worth relative to others. She also notes that ranking is a destructive tendency. But why doesn't he feel the need to rank? It is possible that he was born with this disposition, or that it was drilled into him as a child. But a more likely reason is that he doesn't feel the need to rank because he *knows* it is a destructive tendency. So it seems that Driver's modest person is not all that ignorant: he knows something that is important for living well and acting appropriately. But this doesn't get us very far, because Driver could still be correct in claiming that the modest person is ignorant about the full extent of his self-worth (even though he might not be ignorant about the destructiveness of ranking). It is this particular bit of ignorance that others find charming or attractive, and that produces the good consequences, so it doesn't really matter that his ignorance about self-worth results from the knowledge that ranking is a destructive tendency.

We get a bit further when we ask how it is possible for the modest person to stay ignorant about the full extent of his self-worth (see Kupfer 2003). Driver claims that "the modest person is someone who is disposed to underestimate self-worth to some limited extent, in spite of the available evidence" (2001, 21). But how is this possible? Even if he avoids ranking exercises, he will eventually encounter someone who has done the ranking for him. Consider how often successful people are confronted with facts about their accomplishments. Surely, Roger Federer cannot be ignorant of the fact that he is widely regarded as the greatest tennis player in history. And given the number of rewards and prizes she has received, Malala Yousafzai cannot be ignorant of the fact that many people admire her for her courage. On Driver's account, it would be very difficult for successful or influential people to remain modest for very long. Sooner or later the truth will catch up to them, and then their modesty will be ruined. Yet this seems deeply counter-intuitive. People often become more modest with age, even while becoming less ignorant about their relative self-worth.

Far from a virtue of ignorance, Aristotelians argue that modesty is a virtue of the wise, and that it requires or involves a characteristic set of (true) beliefs, motivations, and attitudes. A modest person has an accurate understanding of the significance of his achievements, but this involves an awareness of his successes as well as his limitations. For example, Federer must know that he is the world's best tennis player (how could he not?), but if he is modest he will also be aware of his own limitations. He will know that he is not the world's best tennis player in every respect, and this makes it possible for him to genuinely admire other players: Nadal for his performance on clay, or Sampras for the power of his serve. In speaking of his admiration for other players, Federer would not be underestimating his self-worth nor understating it; he would simply be telling the truth. Further, if he is modest, Federer will be aware of how little he knows about, say, art, history, and politics. That is, he will know that he is *only* the world's best tennis player. He will not make the mistake of thinking that his opinions about art, history and politics should be taken seriously just because he is the world's best tennis player (which is the kind of thing arrogant people do). A modest person will also be aware that luck played a big part in enabling his success. If he is modest, Federer will be aware that he was blessed with talents and opportunities that very few people have. And he will be aware of the important contribution that other people made to his success.

Further, and more importantly, the modest person will realize that achievement in a specific field is not a measure of self-worth. Being the world's best tennis player doesn't make Federer a better person. Driver seems to think that a person's self-worth depends on their achievements. She claims, for instance, that the modest person stays ignorant of self-worth because he doesn't spend a lot of time ranking, thereby suggesting that more time spent ranking will result in a more accurate estimation of self-worth. She also claims that if Albert Einstein viewed himself merely as *a great physicist* (as opposed to the greatest physicist of the twentieth century), then he would be modest (2001, 19). In the Aristotelian view, this is a mistake. Einstein, if he is modest, would not base his sense of self-worth on his scientific achievements at all. A modest person knows that being successful in one area does not make one a good or excellent person. He will genuinely admire and praise people who are virtuous, who have devoted their lives to worthy causes, managed to overcome hardship, endured suffering and defeat with dignity, and so on. In short, then, and regardless of the magnificence of his achievements, the Aristotelian would argue that a person who is wise – who sees his accomplishments in perspective – must be modest (see Ridge 2000, 281; Winter 2012, 538).

In the Aristotelian view, then, the virtue of modesty involves a characteristic set of motivations and attitudes as well as practical wisdom. A modest person is one who recognizes and appreciates the contributions and achievements of others. And in doing so, he is not underestimating his own worth or overestimating theirs; rather, he sees the truth about others. Far from being a minor virtue, as Driver claims, modesty is an important virtue; one who lacks it reveals an important misconception of what matters in life.[7]

5.3 Pluralistic Virtue Ethics and the Disunity of Virtue

As a virtue ethicist, Christine Swanton is committed to the view that all the virtues express "fine inner states," by which she means appropriate emotions, motivations, attitudes, and intelligence. She also agrees with the Aristotelian claim that virtue requires "a standing commitment to act from virtue" (2003, 28). In her view, the virtues are dispositions to respond well to the demands of the world, but she thinks a closer examination of the virtues shows that they don't all have one thing in common. With regards to practical wisdom, she thinks that although it is characteristically important, it is not a necessary feature of virtue. She agrees with Nietzsche that some virtues require creativity rather than rationality.[8] Our focus in this section will be on Swanton's objection to the unity of virtue thesis (2003, 34–48; 2015a; 2015c).

As we've seen, Aristotelians claim that an understanding of what is good or worthwhile forms a crucial part of practical wisdom. The virtues involve an understanding of, and commitment to, different values. Honesty is a commitment to truth, benevolence to the good of others, and so on, but ultimately, all of these goods can be unified in the sense that they all form part of a good or flourishing human life. In short, then, Aristotelians think that all the virtues involve a commitment to a *single* form of goodness, namely, living a good or flourishing life. Without such a commitment, one cannot have any of the virtues. To illustrate, consider the following case.

> Cassandra has devoted her life to making as much money as possible. She is prepared to do so through whatever means available to her (e.g., lying, deception, fraud, insider trading, etc.). She is indifferent to the demands of justice, and doesn't care about how she harms others. But in addition to her love of money, she also truly appreciates the inherent value of works of art, and she has a vast knowledge of art history. Whenever possible, she makes large donations to underfunded art museums all over the world, because she wants to make sure their artworks are preserved. The question is, does she have the virtue of connoisseurship?

Aristotelians will deny that Cassandra, a thoroughly dishonest, manipulative, and unjust person, has any kind of virtue. Annas (2011, 100–118) argues that a virtuous person is committed to goodness, to living a good life. Given that Cassandra has no such commitment, she has no virtue. Similarly, Hursthouse argues that vicious people cannot act from virtue. They might think they are motivated to act by what is right, but they are mistaken, for they have no idea of what is right or good. They are, she claims, "hopelessly corrupted by the wicked doctrines they have embraced and made their own" (Hursthouse 1999, 147).[9] This leaves the Aristotelian with two options. The first is to argue that although Cassandra possesses connoisseurship as a trait, connoisseurship is not a virtue because it doesn't require practical wisdom, or more specifically, an understanding of what is good or worthwhile. Connoisseurship is a useful trait, in the same way that athleticism, good eyesight, and excellent memory can be useful traits, but it is not a virtue because one can lead a good or flourishing life without being a connoisseur of the arts. The second option is to argue that although connoisseurship is a virtue, it is not a virtue that Cassandra possesses. Works of art are the product of human activity; they express human emotions, attitudes, and beliefs. To truly appreciate the value of works of art one has to have an understanding of and commitment to what is good or worthwhile, which Casssandra clearly lacks.

Against this, pluralists like Swanton argue that virtue cannot be defined in terms of a commitment to a single form of goodness, such as the agent's good or flourishing. The virtues are a collection of distinct traits that involve commitments to distinct forms of goodness. As we've seen in Chapter 2, Swanton identifies four different grounds of virtue. *Value-based virtues*, which include the virtue of connoisseurship, involve responding well to valuable things, such as knowledge, beauty, the environment, works of art, and so on. Some of these virtues might well contribute to the flourishing of their possessor, but if they do, it is not this fact that makes the trait in question a virtue. *Status-based virtues*, such as justice, deference, and politeness require that we recognize and respond appropriately to a person's status as, for example, a parent, a teacher, a political leader, and so on. *Bond-based virtues*, such as love, compassion, and friendship, express an appropriate attitude or commitment to bonds or relationships. Finally, *flourishing-based virtues*, such as charity and benevolence, are aimed at promoting or protecting the good of sentient beings (Swanton 2003, 34–48; 2015c, 212–216).

If pluralists are right, then it follows that a person can be virtuous in some respects but not in others. The intellectual skills required for appreciating valuable things, such as art, knowledge, and science, are very different from intellectual skills needed for promoting or protecting the happiness or welfare of sentient beings. Flourishing-based virtues require some degree of empathy and care, an understanding of and responsiveness to what is good *for* these beings, and so people who don't have the virtue of benevolence will typically not have the virtues of generosity or care either. However, appreciating valuable *things*, such as beauty, science, or artworks, does not require empathy at all. In Cassandra's case, then, a pluralist could argue that although she lacks the virtues of honesty, justice, benevolence (and many more), she at least has the virtue of connoisseurship. She responds well to works of art, because she appreciates them and goes out of her way to protect them.

In response, Annas doesn't dispute Swanton's claim that there is a plurality of goods and values. She accepts that "in exercising different virtues the virtuous person is directed towards different values." However, she thinks "the different virtues can, and should in a good life, be unified by the person's living their life in accordance with a unified conception of goodness." This conception of goodness is "to be discovered and exercised by the person's practical reasoning, which unifies the acquisition and expression of the virtues" (Annas 2011, 115). What the virtuous person is committed to, then, is the sole end of living a good life (*eudaimonia*). Looking at Cassandra's life from this perspective, we see that it is characterized by a certain kind of tension or disunity. She cares about money, and so has acquired traits (dishonesty, manipulativeness, ambition, etc.) to allow her to become as rich as possible. But her love of the arts, specifically her tendency to make donations to struggling art museums, stands in the way of her desire to become as rich as possible. Further, she cares about works of art, but without caring about the people who produce or appreciate them.

In what follows, we will consider the reasons why sentimentalist virtue ethicists reject the Aristotelian view (namely that practical wisdom is necessary for virtue, and that it serves to unify the virtues).

5.4 Sentimentalist Virtue Ethics, Practical Wisdom, and the Impossibility of Perfection

Sentimentalist virtue ethics defines the virtues in terms of emotion rather than reason. A virtuous person is motivated by sentiments that are intuitively good, such as benevolence, gratitude, compassion, and love (see Chapter 2). Sentimentalism is an example of an agent-based theory because it takes virtue to be fundamental. That is, it holds that:

> certain forms of overall motivation are, intuitively, morally good and approvable in themselves and apart from their consequences or the possibility of grounding them in certain rules or principles. Every ethical theory has to start somewhere, and an agent-based morality will want to say that the moral goodness of (universal) benevolence or of caring about people is intuitively obvious and in need of no further moral grounding.
>
> (Slote 2001, 38)

Michael Slote rejects the Aristotelian view on the grounds that a normative theory that seeks to be a "pure" form of virtue ethics cannot make rationality a requirement for virtue. He notes that "[Aristotle] implies that the virtuous individual does what is noble or virtuous because it is the noble – for example, courageous – thing to do, rather than its being the case that what is noble – or courageous – to do has this status simply because the virtuous individual actually will choose or has chosen it" (2001, 5). In the Aristotelian view, a virtuous person is someone who acts for the right reasons and has the appropriate feelings and attitudes when she acts. Slote argues that by defining virtue with reference to the "right" or "appropriate" reasons, feelings, and attitudes, Aristotelians presuppose some standard that is independent of agent-evaluation. As such, their position is not an example of agent-*based* virtue ethics, that is, virtue is not a primary or fundamental concept. We can call this the "purity" objection.

One way Aristotelians can respond to the purity objection is simply to accept that virtue is not (and was never meant to be) a fundamental concept, and if this means that the theory is not as pure as it could be, so be it. Hursthouse (1999, 82–83) explicitly "disavows" the idea that virtue has a foundational role in her theory, and instead claims that although "the concept of the virtuous agent is the focal concept," virtue ethics also relies on many other concepts, including "the *good* of human beings and what (truly) *benefits* them, … the *worthwhile*, the *advantageous*, and the *pleasant*."

The advantage of the Aristotelian view is that it avoids a problem encountered by agent-based theories, namely that an agent who is motivated by good feelings or desires will often go wrong. As we've seen, one of the main reasons why Aristotelians think practical wisdom is required for virtue is that it allows the agent to act well reliably. Correct perception of the relevant features of the situation and a correct understanding of what is beneficial and worthwhile are necessary for right action. In response, Slote argues that a truly benevolent person will make an effort to get the relevant facts right, so that her actions can be really useful (2001, 18, 40). But what makes her admirable or virtuous is the fact that she is motivated by benevolence or care, and not the fact that she has knowledge. A truly benevolent person attains and uses knowledge to achieve her benevolent ends.[10]

Daniel Russell is not convinced by this response. To illustrate why virtue requires practical wisdom, he uses the example of the Nukak people, a group of hunter-gatherers who live in Colombia's forests. In 2003, a Nukak tribe was pushed out of the forests by guerrilla warriors, and Colombian authorities were required to provide aid and assistance. It was obvious that the displaced people needed things like food, water, and shelter, and these were provided by aid workers. Nevertheless, the attempt to help the tribe was considered a failure, for several years later they were leading listless lives, completely dependent on aid. They were not working and did not learn Spanish, and had no plans to return to the forest (Russell 2009, 80–81).

Russell asks us to consider why the aid workers were unsuccessful. They didn't fail because of an absence of benevolent feelings or a true desire to help the tribe. Nor was it caused by a lack of Aristotelian "cleverness," that is, the kind of technical know-how required for executing one's plans (in this case, doing things like setting up a camp, distributing food parcels, and providing clean water). Rather, the failure was a result of a faulty judgment about what would be beneficial to the Nukak people in these circumstances, that is, about what would count as helping them. And this amounts to a failure in practical wisdom, which has to do with the very formulation of a plan and requires deliberation about things like whether independence and integration are worthwhile goals in the circumstances. Russell thinks that Slote's benevolence can accommodate cleverness: benevolent desires naturally move the agent to do certain things, at which point they can reason about how best to achieve these ends. But Slote's commitment to the view that virtue must be fundamental prevents him from incorporating the wisdom or intelligence needed for formulating a plan, or deliberating about which ends are worthwhile. The result is that someone who has benevolence in Slote's sense will often "fail to hit their benevolent marks" (Russell 2009, 80–83).

The question, then, is whether we want to describe the benevolence of the aid workers as a genuine virtue or not. Sentimentalists believe that the aid workers are genuinely benevolent because they acted from good motives (which included obtaining the knowledge and skill needed for successfully executing their plans). Their failure to benefit the Nukak people in the long run does not detract from their admirability. By contrast, Aristotelians argue that the aid workers do not have benevolence as a human excellence because they lacked practical wisdom; they didn't have a correct understanding of which ends are worthwhile or beneficial. What the disagreement boils down to is whether we should see virtue as an admirable trait or whether, instead, we should apply a higher standard, and see it as a human excellence.

Slote deals with this issue in a more recent book, entitled *The Impossibility of Perfection* (2011). He argues that we cannot apply a higher standard, given that perfect virtue is in principle impossible for human beings. Some virtues are "partial," in the sense that they conflict with each other, not only in particular circumstances, but by their very nature. The implication is that having one of these virtues necessarily means having less of another. One example of a pair of partial virtues is prudence and adventurousness. A prudent person will pursue security, for instance by finding a good job, buying a house, and saving money. By contrast, an adventurous person will take risks, enjoys discovering new things and making or bringing about progress. Prudence and adventurousness are incompatible: one cannot pursue security and adventure at the same time, which means that one cannot reach perfection. Prudence necessarily brings with it a deficiency in adventurousness, and adventurousness necessarily brings with it a deficiency in prudence. Another example of a pair of partial virtues is frankness and tact. A tactful person must be less than fully honest, and an honest person cannot be perfectly tactful. These pairs of virtues compete with each other. We necessarily lose something of value if we choose one over the other. It follows that perfect virtue or excellence is impossible for human beings, and that we have to reject the unity of virtue thesis (Slote 2011, ch. 2).

Chapter Summary

- Aristotelians make three claims about the nature and role of practical wisdom: (a) Practical wisdom is necessary for virtue. One cannot have any of the individual virtues without having practical wisdom. (b) The virtues form a unity: a person who has one virtue will also have the others (at least to some degree). (c) A fully virtuous person, one who has practical wisdom, does not rely on moral rules or principles but instead exercises judgment in discerning the morally relevant features of particular situations.

- In response to the first claim, Julia Driver argues that although knowledge is needed for some virtues, it is not necessary for each and every virtue. Virtues like modesty, blind charity, and trust require ignorance about relevant facts.   *
- In response to the second claim, Christine Swanton argues that there are at least four distinct grounds of virtue, each involving its own set of skills. The virtues do not form a unity.
- Michael Slote rejects the first claim on the grounds that a normative theory that seeks to be a "pure" form of virtue ethics cannot make rationality a requirement for virtue. He rejects the second claim on the grounds that some virtues are "partial," which means that having one of them necessarily means having less of another.

The focus of the first few chapters of this book has been on questions about the nature of virtue, virtuous motivation, and practical wisdom, as well as the link between virtue and happiness. In the following chapter we will consider whether virtue ethics can provide a satisfactory account of right action.

Notes

1 For a more detailed account of Aristotle's distinction between these intellectual virtues see Chapter 8.
2 It is interesting to compare Hursthouse's (2006c, 298) discussion of cleverness with Russell's (2009, 1–2, 24–25).
3 For a discussion of the other intellectual virtues needed for acting well, see Hursthouse (2006c).
4 We will discuss the role of duty and moral principles in Chapters 7 and 8.
5 Annas develops the skill analogy in Chapter 3 of *Intelligent Virtue* (2011).
6 Driver thinks the example of modesty also shows that good motives are not necessary for virtue.
7 An interesting challenge to the Aristotelian view is to show whether it is possible for the perfectly virtuous person to be modest. As we've seen in Chapter 3, Aristotelians claim that the best life for human beings is a virtuous life. The virtues are human excellences, and so it follows that a perfectly virtuous person has the best life possible. But a virtuous person also sees things as they are, and so he must know that he is perfectly virtuous, and hence, that he is better than other people in this regard. The question, then, is whether a perfectly virtuous person can be modest. On the one hand, if he is perfectly virtuous then he must also have the virtue of modesty. On the other hand, if he is perfectly virtuous he must know that he is better than others, and so he can't be modest.

8 Swanton discusses this point in Chapter 7 of her book (2003). For a summary of Swanton's position, see Chapters 2 and 3, this volume.
9 As we will see in Chapter 6, Aristotelian virtue ethicists accept that a non-virtuous person can sometimes act virtuously, that is, do what a virtuous person would do in the circumstances. But there is a difference between performing a virtuous action and acting from virtue. Acting from virtue requires virtuous motivation, whereas performing a virtuous action does not.
10 Interestingly, and despite their obvious differences, Slote agrees with Driver that some virtues may well require ignorance. See Slote's (2004) response to Driver.

Further Reading

Annas, Julia. 2011. *Intelligent Virtue*. Oxford: Oxford University Press, chapter 3.
Aristotle. 2009. *The Nicomachean Ethics*. Translated by David Ross, revised by Lesley Brown. Oxford: Oxford University Press.
Badhwar, Neera K. 1996. "The Limited Unity of Virtue." *Noûs* 30(3): 306–329. doi:10.2307/2216272
Driver, Julia. 2001. *Uneasy Virtue*. Cambridge: Cambridge University Press.
Hursthouse, Rosalind. 1991. "Virtue Theory and Abortion." *Philosophy and Public Affairs* 20(3): 223–246.
Hursthouse, Rosalind. 1999. *On Virtue Ethics*. Oxford: Oxford University Press, part III.
Hursthouse, Rosalind. 2006c. "Practical Wisdom: A Mundane Account." *Proceedings of The Aristotelian Society* 106(1): 285–309. doi:10.1111/j.1467-9264.2006.00149.x
Russell, Daniel C. 2009. *Practical Intelligence and the Virtues*. Oxford: Oxford University Press, chapters 1 and 9.
Slote, Michael. 2001. *Morals from Motives*. New York: Oxford University Press.
Slote, Michael. 2004. "Driver's Virtues." *Utilitas* 16(1): 22–32. doi:10.1017/S0953820803001031
Slote, Michael. 2011. *The Impossibility of Perfection: Aristotle, Feminism, and the Complexities of Ethics*. New York: Oxford University Press.
Swanton, Christine. 2003. *Virtue Ethics: A Pluralistic View*. Oxford: Oxford University Press.
Swanton, Christine. 2015a. "Comments on *Intelligent Virtue*: Rightness and Exemplars of Virtue." *The Journal of Value Inquiry* 49(1): 307–314. doi:10.1007/s10790-014-9478-1
Swanton, Christine. 2015c. "Pluralistic *Virtue Ethics*." In *The Routledge Companion to Virtue Ethics*, edited by Lorraine Besser-Jones and Michael Slote, 209–222. New York: Routledge.
Toner, Christopher. 2014. "The Full Unity of the Virtues." *The Journal of Ethics* 18(3): 207–227. doi:10.1007/s10892-014-9165-2
Watson, Gary. 1984. "Virtues in Excess." *Philosophical Studies: An International Journal for Philosophy in the Analytic Tradition* 46(1): 57–74. doi:10.1007/BF00353491
Winter, Michael Jeffrey. 2012. "Does Moral Virtue Require Knowledge? A Response to Julia Driver." *Ethical Theory and Moral Practice* 15(4): 533–556. doi:10.1007/s10677-011-9310-y

6 Virtue and Right Action

It is generally expected that a normative theory should help us decide what to do in a particular situation and allow us to assess or evaluate particular actions. Many moral philosophers take this to mean: it should provide an account of right action. The question, What makes an action right? is widely regarded as a (if not *the*) central question in moral philosophy. W. D. Ross devotes the first half of *The Right and the Good* (2002) to the question of right action, and J. S. Mill spends most of "Utilitarianism" defending the claim that the "greatest happiness principle" (the utilitarian criterion of right action) is "the fundamental principle of morality" (Mill 1998, 134). The question, then, is whether virtue ethics can come up with a plausible account of right action.

Robert Louden, who is one of the earliest critics of contemporary virtue ethics, argues that it is "structurally unable" to give an account of right action, given that it is focused on "being" rather than "doing" (1984, 229). Since the publication of Louden's article, a number of virtue ethicists have tried to prove him wrong by providing distinctively virtue-ethical accounts of right action. However, it is worth noting that the notion of right action tends to feature much less prominently in their work. Julia Annas discusses it very briefly in *Intelligent Virtue* (2011, 41–51), and Christine Swanton only gets around to presenting her account of right action in Chapter 11 of her book, *Virtue Ethics: A Pluralistic View* (2003). Rosalind Hursthouse spends the first chapter of *On Virtue Ethics* (1999) trying to show that virtue ethics can come up with an account of right action, but she notes that "it does this under pressure" (1999, 69). Before we examine some of these accounts, it is useful to consider why so many virtue ethicists seem reluctant or even unwilling to talk about right action. To this end, we begin the chapter with a discussion of a position known as eliminativism, roughly, the view that virtue ethics should not provide an account of right action at all.

6.1 Eliminativism

Some virtue ethicists respond to Louden's challenge by arguing that virtue ethics need not, and indeed *should* not, try to offer an account of right action. In support, they tend to cite the following passage from Elizabeth Anscombe's seminal essay, "Modern Moral Philosophy":

> [T]he concepts of obligation, and duty – *moral* obligation and *moral* duty, that is to say – and of what is *morally* right and wrong, and of the *moral* sense of "ought," ought to be jettisoned if this is psychologically possible; because they are survivals, or derivatives from survivals, from an earlier conception of ethics which no longer generally survives, and are only harmful without it.
>
> (1958, 1)

Modern moral philosophers define a "right action" as an act that is either permissible or obligatory, and a "wrong action" as one that is impermissible, that is, an act one has an obligation to refrain from. Anscombe argues that the idea that someone has a moral obligation to either do or refrain from doing an action simply makes no sense. If a right action is a permissible action, then who (or what) is it that permits it? Who (or what) imposes upon one a duty or obligation to perform (or not perform) certain actions? Talk about right and wrong actions seems to presuppose the existence of a supreme lawgiver, which most people will find problematic. Richard Taylor, who is among the most ardent supporters of eliminativism, explains the problem as follows.

> [W]hat is the idea of moral obligation in modern philosophical thinking? ... It is a presumed obligation to do what is "right," and by the same token to avoid what is "wrong"... . Originally ..., *right* meant permitted by this or that person or group (by the state, for example); *wrong* meant forbidden; and *obligatory* meant required. Later, with the spread of Christianity into the world where rational philosophy had flourished, these terms came to mean permitted, forbidden, and required by God. But then, as belief in God faded, at least among philosophers, the *terms* right and wrong and obligatory were kept, though now divorced from any connection with any lawgiver, such as the state or God, which had given them their original meaning.
>
> (2002, 83)

The problem, then, is that modern moral philosophers use the concepts of moral rightness and wrongness in this traditional sense, but without believing in any source of authority that could ground such statements and serve to make them intelligible (see Hacker-Wright 2010, 209). It therefore seems reasonable to conclude, with Anscombe, that virtue ethicists should discard or "jettison" the concepts of right and wrong action.

What are the implications of getting rid of these concepts? As noted earlier, a criterion of right action is supposed to guide us in our decision-making and allow us to assess actions. Arguably, however, virtue ethics already fulfills these functions by giving us an account of virtue and virtuous action. We can recommend and approve of actions that are kind, honest, or just, and we can oppose or disapprove of actions that are unkind, dishonest, or unjust. Further, replacing the concepts of right and wrong with virtue and vice terms has a distinct advantage, namely that the latter are "thick" concepts, that is, they are both evaluative and descriptive. By claiming that someone did what was honest or kind, for example, I am not just approving of their action but also giving important information about what it is that I approve of. Similarly, by advising someone to "Do what is just" (as opposed to merely "Do what is right") I am both prescribing an action and describing it. Anscombe writes:

> You can do ethics without [the notion "morally ought"], as shown by the example of Aristotle. It would be a great improvement if, instead of "morally wrong," one always named a genus such as "untruthful," "unchaste," "unjust." We should no longer ask whether doing something was "wrong," passing directly from some description of an action to this notion; we should ask whether, e.g., it was unjust; and the answer would sometimes be clear at once.
>
> (1958, 8–9)

Once this point is grasped, the question is: Why do some virtue ethicists nevertheless provide an account of right action?

One can begin to show why such an account is needed by pointing out that we often find it natural, even necessary, to use the concepts of right and wrong action. Consider, for example, a situation where telling the truth will hurt someone's feelings, and so the act of telling the truth will be both honest and unkind. In such a case, saying that x is an honest action (or a kind action) is not necessarily to recommend it as "the thing to do." We need a stronger term whereby to recommend the action, and here "right action" seems appropriate. If, for instance, I think that being kind is more important than being honest in this particular case, I might form the judgment that, "Keeping quiet is the right thing to do here." What do I mean by "the right thing to do" in this context? Well, it could be that I'm using it in the traditional sense, claiming that keeping quiet is either obligatory or permissible (in which case I encounter Anscombe's objection). But I could also use "right" in a different sense, for example:

a   to recommend an action as something that would be good or praise-worthy to do; or

b   to indicate that the action is not deplorable or bad, that it is accep-
    table or "all right"; or
c   to signal that doing x is the correct decision, the best of the available
    options, or the solution to the problem.

Using "right" in any of these senses avoids Anscombe's objection, and it
should also make it clear why some virtue ethicists find it necessary to provide an account of right action. But it also draws attention to the ambiguity
of the concept of right action. As we will see in this chapter, many of the
objections to virtue-ethical accounts of right action stem from a failure to
notice that "right action" is used in a way that differs from how deontologists
and consequentialists use it. When examining these accounts, it is important
to pay attention to the sense(s) in which the term "right action" is used, for as
Daniel Russell writes:

> virtue ethics can be seen as a sort of "protest" against traditional ways
> of thinking about rightness and ethical theory ... . [It] offers not only a
> different account of right action, but indeed a different conception of it,
> and unless we appreciate what is different about it we risk simply beg-
> ging all sorts of questions against it, wondering why the new account
> does not fit the old conception.
>
> (2009, 38)

We will begin by considering an Aristotelian account of right action, and
then go on to consider two alternative views: the agent-based account
provided by Michael Slote, and the target-centered account given by
Christine Swanton.

6.2 A Qualified-Agent Account of Right Action

Aristotelian virtue ethicists think about right action in terms of the actions
and attitudes of the moral expert – the fully virtuous or "qualified" agent
(the *phronimos*). The most influential qualified-agent account of right
action is the one provided by Hursthouse:

(V)   An action is right iff it is what a virtuous agent would characteristically
      (i.e. acting in character) do in the circumstances (1999, 28).

Before we examine this account in more detail it is worth noting that
Hursthouse does not claim that an action is right *because* it is what a virtuous person would do. (V) does not provide an explanation of what
makes an action right. Instead, a qualified-agent view claims that given

their practical wisdom and good character, virtuous agents are moral experts, and so their judgements will correctly capture moral rightness and wrongness (Kawall 2014, 130). In other words, (V) helps us to identify right actions; it asserts that what all right actions have in common is that they are the kinds of action that virtuous agents characteristically perform. The question of what makes a particular action right will have to be answered by referring to the virtuous person's reasons for performing the action. But Aristotelian virtue ethicists don't think it is possible to provide a useful summary of the virtuous person's reasons, or a set of right-making features that can be presented in the form of a set of rules or principles: there is no substitute for practical wisdom.

In thinking about the ways in which virtuous people characteristically act, we may begin by noting that they tend to make the *right decision*, that is, where there is a choice between different actions, they tend to pick the correct one. Further, virtuous agents characteristically perform certain *types of action*. Courageous people face danger and endure suffering, honest people tell the truth and refrain from cheating, and benevolent people help those in need. However, as we have seen in earlier chapters, an honest person cannot be defined as someone who always tells the truth, and neither can a benevolent person be defined as someone who always helps those in need. Rather, a virtuous person acts for *the right reasons* and has *the right attitudes* and *emotions* when they act. Finally, virtuous people pursue *worthwhile ends*, which requires an understanding or correct conception of *eudaimonia*,[1] and because they have *practical wisdom*, they will typically succeed in achieving these ends. If an agent makes the right decision, for the right reason, with the right attitudes and emotions, and succeeds in achieving a worthwhile end, then we can be sure that he has performed a right action. On the other hand, if he fails in all these respects, then he performs a wrong action. However, it should be obvious that in between these two extremes, there is a range of different possibilities.

This draws our attention to an important respect in which virtue-ethical accounts of right action differ from many other such accounts. It is customary to think of actions as either right or wrong. When discussing a particular issue in applied ethics, such as abortion or capital punishment, it is not uncommon for people to be either "for" or "against" the practice. The assumption that an action must be either right or wrong is the result of thinking in terms of permissibility: a given action cannot be more or less permissible, or more or less impermissible. It is either permissible or impermissible. However, if we think of rightness in terms of virtue, then we have to be more nuanced in our judgments. A particular action can be anywhere on a scale from perfectly virtuous (virtuous in every respect) to wholly vicious, and so the question for virtue ethicists is where to draw the line between right and wrong action. In brief, Hursthouse handles this problem by making three suggestions: (a) some actions are right only with qualification; (b) whether or not an agent's reasons, feelings, attitudes, and motives are relevant for rightness depends on the context; and (c) an agent can make the right decision but still fail to perform a right action. In what follows, we will examine three cases where, for very different reasons, an agent fails to perform a fully virtuous action, one that is right without qualification.

6.2.1 The Poorly Motivated Agent

Part of what makes a person virtuous is that they have good motives. For example, a kind person characteristically helps others because he cares about their welfare, and not because he wants to impress someone else. But does an agent's motive also affect the rightness of their action? Consider the case of Roberto, who has a history of being selfish and tight-fisted, and as a result has become quite unpopular with his co-workers. On one particular occasion a charity worker comes by the office to ask for donations for the Cancer Society. Roberto, seeing this as an opportunity to impress his co-workers with his generosity, thereby going some way towards rehabilitating his reputation, makes a sizable donation. He regrets having to make the financial sacrifice, but he thinks it will pay off in the form of increased popularity and more invitations to social events. Does he perform a right action? Does he succeed in doing what a virtuous person would do in the circumstances?

The answer to this question will depend on what is involved in "doing what a virtuous person would do" – does it require merely performing certain actions (where actions are described behavioristically, as "giving to charity" or "rescuing a drowning child"), or does it also require acting from virtuous motives? Hursthouse (2006b, 106–112) thinks it depends on the context, more specifically, on what we are interested in when judging an action. In many contexts, we're just not interested in people's reasons for acting in certain ways. As long as they do certain things, such as paying their rent on time, paying for their groceries, and telling the truth when we ask them for directions, we are confident in describing their actions as right. In these contexts, "right" is used in a fairly thin or undemanding sense, to indicate that the action is the kind of thing that we need people to do in order for society to function well. However, in contexts relating to moral improvement, we use a richer, more demanding sense of "right," which requires the agent not merely to perform a certain type of action but also to do so for the right reasons and with the right attitude and emotions. In these contexts,

[w]hat you *do* does not count as right unless it is what the virtuous agent would *do*, say, "tell the truth, after much painful thought, for the right reasons, feeling deep regret, having put in place all that can be done to support the person on the receiving end afterwards." Only if you get all of that right are you entitled to the satisfactory review of your own conduct ... simply making the right decision, and telling the truth just [isn't] good enough to merit approval.

(Hursthouse 2006b, 108–109)

Returning to Roberto's case, then, we can see how the charity worker herself might describe his action as right. Assuming that he has cash in his wallet and can afford to donate all of it, Roberto has at least three options available to him: to donate all of it, to give nothing at all, or to give only small change. He decides to donate all of it, thereby doing what a generous person would do. However, one of Roberto's long-suffering co-workers, who has had to pay for his lunch on various occasions when Roberto "forgot to bring his wallet," will be interested in his reasons and feelings. She might wonder whether his act of giving is a sign of moral improvement, and if she discovered his true reasons for donating she is likely to conclude that his action is not right, or at least, not right without qualification. It does not merit unqualified approval.

6.2.2 Tragic Dilemmas

Another context in which motives, attitudes and emotions play a role in the assessment of an action is when an agent finds himself in a tragic dilemma, that is, a situation in which he is forced to make a choice between two or more terrible actions. The actions are "terrible" in the sense that they involve, for example, causing a great amount of suffering, breaking a promise, or killing someone – the types of action that a virtuous person would characteristically avoid. Hursthouse (1999, 75) mentions Bernard Williams' case of Jim and Pedro as a possible example. Jim, an explorer, wanders into a village where he finds Pedro about to shoot twenty peasants. Pedro, in an effort to honor the new guest, presents Jim with the opportunity to shoot one peasant whereupon the others will be released. But if he refuses, Pedro will carry on and shoot them all as originally planned (see Williams 1973, 98ff).

In Hursthouse's view, whether Jim kills one peasant or refuses, thereby allowing all twenty to be killed, he would be doing something that can only be described as "terrible." His life will be forever marred, and he will always regret finding himself in the situation. This is what makes it a *tragic* dilemma. But is Jim is forced, not only to do something *terrible*, but to do something terribly *wrong*? Hursthouse doesn't think so. The statement "Jim kills a peasant" (or, for that matter, "Jim refuses to kill a peasant and walks away") does not provide a full description of what the agent does. A full description will include reference to the way he acts – his feelings, attitudes, and motives. And this leads to the conclusion that although Jim is forced to make a choice between two terrible actions, he is not forced to act *wrongly*. If he is a virtuous person, then he will not act indifferently or gladly, as the vicious do, but with immense regret and pain (see Hursthouse 1999, 73–74). In this kind of case, then, the agent's inner states are relevant when assessing their action.

This leads to the further question: Can a virtuous agent perform a right action in a tragic dilemma? Hursthouse thinks some tragic dilemmas are resolvable. Say, for the sake of argument, that a virtuous agent would see that killing one person is preferable to allowing all twenty to be killed. A straightforward application of (V) would then support the conclusion that if Jim decides to shoot one person and does so in a way that is characteristic of a virtuous agent (that is, with immense regret and pain), then he performs a right action. Somewhat surprisingly, Hursthouse rejects this conclusion, for she thinks it is a mistake to give "this terrible deed, the doing of which mars the virtuous agent's life, a tick of approval, as a good deed" (1999, 78). Although she allows that the virtuous agent can make the right decision (that is, resolve the dilemma correctly), she denies that he thereby performs a right action.

To understand Hursthouse's view, it is important to note that she doesn't think "making the right decision" or "doing what one ought to do" is equivalent to "performing a right action." She distinguishes between two ways in which we use the term "right." We sometimes say "X is right" to recommend an action as the correct or preferable thing to do, the best of the available actions. But we can also say "X is right" as a way of giving the action a "tick of approval" as a good or excellent action. An act that is right in this sense is "an act that merits praise rather than blame, an act that an agent can take pride in doing rather than feeling unhappy about, the sort of act that decent, virtuous agents do and seek out occasions for doing" (Hursthouse 1999, 46). Hursthouse thinks one can make the correct decision but still not act in a way that warrants a tick of approval. And this is what happens in tragic dilemmas that are resolvable. One of the available actions is preferable to the others, and hence "right" in the sense of what ought to be done, but it is not "right" in the sense of being a good or virtuous action. Hursthouse therefore adds a qualification to her original specification of right action:

An action is right iff it is what a virtuous agent would, characteristically, do in the circumstances, except for tragic dilemmas, in which a decision is right iff it is what such an agent would decide, but the action decided upon may be too terrible to be called "right" or "good." (And a tragic dilemma is one from which a virtuous agent cannot emerge with her life unmarred.).

(1999, 79)

By adding this qualification, Hursthouse acknowledges that a virtuous person can find herself in a situation where it is impossible to perform a right (good or excellent) action.

6.2.3 *"Past Wrongdoing" Dilemmas*

A different kind of moral dilemma occurs when an agent finds himself in a difficult situation because of some character defect or past wrongdoing. Hursthouse (1999, 50–51) gives the example of a distinctly non-virtuous man who impregnates two women, A and B, after convincing each that he intends to marry her. He now finds himself in an irresolvable dilemma, for he can only marry one of them. But Hursthouse asks us to consider a situation where a solution to the dilemma presents itself: B decides she no longer wants to marry him, and finds another suitor who is delighted to adopt the child. A, on the other hand, and despite learning of his deceit, still wants to marry him. The philanderer decides to marry A, for he realizes it would be worse to abandon A than to abandon B. The question, then, is: Does he perform a right action?

Some critics argue that (V) does not apply to this kind of case, simply because a virtuous agent would not find himself in this situation in the first place (Harman 2001, 120–121). But Hursthouse thinks (V) does allow for action assessment: it tells us that it is impossible for the philanderer to perform a right action in these circumstances. She thinks this is exactly the result we want, that is, if we keep in mind that a "right action" is an act that warrants a "tick of approval." By claiming that marrying A is not a right action, she does not imply that he ought not to marry A. She simply means that he doesn't perform a good deed; he cannot review his conduct with satisfaction (Hursthouse 1999, 50).

This response has not completely satisfied her critics. Robert Johnson (2003) argues that a non-virtuous agent can perform a right action, even if he finds himself in a situation that no virtuous person could be in. He gives the example of a chronic liar who wants to improve his character, and so goes to see a therapist who advises him to write down all his lies, think about his reasons for lying, and remind himself why telling the truth is important. Johnson argues that (V) gives the wrong result, namely that the liar cannot perform a right action (since no virtuous person would have to deal with the problem of chronic lying in the first place). In Johnson's view, there can be "something truly excellent in a moral respect about the reformations of the liar" (2003, 825).

Some Aristotelians respond to this objection by revising (V), for example, by defining right action in terms of what the virtuous agent would advise one to do, or would approve of one doing (see Kawall 2002; Kawall 2009; Tiberius 2006; Svensson 2010). A different approach is to retain (V) and to insist that the reforming liar's actions are not right. This is not to say that he acts wrongly, for his actions are not characteristic of the vicious. We can admit that there is a definite improvement in his behavior, and hence, that he deserves some praise and encouragement. And we can account for Johnson's intuition that there is *something* truly excellent about his behavior by noting that his actions do reveal a certain amount of courage and determination. But the central virtue in question here is honesty, and by writing down his lies (and so on), the reforming liar does not act in a way that is characteristic of an honest person, at least not yet.

If we accept that (V) allows us to assess the actions of the non-virtuous agent, a further question arises, namely, whether it provides action guidance. We can derive the following action-guiding principle from (V):

(AG+) Do what a virtuous agent would characteristically do in the circumstances.

This principle generates a list of more specific virtue-rules, such as "Do what is charitable" and "Do what is honest" (see Hursthouse 1999, 36–39). In previous wrongdoing dilemmas, where nothing the agent can do will count as characteristic of the virtuous agent, (AG+) does not provide guidance. In such cases the agent can turn to (W), which is the corollary of (V), and its corresponding action-guiding principle, (AG−):

(W)   An action is wrong iff it is what a vicious agent would characteristically do in the circumstances.

(AG−)   Do not do what a vicious agent would characteristically do in the circumstances.

(AG−) generates a list of more specific vice-rules, such as "Do not do what is dishonest, uncharitable, or mean," and these rules arguably provide action guidance to non-virtuous agents. To demonstrate, consider, again, the case of the philanderer, who has at least three options: Option 1 is not to support either of them, Option 2 is to fail to support A and to pursue B, despite the fact that B is no longer interested in him, and Option 3 is to respect B's wishes and instead to support A. Each of these options involve acting poorly, because they involve failing to support someone he has impregnated. But his options are not equally bad. By choosing Option 1 he will manifest an indifference to A, who still wants and needs his support. But Option 2 is even worse, because he will display insensitivity and disrespect towards B, who doesn't want or need his support, as well as cruelty towards A, who (despite everything!) was still prepared to marry him. The vice-rule, "Do not do what is uncaring or indifferent" points to Option 3 as the least bad, and therefore correct one. By marrying A, the philanderer will take the first step on the road to becoming a more responsible (and thereby more virtuous) person. Similarly, the best the chronic liar can do is to avoid continuing to act viciously. But his actions are not yet characteristic of a virtuous person.

In summary, then, a qualified-agent account of right action is both complex and nuanced. When "right action" is used in the sense of an action that merits approval, one that an agent can feel proud of and look upon with satisfaction, then it requires that the agent make the correct decision, is motivated by the right reasons and emotions, has the right attitude, and succeeds in attaining a worthwhile end. In what follows, we will consider two alternative virtue-ethical accounts of right action. The first, an agent-based account, specifies right action in terms of motives, whereas the second, a target-centered account, specifies it in terms of success in action.

6.3 An Agent-Based Account of Right Action

As we've seen in earlier chapters, Slote develops an agent-based virtue ethics which is inspired by the sentimentalism of David Hume, Francis Hutcheson, and James Martineau. Slote's view is agent-based as it takes good character to be the fundamental source of moral value. In his view, the admirability of good character is not dependent on any further properties, such as its consequences or its being needed for happiness (*eudaimonia*). Good character is intrinsically valuable or admirable, and all other ethical concepts, including right and wrong action, are to be understood in terms of the virtues (Slote 2001, 5).

In his book *Morals from Motives* (2001), Slote presents the following criterion of right and wrong action:

(M)   An action is right if it comes from good overall motivation and wrong if it comes from bad (or insufficiently good) motivation (see Slote 2001, 14, 33).[2]

It is useful to compare an agent-based account of rightness with the account given by objective consequentialists. What they have in common is that they reject the claim that an action can be right or wrong in itself. That is, they agree that we cannot judge an action as wrong purely on the grounds that it involves, say, telling a lie or killing an innocent person. But this is where the agreement ends. Objective consequentialism is a version of evaluational externalism: it holds that the rightness of an action depends on actual consequences. By contrast, agent-based virtue ethics is an example of evaluational internalism, for it claims that what makes an action right is the fact that it proceeds from a good motive (see Driver 2001, xiv–xv). Having good or virtuous motives involves aiming at the ends of virtue. In the case of benevolence, for example, it involves aiming at the good of others, so an action will be right if the agent makes a sincere attempt to benefit others, regardless of whether they succeed. But not all virtues involve aiming at good consequences. For example, the virtue of honesty involves aiming at the truth, and so an act is honest (and therefore right) if the agent is sincere in their attempt to establish and communicate the truth, regardless of whether they actually succeed in doing so.[3]

6.3.1 Moral Luck, Motives, and Consequences

Slote's main argument in support of an agent-based account of right action is that it allows us to avoid the problem of moral luck. We have an instance of moral luck whenever luck makes a moral difference. A common example is when someone receives moral praise or blame for acting in ways that are beneficial or harmful, despite the fact that they are not fully in control of the consequences of their actions. Moral luck presents a problem because it conflicts with the intuition that a person should not be praised or blamed for what is not under his control, that is, for what happens accidentally or despite his best intentions and efforts (see Nagel 1991, 24–38). Slote appeals to this intuition by noting that a fully benevolent agent – one who makes every effort to find out relevant facts and is careful in acting – cannot be criticized as acting immorally if he fails to help the people he seeks to help. Likewise, a poorly motivated person who accidentally or unintentionally produces a good result does not deserve praise (Slote 2001, 34). He writes:

> [M]otive is fundamentally at least relevant to the *moral* character of any action. For if we judge the actions of ourselves or others simply by their effects in the world, we end up unable to distinguish accidentally or ironically useful actions (or slips on banana peels) from actions that we actually morally admire and that are morally good and praiseworthy.
>
> (Slote 2001, 39)

An agent-based account of rightness avoids the problem of moral luck by evaluating an action based on the agent's motive rather than actual consequences.

A possible advantage of this approach is that it allows for right action in some moral dilemmas. Consider, again, the case of Jim and Pedro. From a deontological perspective, the case presents us with a (possibly irresolvable) moral dilemma: Jim has a duty not to kill an innocent person and he has a duty to save nineteen people, but he cannot do both. And so he is doomed to moral failure. Consequentialists resolve such dilemmas by claiming that the right thing to do is whatever would have the best consequences. Hursthouse, in turn, argues that although Jim could make the right decision, he cannot perform a right action, given that he is forced to do something terrible, something that will scar him for life. From an agent-based perspective, the rightness of Jim's action, whether it be shooting the one peasant or refusing to do so, will depend on whether it comes from benevolence rather than malice or indifference. So if Jim is motivated to shoot one of the peasants by a sincere desire to prevent the death of all the others, then his action will be benevolent rather than malicious. But it is also possible that his concern for their welfare motivates Jim to refuse to shoot one of the peasants. He might sincerely (even though mistakenly) believe that the peasants will be better off in the long term if he walks away. It follows, then, that if Jim is a benevolent person then it is possible for him to avoid wrongdoing and, indeed, to perform a right action.

This response invites the following objection: according to an agent-based view, it doesn't matter what you do, or how bad the results of your actions are, as long as you "mean well." Consider the case of Rosalia, who is moved by a desire to help Ethel, but ends up not merely failing to help but actually harming her. It seems to follow from (M) that Rosalia performs a right action, a conclusion that many people find deeply counterintuitive. Slote handles this kind of case by noting that we should not be too quick to judge that the agent acts from a truly good or admirable motive. Rosalia may not manifest true benevolence at all. He explains:

> Benevolence ... isn't benevolence in the fullest sense unless one cares about who exactly is needy and to what extent they are needy, and such care, in turn, essentially involves wanting and making efforts to know relevant facts, so that one's benevolence can really be useful.
>
> (Slote 2001, 18; see also Slote 2010, ch. 7)

If, as seems likely, Rosalia's failure is a result of her not acting from a truly benevolent motive, then her action cannot be described as right or admirable. Note, however, that it doesn't necessarily follow that she acts wrongly. Her action will be wrong only if it comes from a deplorable character trait, such as carelessness or insensitivity. Say, for example, Rosalia is a rich socialite who, moved by the plight of a homeless woman, offers to take her to a beauty salon to have her hair and nails done. Rosalia would no doubt claim that she means well, but her action is wrong because it comes from insensitivity and a clear lack of empathy. But many agents who fail to act from benevolence in its fullest sense do not have bad or inferior motives, in which case their actions will be neither right nor wrong but (merely) acceptable.

6.3.2 Rightness and Goodness

A common objection to an agent-based account of rightness is that it fails to account for the commonsense distinction between a right action and one that is well-motivated. Consider the example of a mother who is motivated by benevolence (in its fullest sense) to give her child para-cetamol for a bad headache. Unbeknown to her, however, the child is allergic to the drug and becomes very ill. According to an agent-based account, the mother's action is right because her motive is good. Many people find this conclusion odd. It would be entirely appropriate for the mother to regret giving the medication, to think that she should not have done so, or that it was a mistake – the wrong thing to do. It seems more plausible to claim that the action is wrong, even though the mother herself is not blameworthy. That is, we want to separate the evaluation of the action (as right or wrong) from the evaluation of the agent (as good or bad, praiseworthy or blameworthy).

The same problem appears in cases where a poorly motivated agent brings about a good result. Ramon Das gives the following example.

> A man dating a woman with a young child dives into a swimming pool to save the child from drowning. He cares not at all for the child, and is motivated exclusively by a desire to impress the woman as a means, let us suppose, to sleeping with her.
>
> (2003, 326)

The agent-based view, namely that the man acts wrongly, conflicts with the intuition that many people have, which is that he does the right thing but for the wrong reason.

Of course, the mere fact that some people find a conclusion counter-intuitive does not show that it is mistaken. To evaluate Slote's position, we need to consider his reasons in support of it. As we've seen, Slote argues that if we judged actions based on their consequences, morality would be vulnerable to moral luck. The mother in the above case does not deserve blame, so her action cannot be wrong. And the rescuer does not deserve praise, and so his action cannot be right. However, the problem with this reasoning is that it confuses "rightness" with "goodness" (or praiseworthiness) and "wrongness" with "badness" (or blameworthiness). When assessing an action as wrong we are not necessarily blaming or criticizing the agent. We are simply saying that he should not have done what he did. To be sure, an evaluation of an action as wrong is often *accompanied* by criticism of the agent, given that people who act wrongly usually do so intentionally or from some character flaw or weakness. But this is not always the case. We can judge a specific action as wrong, as something that ought not to have been done, while at the same time acknowledging that the agent is not to blame. Equally, we can judge an action as right and still criticize the agent for acting from a bad motive (see Jacobson 2002; Brady 2004; Van Zyl 2011b).

The distinction between a right action and a good or praiseworthy action has important implications for the problem of moral luck. Moral luck is a problem because it involves holding an *agent* morally responsible for an action that is not wholly within her control. As Nagel puts it, we have an instance of moral luck "where a significant aspect of what some-one does depends on factors beyond his control, yet we continue to treat him in that respect as an object of moral judgment" (Nagel 1991, 26). Consequentialists (or, for that matter, anyone who thinks consequences affect rightness) could therefore respond to the problem of moral luck by pointing out that when they judge the mother's action as wrong, given its bad consequences, they are not treating *her* as "an object of moral judgment" but simply claiming that the *act* in question ought not to have been done. Whether the agent is blameworthy or criticizable is a separate matter. Consequentialists need not be embarrassed by the fact that an action can have unforeseen or unintended consequences and thus be right or wrong as a matter of luck or accident. The possibility that one's action can turn out to be wrong as a matter of bad luck is only problematic when "wrong" is taken to imply blameworthiness, and consequentialists have generally been careful to distinguish wrongness from blameworthiness.[4]

The disagreement about moral luck turns out to be largely a disagreement about language. Slote uses "right" to imply praise, whereas his critics use it in the sense of what is "permissible" or "obligatory," or alternatively, "the cor-rect or appropriate thing to do." This is why Slote thinks luck does not affect rightness, whereas his critics think it can. So the disagreement can be resolved by simply pointing out these differences. However, if we go along with Slote's usage and accept that "right" implies praiseworthiness and is not equivalent to "what ought to be done," then an agent-based account of right action becomes vulnerable to a different objection, namely that it fails to provide action guidance.

6.3.3 The Problem of Action Guidance

An agent-based account of right action (M) states that an action is right if it comes from good overall motivation and wrong if it comes from bad motivation. If "right" means "good" or "praiseworthy," then (M) does not provide an answer to the question of what I ought to in a particular situation. But it seems reasonable to assume that (M) implies the following action-guiding rules:

(M+)   One ought to act from a good overall motive; and
(M−)   One ought to refrain from acting from a bad overall motive.

If the agent follows (M+) he will perform a right action, and if he follows (M−) he will do what is acceptable and thereby avoid wrongdoing. For many of us, these rules will provide adequate action guidance: I should act upon my desire to help others, and I should resist acting on my desire for revenge. The difficulty for agent-based virtue ethics is to show that it can guide a person who is poorly motivated. Given that one cannot change one's motives at will, a poorly motivated agent cannot act from a good motive. Here (M+) does not provide guidance, so it follows that the agent cannot do what is right. Agent-based virtue ethics therefore seems to violate the principle that "ought" implies "can" (see Slote 2001, 15–16). Jason Kawall explains this objection as follows.

> The worry is that the ordinary or vicious agent would need to have an overall good motive that would be expressed in her action. But then it seems there would be actions agents ought to perform, but cannot because they do not have the correct motives.
>
> (2014, 133)

In response to this objection, Slote argues that one is never forced to perform a wrong (bad or blameworthy) action:

> Presumably, one cannot change one's motives or character at will. But a thoroughly malevolent individual who sees a person he can hurt may still have it within his power to refrain from hurting that person, even if we can be sure he won't in fact exercise that power. And the act of refraining

would fail to express or reflect his malevolence and would therefore not count as wrong.

(2001, 17)

In effect, Slote's argument is that in cases where (M+) does not apply (because the agent doesn't have good motives to act from), he should turn to (M−) for guidance. (M−) provides guidance because it is possible for a poorly motivated agent to refrain from acting from a bad motive. Although this might be true in many cases, it will sometimes be impossible to avoid acting from bad motives. Daniel Doviak gives the following example.

> Imagine a wicked person who enjoys inflicting pain on other people and who cannot find it in himself to benefit others out of a caring motive. Suppose that on a particular occasion this wicked individual has the option of either harming or not harming an innocent person. Suppose that if the wicked agent were to harm the innocent person, he would harm out of malevolence, and that if he were *not* to harm the innocent person, he would do so only out of fear of being caught and imprisoned.
>
> (Doviak 2011, 262)

In this case, the wicked agent is incapable of performing a right action, for he doesn't have good motives to act from. Indeed, as Kawall (2014, 133) points out, he can't even perform an acceptable action because his motives are bad. An agent-based account leads to the conclusion that the wicked agent finds himself in an irresolvable moral dilemma: he cannot avoid wrongdoing. But this view is not plausible at all, for it seems obviously true that the wicked man ought to refrain from harming the innocent person.

In summary, there are two serious objections to an agent-based account of right action. The first is that it fails to accommodate the commonsense distinction between the rightness of an act and its being well-motivated (good or praiseworthy). The second is that it fails to provide action guidance to a poorly motivated agent. In his more recent work, Slote (2010, 93) tries to avoid both these objections by reformulating the criterion of right action as follows:

(ME) An action is right if it expresses or exhibits good motivation and wrong if it expresses or exhibits bad (or insufficiently good) motivation.

The corresponding action-guiding rules can be formulated as follows:

(ME+) One ought to act in ways that express or exhibit good motives; and
(ME−) One ought to refrain from acting in ways that express or exhibit bad motives.

This modification allows Slote to distinguish between an action that is right (because it exhibits good motivation) and one that is good (because it actually comes from good motivation). In the case of the mother who gives the child paracetamol, it supports the conclusion that although the mother is well-motivated, her action does not exhibit good motives because it results in harm to the child. Similarly, in the case of the drowning child, the man's act of saving the child, though poorly motivated, is not wrong because it doesn't exhibit his poor motives. He does exactly what a benevolent person would do in the circumstances. Arguably, the modification also allows Slote to avoid the action guidance objection, for it is possible to be poorly motivated and yet to act in ways that do not display or manifest poor motivation (see Slote 2010, chs. 6 and 7).

6.4 A Target-Centered Account of Right Action

Christine Swanton provides a target-centered account of right action as an alternative to both qualified-agent and agent-based accounts. In this view, a right action is one that successfully hits the targets of the relevant virtue(s). Her account has two central theses:

(T1)   An action is *virtuous* in respect V if and only if it hits the target of virtue V.

(T2)   An action is *right* if and only if it is overall virtuous (Swanton 2003, 228).

We can begin by considering Swanton's account of a virtuous action (T1). Swanton defines virtue as "a good quality of character, more specifically a disposition to respond to, or acknowledge, items within its field or fields in an excellent or good enough way" (2003, 19). Thus, for example, courage is a disposition to respond well to the demands made on us by dangerous situations. A *virtuous action* (in respect of courage) is a successful response to these demands, one that "gets it right."

Swanton draws on Aristotle in this regard. He claims, for example, that a liberal person will give the right amounts to the right people and in the right circumstances; he will spend money on the right objects (rather than squandering it) and in the right way, namely, with pleasure rather than grudgingly (Aristotle, *The Nicomachean Ethics* 1120a25–30). Although it is tempting to think of a virtuous action as whatever a virtuous person would do, Aristotle accepts that a virtuous agent could fail to act virtuously in a given situation. A courageous person may on occasion be so affected by tiredness or grief that he fails to respond well to a dangerous situation, thereby acting out of character. Qualified-agent accounts try to avoid this problem by defining virtuous action as what a virtuous person would *characteristically* do (Hursthouse 1999, 28) but it can still be asked: What makes the action the kind of thing a virtuous person would characteristically do? or: Which feature(s) of this action alerts us to the fact that the virtuous agent has acted in character? In Hursthouse's view, depending on the context, various features can be relevant: the nature of the decision, the agent's reasons, emotions, and attitudes, as well as the successful achievement of a worthy end.

By contrast, Swanton's response is more specific. In her view, the act in question involves a successful response to items in the field of a virtue (or stated otherwise, a virtuous act in respect V is one that *hits the target* of virtue V). Thus, for example, hitting the target of benevolence involves successfully promoting human welfare, and honesty involves telling the truth appropriately, and not lying or misleading. The idea of hitting the target of a virtue is a relatively simple idea, but Swanton (2003, 234ff) notes that it is complicated by several features:

a   *Hitting the target of virtue may involve several modes of moral response.* Benevolence requires responding to the needs of others by promoting their welfare. But Swanton thinks it can also require other modes of responding, such as seeing others "through a loving rather than a hostile gaze" and expressing "appropriate forms of closeness ... [so as] not to appear cold and unfeeling" (Swanton 2003, 234). Similarly, a compassionate response involves an attempt to understand as well as relieve someone's suffering.

b   *The targets of some virtues are internal.* The virtue of determination requires trying hard and not giving up, and so one can reach this target without reaching one's goals (Swanton 2003, 235). It would therefore be a mistake to think that Swanton offers a purely "external" criterion of right action, one that a person is able to meet no matter what kind of motives, disposition, or character they act from.

c   *Some virtues have more than one target.* Courage has an internal target (controlling one's fear) as well as an external target (handling a dangerous or threatening situation successfully).

d   *Targets may vary with context.* In some contexts, the target of generosity is simply to alleviate need. If, following an earthquake, many people donate to a charity organization that actually makes a difference to the victims' lives, it is appropriate to describe their donations as generous, regardless of their inner states. But in contexts that are more intimate, for instance when helping a friend who has been affected by the earthquake, the target of generosity may be to alleviate need with the right attitude.

e   *Some targets of virtue are to avoid things.* For example, the target of modesty is to avoid drawing attention to oneself, talking about oneself excessively, boasting and so on.

A further complication is that an action can be virtuous in one regard but fail to hit the targets of other virtues that are relevant in the context. An action could be both "just and malicious," or "assertive and hurtful" (Swanton 2003, 242). It is for this reason that Swanton includes (T2), which links rightness to overall virtuousness. An action is right if it is virtuous in *all* relevant respects.

The question arises as to how stringently (T1) should be applied. Must the act be the best one possible, or need it only be "good enough" in order to hit the target of the virtue? The first view makes the target of a virtue very stringent, whereas the latter view allows for a range of acts, from the truly splendid and admirable to acts that are merely acceptable, to be assessed as right. A target-centered approach can accommodate either of these views, but Swanton opts for the first, for she finds it natural to think of the targets of a virtue as best acts (relative to the virtue). Swanton (2003, 239–240) proposes the following categories.

a   right actions (actions that are overall virtuous);
b   wrong actions (actions that are overall vicious); and
c   actions that are "all right" (neither overall virtuous nor overall vicious).

6.4.1 The Problem of Moral Luck: Virtuous Action and Action from Virtue

A possible objection to Swanton's account is that it is vulnerable to the problem of moral luck. If the rightness of an action is determined by its success in hitting the targets of relevant virtues, it is possible for a virtuous agent to fail to act rightly through no fault of her own. In the case of the well-motivated mother who administers medication to a child who then has an allergic reaction to it, a target-centered account supports the view that the mother fails to perform a right action. Her action clearly fails to hit the target of benevolence.

People's intuitions on this kind of case differ. As we've seen, those who are drawn to an agent-based account would argue that her action is right because it is well-motivated. If she had good reason to believe that her action would have the desired result, it seems inappropriate, even unfair, to criticize her for failing to do what is right. Others think we cannot plausibly call such an action right, given the terrible consequences it has. Swanton thinks we can accommodate both these intuitions by taking note of a distinction Aristotle makes between *virtuous action* and *action from virtue*. "Virtuous action" pertains to *what* is accomplished; it involves a form of success in responding to the demands of the world. By contrast, an agent "acts from virtue" when the source of the action is the agent's virtue or good character. According to Aristotle, an agent acts from virtue:

> (1) if he knows what he is doing, (2) if he chooses it, and chooses it for its own sake, and (3) if he does it from a fixed and permanent disposition.
>   (*The Nicomachean Ethics* 1105a30–1105b2; see also 1105a9–b2)

People who act from virtuous motives often succeed in performing virtuous actions. But because they do not fully control outcomes and circumstances, there are exceptions, and the example of the mother is a case in point. Here a target-centered account supports the view that although the action is not right, the agent is not blameworthy. A further implication of this distinction is that acting virtuously does not necessarily require virtuous motivation. Someone who acts from selfish motives can still succeed in helping others and thereby act rightly (that is, if we assume that beneficence is the only relevant virtue in the context).

Swanton notes that the requirements for acting from (a state of) virtue and acting virtuously are demanding in different ways. Acting from virtue requires "fine motivation (including having fine ends), fine emotions, practical wisdom, and the possession of a stable *disposition* of fine emotions, feelings, and other affective states" (Swanton 2003, 238). Acting virtuously requires successfully hitting the target of a virtue, and one may fail to do so through sheer bad luck or incomplete knowledge.

6.4.2 How Motive Affects Rightness

Some virtue ethicists tend to blur the distinction between a right action and one that is well-motivated by using "right action" not merely in the sense of what may or ought to be done, but also in the sense of a "good deed" – an act that gets a "tick of approval," as Hursthouse puts it. In this view, the agent's motivation and attitude can affect the rightness of her action. By contrast, Swanton follows a well-established tradition in ethics, which includes philosophers such as W. D. Ross, J. S. Mill, and H. A. Pritchard, that distinguishes between "right action" and "good action." Ross notes, for instance, that:

> moral goodness is quite distinct from and independent of rightness, which ... belongs to acts *not* in virtue of the motives they proceed from, but in virtue of the nature of what is done.
>
> (Ross 2002, 156)

Unlike Ross and Pritchard, however, Swanton thinks that motive can sometimes affect rightness, and in this regard, her position more closely resembles that of Hursthouse and Slote. Swanton gives an account of right action in terms of success in hitting the targets of virtue, which implies that it is possible for a poorly motivated agent to perform a right action. However, as noted earlier, she points out that some virtues have targets that are internal. In situations where these virtues are salient, the agent has to have certain inner states (feelings, beliefs, or motives) in order to succeed in acting rightly.

Consider the example of benevolence. The relevant targets of benevolence are sometimes external, for example, when a wealthy business person gives a large sum of money to help establish a successful charity organization. In such a case, a selfish motive does not affect the rightness of the action. But contrast this to a more intimate context: Susanna takes excellent care of her elderly father. Secretly, however, she cannot stand him; were it not for the fact that he is rich and she is hoping to inherit his wealth, she would not try so hard to please him. Insofar as Susanna successfully promotes human welfare and displays the appropriate kind of behavior and demeanor, she hits the (external) targets of benevolence. Arguably, however, she misses an important (internal) target of benevolence, which is to have genuine concern for another. It is not merely that she does what is right from an inferior motive. Rather, she fails to act rightly because she misses one of the targets of benevolence. In this way motive and other internal states can affect rightness.

6.4.3 Two Kinds of Failure

Compare the case of Susanna with the case of Tessa, who also takes excellent care of her elderly father, but genuinely cares about him. On one occasion she is in a great hurry and forgets to give him his medication, thereby causing him significant pain and discomfort. According to a target-centered account, Tessa fails to act rightly, despite her good motives. Like Susanna, she misses one of the targets of benevolence. This result may elicit the following objection: A target-centered account gives an identical judgment in both cases, namely that the agent fails to act rightly. This is odd, given the important differences between the two cases. (In the first, there is a bad inner state but a good outcome, and in the second a good inner state but a bad outcome.)

In response, a supporter of a target-centered view could again emphasize the distinction between right (virtuous) action and action from virtue. While judgments of right and wrong have traditionally received the most attention, suggesting that they are more important than judgments of the agent, this is a mistake that we should try to correct. In Tessa's case, we have to admit that she failed to act rightly. But this is a very small part of the evaluative picture. We should also consider whether she is blame-worthy, and whether she has any reason to feel guilty or ashamed about what she did (or failed to do). Depending on the exact circumstances, responses involving blame, guilt, and shame could be inappropriate; instead, Tessa should acknowledge her mistake and try to learn from it. But the most important part of our evaluation in this case would be to appreciate her character, as manifested in her behavior over time. If she has taken good care of her father for many months, it would be inappropriate to focus too much attention on a single mistake. By contrast, in Susanna's case, although she, too, acts wrongly on a particular occasion, the rest of the story (whether she acts from virtue, whether she has reason to feel guilty or ashamed, and whether we should focus on her strengths while excusing her failure or weaknesses) looks very different.

6.4.4 The Case of the Drowning Child

How would we apply a target-centered account to Das's case of the man who rescues a child to impress its mother? It is obvious that he doesn't act from virtue, but does he perform a right action? His action hits one of the targets of benevolence: he saves the child from drowning. But recall that Swanton thinks the virtue of benevolence also involves other modes of responding, such as seeing the person in the right way (through a loving rather than hostile gaze), displaying respect, and displaying appropriate forms of closeness. The rescuer's action clearly fails to hit the target of benevolence in these ways, so does this lead us back to the conclusion, which many people find counterintuitive, that he fails to act rightly?

A target-centered account allows us to resist this conclusion by noting that what counts as the target of a particular virtue depends on context. What is most salient or important in this case is that the child be saved from drowning. Seeing the child in the right way or displaying respect while saving him from drowning is just not important here. So although the rescuer doesn't act from virtue, his action is right because it succeeds in hitting the relevant target of benevolence.

6.4.5 Tragic Dilemmas

As we've seen, Hursthouse argues that a virtuous person cannot emerge from a tragic dilemma having done what is right, for the actions he is forced to perform are too terrible to be given a tick of approval. He would make the right decision (i.e., resolve the dilemma correctly), but a right decision is not the same as a right (good) action (see Hursthouse 1999, 77–78). A target-centered account supports a different conclusion. Swanton accepts that the targets of different virtues can come into conflict in a particular situation, and that one might be "faced with alternatives all of which are extremely repugnant." Nevertheless, she thinks it is possible to do what is right in a tragic dilemma (see Swanton 2003, 247; Swanton 2010).

We can use the case of Jim and Pedro to illustrate how this is possible. Imagine that Jim decides to kill one peasant, and that the outcome of this is that Pedro spares the other nineteen. Does he succeed in hitting the targets of the relevant virtues? Aristotelians claim that it is impossible for Jim to act virtuously. As Daniel Russell argues, the agent's benevolence must be frustrated in a tragic dilemma. Jim simply cannot do what a benevolent person has reason to do, which is to save all twenty people. Russell goes on to consider how a virtuous agent will assess their own actions in such an awful situation:

> [She] does not count her action as right, because she recognizes that, among all the ways in which her benevolent *exercise of will* may extend into the world, there is none that is a really *benevolent thing* to do. She has not done the "wrong thing", since she has acted well, but the benevolent person may well hold that there simply was no benevolent thing, and therefore – precisely because of her benevolence – that there was no right thing to do in that situation.
>
> (Russell 2009, 69)

Part of the reason why Russell thinks that a virtuous person cannot do the right thing in a tragic dilemma is that, like Hursthouse, he uses "right action" in the sense of an act that gets a "tick of approval," "the sort of act that decent, virtuous agents do and seek out occasions for doing" (Hursthouse 1999, 46). Swanton doesn't use the term in this sense, but even then, what are we to make of the claim that there simply is no truly benevolent thing to do in this situation?

A target-centered account draws our attention to the distinction between the *aims of the virtuous person* and the *targets of virtue*. If Jim is benevolent, *his* aim will be to save all twenty peasants. However, given that saving all twenty is not possible in this context, the target of *benevolence* can only be to save nineteen. So, even though we have to agree with Russell that *Jim's* benevolence must be frustrated, *his action* will count as benevolent if it succeeds in saving the nineteen. The same point can be made with regards to non-malevolence. A non-malevolent person would not want to harm anyone, but the target of non-malevolence in this context can only be to do as little harm as possible (see Van Zyl 2014).

Chapter Summary

- Eliminativists reject the use of deontic terms, such as right and wrong action, moral obligation (or duty), permissible and impermissible actions, on the grounds that these terms presuppose the existence of a supreme lawgiver. Instead, they argue that virtue ethics allows us to assess actions using character-based notions, such as kindness, honesty, fairness, and generosity, and that this is all that is needed.
- Aristotelian virtue ethicists like Rosalind Hursthouse and Daniel Russell support a qualified-agent account of right action, according to which an action is right if it is what a virtuous agent would characteristically do in the circumstances. Hursthouse makes a distinction between right action as an act that deserves a tick of approval, and a right or correct decision, and argues that it is possible to make the right decision without thereby performing a right action.
- Michael Slote puts forward an agent-based account of rightness. An earlier version of his view ties rightness to the agent's motives. In his later work, and in an attempt to avoid objections to this view, Slote defines rightness in terms of the motives expressed or exhibited by the action.
- Christine Swanton develops a target-centered account of right action. She makes a distinction between a *virtuous action*, that is, an action that succeeds in hitting the target of virtue, and an *action from virtue*, that is, an action that is motivated by virtue. On this view, what makes an action right is that it succeeds in hitting the target of the relevant virtue(s).

Although there are clear differences between these three accounts of right action, it is important to keep in mind that they have a lot in common. All three accounts reject the view that right action can be defined solely in terms of (actual or expected) consequences. And all three reject the view that doing what is right is a matter of adhering to a set of moral rules or principles. Instead, they define right action in terms of virtue or virtuous action, which is why their main interest is in giving an account of the nature of virtue. In the following chapter we will consider a frequent objection to virtue ethics, namely that its focus on character rather than action means that it doesn't help us answer the question: What ought I to do in this situation?

Notes

1   The term "*eudaimonia*" can be translated as "a good human life" or "true happiness for human beings." See Chapter 3.

2 Slote sometimes uses "right" as interchangeable with "fine," "admirable," and "noble," but at other times he uses "right" in the sense of what is morally acceptable or "all right." Although there is some disagreement about Slote's use of moral terms, a plausible view, suggested by Jason Kawall (2014, 131–132) is that Slote gives an account of moral acceptability in addition to an account of right (fine or admirable) action. Slote claims that "an act is morally acceptable if and only if it comes from good or virtuous motivation involving benevolence or caring (about the well-being of others) or at least doesn't come from bad or inferior motivation involving malice or indifference to humanity" (2001, 38).

3 In this regard, agent-based theories of right action differ from subjective consequentialism, which ties rightness to intended or expected consequences.

4 For example, G. E. Moore (1966, 187–188) argues that those who claim that it is intolerably harsh to judge an action as right or wrong based on its actual consequences (given that these are not entirely within the agent's control), make the mistake of confusing the question of what is deserving of moral praise or blame with the question of what is right or wrong. He notes that there is no reason to think that what is right is always praiseworthy, and that what is wrong is always blameworthy.

Further Reading

Anscombe, G. E. M. 1958. "Modern Moral Philosophy." *Philosophy* 33(124): 1–19. doi:10.1017/S0031819100037943

Das, Ramon. 2003. "Virtue Ethics and Right Action." *Australasian Journal of Philosophy* 81(3): 324–339. doi:10.1080/713659702

Doviak, Daniel. 2011. "A New Form of Agent-Based Virtue Ethics." *Ethical Theory and Moral Practice* 14(3): 259–272. doi:10.1007/s10677–10010–9240–0

Hacker-Wright, John. 2010. "Virtue Ethics without Right Action: Anscombe, Foot, and Contemporary Virtue Ethics." *Journal of Value Inquiry* 44(2): 209–224. doi:10.1007/s10790-010-9218-0

Hursthouse, Rosalind. 1999. *On Virtue Ethics.* Oxford: Oxford University Press, Part I.

Hursthouse, Rosalind. 2006b. "Are Virtues the Proper Starting Point for Morality?" In *Contemporary Debates in Moral Theory*, edited by James Dreier, 99–112. Malden, MA: Blackwell.

Kawall, Jason. 2014. "Qualified Agent and Agent-Based Virtue Ethics and the Problems of Right Action." In *The Handbook of Virtue Ethics*, edited by Stan van Hooft, Nafsika Athanassoulis, Jason Kawall, Justin Oakley, Nicole Saunders, and Liezl van Zyl, 130–140. Abingdon and New York: Routledge.

Johnson, Robert N. 2003. "Virtue and Right." *Ethics* 113(4): 810–834. doi:10.1086/373952

Slote, Michael. 2001. *Morals from Motives.* New York: Oxford University Press.

Slote, Michael. 2010. *Moral Sentimentalism.* Oxford: Oxford University Press.

Smith, Nicholas Ryan. 2017. "Right-Makers and the Targets of Virtue." *The Journal of Value Inquiry* 51(2): 311–326. doi:10.1007/s10790-016-9571-8

Swanton, Christine. 2003. *Virtue Ethics: A Pluralistic View.* Oxford: Oxford University Press, Chapter 11.

Taylor, Richard. 2002. *Virtue Ethics: An Introduction.* Amherst, NY: Prometheus Books.

Van Zyl, Liezl. 2014. "Right Action and the Targets of Virtue." In *The Handbook of Virtue Ethics*, edited by Stan van Hooft, Nafsika Athanassoulis, Jason Kawall, Justin Oakley, Nicole Saunders, and Liezl van Zyl, 118–129. Abingdon and New York: Routledge.

7 Applying Virtue Ethics

One of the earliest objections to virtue ethics was that it doesn't provide action guidance. Virtue ethics, it was claimed, is focused on character rather than action, and so it doesn't help us answer the question: What ought I to do in this situation? (see Louden 1984). In the previous chapter we examined three distinctively virtue-ethical accounts of right action, which should make it clear that it is a mistake to think that virtue ethics is concerned (only or mainly) with character and not with action. Nevertheless, many of its critics still object that we cannot apply virtue ethics to practical moral problems. One of their reasons in support of this view is that virtue ethics, unlike consequentialism and deontology, doesn't give us a set of rules or principles that can be applied to particular situations. In response, Rosalind Hursthouse and others have argued that virtue ethics does provide a set of action-guiding rules, the v-rules. But critics still complain that these are not the right kind of rules. Our aim in this chapter is to consider some of the problems that arise when trying to apply virtue ethics to moral problems. Our focus will be on Aristotelian virtue ethics, but much of what we have to say on this matter will be true of other forms of virtue ethics as well.

7.1 Virtue Ethics and Action Guidance

Does virtue ethics provide action guidance? "Providing action guidance" is usually understood as a matter of helping us pick out, from a list of possible actions, the ones that are right. Discussions in applied ethics typically go something like this: First, we are given a description of the situation the agent finds himself in. Then we are presented with a short list of available actions – the agent can do x, y, or z. Finally, the question is posed: What is the right thing to do in the situation – x, y, or z? It is at this point that an account of right action is applied. Standard forms of consequentialism and deontology each have a distinctive *decision procedure*. In the case of consequentialism, it involves looking at likely (short- and long-term) consequences of each alternative, and figuring out which is most likely to produce the best outcome, all things considered. Deontology, in turn, asks us to identify the moral rules that are relevant in the situation, and actions that violate a moral rule would normally be impermissible. One thing that can complicate the matter is when it is unclear how or even whether a given rule applies in the situation. Take, for example, a rule like "It is always wrong to kill an innocent person." In many situations it will be unclear whether the entity in question (say, an embryo or an animal) is a person, and so the discussion will then turn to the correct conception of personhood. Another complication, which often presents itself in conjunction with the first, occurs when two or more moral rules are in conflict. An action can be one of telling the truth and breaking a promise, in which case one has to figure out whether the rule about telling the truth is more or less stringent than the rule about keeping promises.

Admittedly, these two explanations of how to apply consequentialism and deontology are vastly oversimplified, but they are nevertheless useful when introducing newcomers to applied ethics. However, when we turn to the question, How do we apply virtue ethics?, an obvious answer, or even a starting-point to an answer, doesn't present itself. People who are reasonably familiar with the central ideas and concepts of virtue ethics often complain that they still have no idea how to apply the theory. The problem, as Annas notes, is that "virtue doesn't sound like the kind of thing you *can* apply. It sounds like an ideal of character that you aim to reach, rather than a tool you can use to work out what you ought to do" (2015a, 1). For example, "kindness" is not an abstract rule or principle that I can bring to mind and then apply to a particular situation. Rather, kindness is a character trait. If a person is kind, they carry their kindness with them: it is part of who they are as a person. They don't encounter a situation and then appeal to kindness or wonder how to apply kindness. Rather, their kindness will manifest itself in their actions, feelings, and thoughts. A kind person just is someone who cares about the welfare of others, who notices when they need help, and who figures out a way to do so. Likewise, unkindness is a character trait that manifests itself in unkind actions, thoughts, and feelings. So it is difficult to see how one would apply kindness when making a moral decision, especially if one doesn't possess the virtue of kindness. What virtue ethics needs, it seems, is a *decision procedure*, a tool that can be used by the non-virtuous to identify what ought to be done in a particular situation.

As we saw in Chapter 6, Aristotelian virtue ethicists support a qualified-agent account of right action. In this view, an action is right if it is what a virtuous person would characteristically do in the circumstances (Hursthouse 1999, 28). This suggests an obvious way in which one might want to apply virtue ethics, namely, to consider what the virtuous person would do in the circumstances. Roughly, the idea is that if I'm not virtuous myself, then I should look towards someone who is, and try to figure out what he would do in my situation.

The first problem we encounter when trying to put it to use is an epistemological one: given that I am not fully virtuous, how do I know what a fully virtuous person would do in my situation? As we've seen in Chapter 5, Aristotelians claim that the virtuous agent has practical wisdom, and that this allows him to discern moral reasons that may be inaccessible to the non-virtuous agent. These reasons cannot be "codified" or captured in the form of a set of general moral principles and rules that anyone, including the non-virtuous, can apply to particular situations. If this is the case, then it looks like the instruction to do what a virtuous person would do in the situation provides no guidance at all. Robert Louden puts this objection as follows.

> We ought ... to do what the virtuous person would do, but it is not always easy to fathom what the hypothetical moral exemplar would do were he in our shoes ... . Furthermore, if one asks him why he did what he did, or how he knew what to do, the answer – if one is offered – might not be very enlightening. One would not necessarily expect him to appeal to any rules or principles which might be of use to others.
>
> (Louden 1984, 229)

As a decision procedure, it seems, Hursthouse's criterion of right action is not very useful. In response to this objection, Hursthouse begins by noting that if we really don't know what a virtuous person would do, then we should find one and ask him for advice. This is something we already do, and it forms an important part of our moral development:

> [W]hen I am anxious to do what is right, and do not see my way clear, I go to people I respect and admire: people who I think are kinder, more honest, more just, wiser, than I am myself, and ask them what they would do in my circumstances.
>
> (Hursthouse 1999, 35)

A further point that she makes in this regard is that it is simply false to say, as some critics do, that if I am less than fully virtuous, then I will have no idea what a virtuous person would do. Although the notion of "what a fully virtuous person would do in this situation" is quite abstract and vague, most of us are reasonably familiar with the standard virtues, like kindness, honesty, courage, and justice, as well as the standard vices, like cruelty, dishonesty, cowardice, and injustice, such that we are able to handle most of the decisions we have to make in the course of our everyday lives. I don't need to be an expert to know that telling a blatant lie to acquire an unmerited advantage would be dishonest and unjust and therefore wrong. And when I'm tempted to take a family bag of cookies off to bed to eat all by myself, I might think to myself "Don't be greedy," which is all the action guidance I need. In effect, what we use or appeal to when making many of our decisions are what Hursthouse refers to as virtue- and vice-rules (or v-rules). She claims that virtue ethics comes up with a large number of rules: "Not only does each virtue generate a prescription – do what is honest, charitable, generous – but each vice a prohibition – do not do what is dishonest, uncharitable, mean" (Hursthouse 1999, 35–36). In this sense, then, virtue ethicists do not agree with the claim that morality cannot be codified. If we accept this, the next important question is whether the v-rules are the right kind of rules. Do they provide adequate action guidance?

7.2 Codifiability: D-rules and V-rules

Many virtue ethicists have come to endorse the v-rules as part of the response to the action guidance objection (see Annas 2015a, 7; Swanton 2015a). But critics of virtue ethics remain dissatisfied. To see why, we need to consider how the v-rules differ from the kind of rules that deontologists come up with (let's call them the "d-rules").

Deontologists subscribe to the *"strong codifiability thesis,"* that is, the view that the task of normative theory is to provide a set of universal moral rules that can be used as a decision procedure (see Hursthouse 1999, 39–40, 56–59). D-rules usually take the following form: "In situation x, one should do y." Possible examples include: "Whenever you can help someone without undue cost to yourself, you should offer to help" and "Whenever you've made a promise to someone, you should keep it." In its simplest terms, applying a d-rule is a matter of identifying the situation as one in which the rule applies, and then performing the action that is specified by the rule.

The v-rules are quite different. First, they don't include reference to a situation. They just say, "Be kind," "Don't be cruel," and so on. Furthermore, v-rules don't tell us what we ought to do. Unlike the rules of deontology, v-rules don't include reference to a specific action. We should be kind and not be cruel, but what exactly should we *do* in order to be kind and not be cruel? So although virtue ethics provides us with a set of rules, it still doesn't give us a decision procedure. This has led its critics to conclude that virtue ethics cannot avoid the action guidance objection: it is not a complete normative theory because it needs to be supplemented by a list of action-guiding rules, that is, rules that have the same structure as d-rules.

Virtue ethicists strongly oppose the suggestion that the virtues have to be supplemented by a set of d-rules. But this is not because they think the v-rules can do exactly what the d-rules can do. Instead, they altogether reject the strong codifiability thesis. Given the complexity of moral life, they argue that normative theory can only offer a set of rules that apply "for the most part." So they accept that the v-rules are vague and general, but think that this is exactly how they should be. Hursthouse writes:

> Acting rightly *is* difficult, and *does* call for much moral wisdom, and the relevant condition of adequacy, which virtue [ethics] meets, is that it should have built into it an explanation of a truth expressed by Aristotle, namely, that moral knowledge – unlike mathematical knowledge – cannot be acquired merely by attending lectures and is not characteristically to be found in people too young to have had much experience of life.
>
> (1991, 231)

To understand their reasons for rejecting the strong codifiability thesis, it is useful to consider just how one might go about the process of supplementing the virtues with a set of action-guiding rules (that is, rules that have the same structure as the d-rules). Take, for example, the v-rule "Be brave" (or "Do what is brave"). One situation in which we can be brave is in battle, and one way of acting bravely is not to run away when the enemy approaches. If we accept this, then we can supplement the v-rule with a more specific rule, one that makes reference to both a situation and an action: "Whenever you're in battle and the enemy is approaching, don't run away." A few problems immediately present themselves. To begin with, we will have to specify the situation more carefully to allow for exceptional cases in which running away *is* the brave thing to do. (So, for example, one might have, "Whenever you're in battle and the enemy is approaching, don't run away, except when ...") Further, given that there are so many different kinds of situation that call for bravery, the v-rule, "Be brave," will generate a possibly infinite list of d-rules. And the same will be the case for all the other virtues. Finally, we will have to accept that d-rules can come into conflict, in which case we also need a method for resolving such conflicts. Of course, these are problems – or complications – that deontologists have been struggling with for many years, and that we might just have to accept as par for the course. So why don't virtue ethicists just give up the fight and embrace the idea that the virtues need to be supplemented with a list of action-guiding rules?

Julia Annas (2015a) gives the following explanation of why v-rules don't include reference to a situation. She notes that a virtue is always exercised within a situation of some kind. I can't be kind or brave in the abstract, rather, I am brave in fending off this dog attacking me. However, virtue is not defined in terms of kinds of situation. Although a child might think that bravery is defined by certain kinds of action in situations of conflict such as those that occur in war and sports, they soon come to learn that one can be brave in situations that are completely different in nature, such as going to the dentist, speaking in public, and dealing with an illness or injury. If we described virtue in terms of the situations in which they are exercised we could never learn them, because the situations often have nothing in common. Instead, we understand what makes someone brave in all these completely different situations by noting the way the person deals with the situation. With courage, this is facing or enduring danger or difficulty for the sake of a worthy end. A courageous person is someone who is able to identify a noble or worthy end and has learnt how to overcome fear in pursuit of that end.

In response to critics who demand that moral rules include reference to a specific action, Annas argues that it is a mistake to expect a normative theory to guide our actions by telling us what to do:

> Suppose (unrealistically!) someone always does what his mother tells him to do. He always follows her orders; if he fails to do so he feels guilt, regret, and so on. We take this to be immature, a case of arrested development; at his age, we say, he should be making his own decisions. Now, why should this picture become all right when we replace Mom by a decision procedure? Presumably, a decision procedure, supported by a theory of right action, can be expected to be correct more often, and more reliably, than Mom can; but how could this remove the worry?
>
> (Annas 2004, 65–66)

In short, then, virtue ethicists argue that it is a mistake to demand of a normative theory that it should tell us what to do. Instead, they think of action guidance as a matter of directing our development into becoming virtuous agents who can figure out for ourselves what we ought to do (see Hursthouse 1999, Russell 2009). Annas explains this as follows:

> You are being directed to respond to this situation honestly, rather than dishonestly or indifferently. And this focuses your thoughts in a way that they are left hanging by a rule like "Don't lie," which needs all sorts of further work before we can do anything with it. Being told to be honest,

or compassionate or fair, far from being empty, gives you a perspective on the situation which makes clear what the most salient aspects of it are.

(Annas 2015a, 7)

To illustrate this point, consider the example of kindness. Parents often teach their children to be kind by telling them to be gentle, perhaps while showing them how to pat the kitten or hold the new baby. They might do this a few times, and in different ways, until they're sure the child gets it. But what is involved in "getting it" is surprisingly complex. It is not merely a matter of learning that one should stroke a kitten like this, or hold a baby like that. What the parents are trying to teach the child is that living beings are fragile, some more so than others, that we have the power to hurt them, but also to bring comfort, that their feelings matter, that hurting others, even inadvertently, is a bad thing whereas bringing comfort and joy is a good thing, and so on. Given this complexity, it is quite remarkable that so many children begin to acquire the virtues at a fairly young age. A parent might remind the child to be gentle while playing with a younger sibling, and they don't usually interpret this to mean: stroke the sibling on the back, like you did with the kitten, but rather: be mindful of their frailty, be careful not to hurt them. By reminding the child to be gentle, the parent is drawing her attention to the sibling's vulnerability, while giving her some room to figure out for herself how to respond appropriately to this vulnerability. (Though admittedly, some children do need to be given very specific instructions.) Eventually, the child will figure out for herself that the rule, "Be kind" also applies to situations that don't involve physical contact; one can be kind in the way one communicates with others, for example, when conveying bad news or comforting them when they are upset. In time, being kind becomes a settled part of the child's character, so that she won't need to be reminded every time that a kind response is called for. She becomes someone who is careful not to hurt others, and who regards their interests as something worth protecting. "Be kind" is not a rule that one picks from an inventory of rules, and then applies to a particular situation to get the correct solution. Rather, kindness is a skill that takes time, experience, and intelligence to develop.

To see how an adult might "apply" virtue ethics in everyday life, consider the example of Marthinus, who is enrolled in a course of study but finds it extremely difficult. He worries that he might fail, thereby wasting time and money and causing himself (and his parents) a significant amount of stress and embarrassment. He wonders whether it would be best to quietly withdraw and do something else instead. It occurs to Marthinus (or perhaps a friend reminds him) that he should be courageous in facing this decision. Like most people, he has a general sense of what courage is: it involves overcoming fear (of suffering, failure, loss, and so on) for the sake of a worthwhile end. Thinking about what courage demands in his present situation will direct his attention to the following sorts of question: Is completing this course a worthy end? Is it an end I can realistically achieve? What will I have to sacrifice to make it possible? It would be foolish, rather than courageous, to continue if completing the course is not a worthwhile goal, if it is impossible to achieve, or if it requires sacrificing other things that are more important. Thinking about how to be courageous in this situation is difficult, for it requires thinking about what is important or worthwhile. But note that this way of making decisions has an important advantage over other decision-making procedures (such as applying a d-rule, or doing what one's mother tells one to do). If, after giving it some thought, Marthinus decides that completing the course is both possible and worthwhile, he has not merely picked out the correct solution to the problem he started out with. He has figured it out for himself, which means that he will be committed to this course of action. That is, he will do the right thing for the right reasons, rather than because it is the outcome of applying a decision procedure.

In what follows, we will consider Hursthouse's discussion of the morality of abortion as an example of the guidance that virtue ethics gives us in dealing with difficult moral dilemmas.

7.3 Virtue Ethics and Abortion

In an influential paper, "Virtue Theory and Abortion," Hursthouse (1991) applies virtue ethics to the morality of abortion. Applied ethicists have generally approached the matter by focusing on questions to do with women's rights (e.g., Does the right to bodily integrity include a right to abortion? and: Does the right to self-determination override the fetus's right to – or interest in – life?) as well as questions about the status of the fetus (e.g., Is the fetus a person? and: Do we have a duty not to kill it?). Hursthouse accepts that virtue ethics cannot contribute much to these debates, but she claims that neither of these issues is relevant to the morality of abortion. First, with regards to women's rights, she points out that even if we were to accept that women have a right to an abortion, it doesn't follow that having an abortion is a morally acceptable thing to do, for in exercising a right one can still do something cruel, inconsiderate, callous, or light-minded. Hursthouse takes the central question about the morality of abortion to be: "In having an abortion in these circumstances, would the agent be acting virtuously or viciously or neither?" (1991, 235). In short, then, Hursthouse thinks we can set aside the question about whether women do (or should) have the right to have an abortion, and instead focus on the question that many pregnant girls and women are actually faced with: Should I have an abortion? (or: Is it the best thing to do in my situation?)

This brings us to the second issue mentioned above: the relevance of the status of the fetus. Many people think the answer to the question of whether one should have an abortion will depend, at least in part, on whether the fetus is a person. If it is, then the fetus, like any other person, has a *prima facie* right to life, which means that killing it would almost always be wrong. Somewhat controversially, Hursthouse argues that the metaphysical question about the status of the fetus is irrelevant to the morality of abortion (1991, 235–236). Her reasoning in support of this claim goes roughly as follows. The question, for virtue ethics, is when, if ever, a virtuous person would have an abortion when faced with an unwanted pregnancy. A virtuous person has practical wisdom, and this requires knowledge of the relevant facts as well as good judgment. The relevant facts include familiar biological facts about human reproduction, such as how pregnancy comes about, how long it lasts, the impact it has on the mother's body, the way in which the fetus grows and develops, the fact that childbirth can be dangerous and painful, as well as facts about human psychology and social life, such as parents' feelings towards their offspring, the nature of family relationships, and so on. But the wisdom or knowledge that the virtuous person possesses does not include an answer to the metaphysical question of whether the fetus is a person: "[T]he sort of wisdom that the fully virtuous person has is not supposed to be recondite; it does not call for fancy philosophical sophistication, and it does not depend upon ... the discoveries of academic philosophers" (Hursthouse 1991, 235).

This response is not very convincing, but a virtue ethicist can give another, more straightforward reason why we need not concern ourselves with the metaphysical status of the fetus. Unlike deontologists, virtue ethicists are not interested in whether the d-rule, "It is always wrong to intentionally kill an innocent person," applies to embryos and fetuses, for they altogether reject this approach to morality. Instead, the question we need to ask is whether opting for abortion in a particular situation would be virtuous (responsible, unselfish, kind) or vicious (selfish, cruel, callous, light-minded). And to answer this question, we only need to consider the relevant biological, social and psychological facts about human reproduction and parenthood and ask: "What is the mark of having the right attitude to these facts and what manifests having the wrong attitude to them?" (Hursthouse 1991, 237).[1]

Hursthouse thinks there are a number of things the virtue ethicist can confidently say about the morality of abortion. To begin with, she can point out that anyone who believes that an abortion is a trivial matter is deeply mistaken:

The fact that the premature termination of a pregnancy is, in some sense, the cutting off of a new human life, and thereby ... connects with all our thoughts about human life and death, parenthood, and family relationships, must make it a serious matter. To disregard this fact about it, to think of abortion as nothing but the killing of something that does not matter, or as nothing but the exercise of some rights one has, or as the incidental means to some desirable state of affairs, is to do something callous and light-minded, the sort of thing no virtuous and wise person would do. It is to have the wrong attitude not only to fetuses, but more generally to human life and death, parenthood, and family relationships.

(Hursthouse 1991, 237–238)

Further, a virtue ethicist would note that parenthood is an intrinsically worthwhile pursuit, one that constitutes, at least in part, a good or flourishing life for many people. It is often the single most important and meaningful thing they will ever do. Of course, parenthood is not the only worthwhile pursuit, and it can conflict with other pursuits that are equally worthwhile. A virtuous person could therefore decide to avoid parenthood, and the best way to do this is to take the necessary steps to avoid an unwanted pregnancy. However, Hursthouse argues that someone who is already pregnant and then opts for an abortion for the sake of a worthless pursuit, thereby manifests "a flawed grasp of what her life should be, and be about – a grasp that is childish, or grossly materialistic, or shortsighted, or shallow" (1991, 241). Having an abortion for trivial reasons can be callous, self-centered or cowardly, and therefore wrong.

While she thinks having an abortion is always a matter of some seriousness, Hursthouse argues that there are many cases in which terminating a pregnancy is not vicious. For example, when a woman is in poor physical health, or living in poverty and forced to do very physically demanding jobs, she cannot be described as irresponsible or light-minded if she seeks an abortion:

That they can view the pregnancy only as eight months of misery, followed by hours if not days of agony and exhaustion, and abortion only as the blessed escape from this prospect, is entirely understandable and does not manifest any lack of serious respect for human life or a shallow attitude to motherhood.

(Hursthouse 1991, 240)

Opting for an abortion can sometimes manifest appropriate humility, for instance when a young woman (or girl) judges, correctly, that she is not ready for parenthood yet. But although opting for an abortion is sometimes the right decision, Hursthouse doesn't think it is ever something to be celebrated or desired as a worthy end. An abortion always brings about an evil, for it involves cutting off a new life, and cannot be described as a right action (that is, an action that merits a "tick of approval"). And although some women find themselves in the situation through no fault of their own, many unwanted pregnancies are the result of irresponsible or careless behavior. (They present us with what we referred to in Chapter 6 as "past wrongdoing" dilemmas.) Consider, for example, a woman who has multiple sexual partners and is careless about contraception and then ends up pregnant, not knowing who the father is and not having any means to support a child. Deciding to terminate might well be the right decision in the circumstances, but it is not an action that deserves a tick of approval as a right or virtuous action:

> even in the cases where the decision to have an abortion is the right one, it can still be the reflection of a moral failing – not because the decision itself is weak or cowardly or irresolute or irresponsible or light-minded, but because lack of the requisite opposite of these failings landed one in the circumstances in the first place. Hence the common universalized claim that guilt and remorse are never appropriate emotions about abortion is denied.
>
> (Hursthouse 1991, 243)

A further question about the morality of abortion relates to the stage of the pregnancy: Is a late abortion worse than an earlier one? Hursthouse responds by noting that given the facts about gradual fetal development, it is appropriate for our attitudes and feelings towards the fetus to change as it develops. A miscarriage in the later stages of pregnancy is commonly – and appropriately – regarded as a far greater loss and source of grief than an early miscarriage. One might think this reflects the fact that at some stage the developing fetus becomes a person, or comes to possess certain qualities that gives it greater inherent worth (such as consciousness, the ability to feel pain, etc.). But Hursthouse once again tries to avoid the personhood issue. Instead, she claims that describing a miscarriage as *tragic* becomes more and more appropriate as the fetus grows, "for the mere fact that one has lived with it for longer, conscious of its existence, makes a difference" (Hursthouse 1991, 239). In the same way, she argues that it is much more "shocking" for a woman to have a late abortion for trivial reasons than it is to have an abortion for the same reasons in the early stages of pregnancy. To justify a late abortion, a pregnant woman would have to have a very good reason. One possible such reason is that the pregnancy is threatening the mother's life or health, or that the fetus has been diagnosed with a severe abnormality.

Although Hursthouse herself does not discuss the difficult question about the morality of abortion in the case of fetal abnormality, it is interesting to consider how one might apply virtue ethics in such cases. The question the parents will have to consider is whether it would be selfish and callous (or the reverse) to terminate a wanted pregnancy solely on the grounds that the fetus has been diagnosed with an abnormality.[2] To make a good decision, the parents need to consider relevant medical facts, such as the nature and severity of the abnormality, the availability of treatment, and, in cases where the baby is likely to only live for a short time, the availability of palliative care. They will also have to consider whether it will be possible for them to satisfy the child's needs, given their circumstances: in particular, their access to resources such as special education and therapy, their financial and social situation, and their responsibilities to any other children they might have. Most importantly, they will have to think carefully about what it means to be a good parent and about the things that are important in life. Parents often have expectations about the kind of life their offspring will have (playing sports, attending a mainstream school, and going to college), and the prospect of having a child who may not be able to participate in these activities forces them to rethink what is important in life. In some cases it will clearly be selfish and callous to terminate the pregnancy; for instance, if it is done not because the child is likely to undergo severe or prolonged suffering but solely because he or she will be "different" or "imperfect."

The diagnosis of severe fetal abnormality presents parents with what Hursthouse refers to as a "tragic dilemma" (1999, 63ff). As we've seen in Chapter 6, some tragic dilemmas are resolvable, that is, one of the options available to the parents will be preferable to the others in the sense that it will be what a virtuous person would choose to do in the situation. For example, if caring for a child who needs constant attention or support will seriously undermine the parents' ability to support their other children, the decision to abort might well be the right one. And if the unborn baby is enduring (or will endure) extreme or constant pain or discomfort, with little prospect of having enjoyable or meaningful experiences, then opting for an abortion might well be the right thing to do. However, it doesn't follow that undergoing an abortion for these reasons will count as a right (good or virtuous) action. The action will inevitably leave a good or virtuous parent with feelings of immense sorrow and pain, which means that in Hursthouse's view, we cannot describe it as right or virtuous, as meriting a tick of approval, even though the parents may be entirely blameless.

Most objections to Hursthouse's approach focus on her claim that the status of the fetus is irrelevant to the morality of abortion. Hursthouse claims that her discussion is focused on the morality of abortion rather than the "rights and wrongs of laws prohibiting or permitting it" (Hursthouse 1991, 234). Now, we can accept Hursthouse's point that one can act viciously in exercising a *legal* right. However, one might still wonder whether a discussion of the morality of abortion solely in terms of virtue and vice can be complete. In particular, it is questionable whether the virtue ethicist can successfully sidestep questions about the status of the fetus and our duties to the unborn. If the fetus has a moral right to life, then killing it would normally be unjust and therefore vicious. R. Jo Kornegay (2011) argues that Hursthouse's discussion *presupposes* that terminating a pregnancy is morally permissible. That is, she *assumes* that the moral status of the fetus is lower than that of an infant or adult, such that the right to life, as well as the corresponding duty not to kill it, does not extend to the fetus. Many of the reasons that Hursthouse gives for justifying abortion would not apply to infanticide or homicide. Consider, for example, Hursthouse's claim that a woman who thinks that having another baby will seriously undermine her ability to be a good mother to her other children, has a good reason for abortion (1991, 241). Clearly, the same reason would not justify infanticide. Kornegay therefore concludes that "Hursthouse must attribute sufficiently low status to the fetus to avoid the implication that abortion is *prima facie* an unjust killing (i.e. it violates a robust fetal right to life)" (2011, 57).

Kornegay's objection draws our attention to the question discussed earlier on, namely, whether the virtues (and the v-rules) need to be supplemented by a list of d-rules. It seems that virtue ethics cannot escape the question of whether we have a duty not to kill an embryo or fetus. It is only if we accept that there is no such duty, or that the duty is not sufficiently strong to override other concerns, that it becomes appropriate to ask whether it would be virtuous or vicious to have an abortion in a particular situation. If we don't have any duties towards an embryo or fetus, then it seems that we are free to do with it as we please. Our actions might be described as shortsighted, selfish, irresponsible – the kind of thing that a vicious person would do, but not as *impermissible*. Duties place demands on us, so it seems that if we don't have any duties towards the unborn, then anything is permitted. In what follows, we will consider whether virtue ethics can account for the force of duty, and then return to these questions about the morality abortion.

7.4 The Demands of Virtue

An important question for virtue ethics is whether it can account for the force of duty. Julia Annas puts the question as follows:

Does virtue cover only part of ethics, giving no account of duty and obligation? At first it might seem so. Duty and obligation come with *demand*: a duty is what I have to do, must do, am required to do. I must do it whatever I think about the matter, and whether my desires, feelings and aspirations go along with it or not. Just this point is what is definitive about duty: the demand it makes is indifferent to your character. How can virtue, which is all about character, generate anything with the strong kind of demand made by duty?

(2015a, 8)

In response to this question, Annas begins by drawing a distinction between two kinds of duty. The first kind, role-specific duties, are duties that we have in connection with the roles we occupy and the institutions we belong to. We have duties as a teacher, soldier, or parent, or as a member of a university, corporation, or club. These duties are defined by the role in question, and they make demands on the person who has assumed that role, quite irrespective of the person's character, desires, or feelings. Annas uses the example of the crossing-guard who has a duty to be mindful, in various prescribed ways, of the safety of the children entrusted to his care. This duty makes a demand on the crossing-guard irrespective of whether he enjoys helping the children in his care (Annas 2015a, 9; 2015b, 614). Virtue ethicists have no trouble recognizing the existence of role-specific duties or the demands they make. They will accept something like "Teachers have a duty to do x" as a good reason why a particular teacher should do x. And we can commend a teacher who does her duty in a way that is characteristic of a virtuous person – diligently, enthusiastically, proudly, compassionately, and so on.[3]

In addition to role-specific duties, deontologists also recognize non-role specific (or general) duties. These are moral duties that we are thought to have purely in virtue of being a human being, such as the duty not to kill innocent people, the duty to help people in need, and the duty to keep promises. Kantians claim that duties make a categorical demand on us, that is, a demand that is independent of our desires, preferences, and goals. As Annas (2015b, 613) explains, a categorical demand is external to the agent; it presents as a demand that has the special force that no demand could have if it depended on the agent's desires, goals, or preferences. If we didn't have such duties, it seems, we would be able to do whatever we liked. We might be assessed as more or less virtuous or vicious, or worthy of praise or blame, but the stronger reprimand, namely that we failed in our duty, or disobeyed a moral command or imperative, would not apply. Many people find it obvious that there are such demands on us, things we must do (or refrain from doing) regardless of our desires, goals, or plans. It is this kind of duty that appears to present a problem for virtue ethics, which is thought to be more a matter of self-improvement and aspiration than of demand.

To examine the claim that we have duties of this second kind, Annas uses Peter Singer's (1972) example of the drowning child: you are walking by a pond and see a small child who will drown if not pulled out soon. There is no danger to you in going in to rescue the child, but you are wearing your new expensive clothes, and these will be ruined (Annas 2015a, 9). It is clear that you should save the child, and that the damage to your expensive clothes is not a good reason for ignoring the child's plight. But ethicists give different answers to the question, Why should you save the child? Deontologists claim that you have a duty to do so, whereas virtue ethicists point out that it is what a virtuous person would do. Is the deontologist's answer better at capturing our intuition that there is a strong demand on you to save the child, a demand that is independent of your desire to spare your clothes and also independent of your desire to be a good person?

Annas does not think so. She agrees that there is a strong demand to save the child, and that the demand does not depend on whether you want to save the child or would rather spare your clothes. But she challenges the further thought, namely that "where there is a strong demand of this sort, so strong that someone who ignores it is clearly doing wrong, then there must be a duty" (Annas 2015a, 10). Many of the demands on us have their origin in some or other role-specific duty. For example, when someone takes up the well-defined role of being a judge, they take on a clear set of duties. These duties are defined by the relevant institution, and make strong demands on the occupants of the role. But Annas thinks it is a mistake to assume that a strong demand (in this case, to save the child) can only come from duty. What would be the origin of such a duty? Some would argue that one has a duty to save the child because of one's role as a human being, but Annas is not convinced by this. Human beings can occupy various roles, but being a human being is not a role one can occupy, and there is no institution or authority figure that can define one's duties as a human being.

Annas thus warns that we should resist the phenomenon of "duty creep," which she describes as follows.

> When we find cases where there is a strong demand, and you would be wrong to think that the action is merely optional, we feel a tendency to think that there must be a duty, and when we ask what the source of this is, we are thrown back on inventing non-existent roles to produce the duty. Duty creep is a product of the thought that strong demand can only come from duty.
>
> (Annas 2015a, 10)

Where, then, does the demand to save the child come from? Annas asks us to consider the case where a passer-by does not save the child. She thinks it would be strange to react by wondering how this person could have failed to recognize his duty to save the child. Instead, the obvious – and appropriate – reaction is: "Who could do that? What kind of person could do something so callous?" (Annas 2015a, 11). In other words, what we have is a failure of character, rather than a failure to understand what the person's duties are. It is virtue, rather than duty, that makes the demand:

> [W]hat kind of person needs a duty to get her to rescue the child? We don't need a duty in this case; once we bring it in we can see that it is redundant. A despicable person will fail to rescue the child, and an ordinarily virtuous person will save her. What is added here by duty? Why would I need a duty to get me to stand up bravely to a bully, make a fair division between people, give time to friends who are moving house? The work is being done by virtue, and this makes us see – and this is the important point – that virtue is *strongly demanding*. When I am faced by a bully, courage does not present the optional course of standing up to him; it *demands* it. Justice *requires* me to make a division which is fair, generosity *requires* me to give time to friends when they need it ... . I respond to the *demands* of virtue, without needing to reach beyond virtue for duties or obligations.
>
> (Annas 2015a, 11. See also her 2015b, 611)

We can now return to the question about the morality of abortion, and ask whether Annas' discussion of demands and duties sheds any light on the matter. Consider, first, the options open to deontologists. One option is to argue that a pregnant woman does not have any duties to the fetus, given that it is not a person. But if this is the case, then it would be morally permissible for her to do with it whatever she likes. Depending on her plans, goals, and desires, she might choose to nurture it, kill it, or disregard it entirely. The other option is to argue that a pregnant woman does have certain duties towards the fetus. The thought might be that there is a demand on her to take the pregnancy seriously, which means that there must be some kind of duty at play. But the challenge is to explain the origin of such a duty. Does she have these duties in virtue of occupying the role of human being? Or has she somehow assumed the role and accompanying duties of a mother, for example by consenting to sexual intercourse, or by failing to take contraception? (What if she did not consent, or did take contraception?) And further: what exactly are these duties? Does she only have a duty not to kill the fetus? Or does she also have a duty to protect it from harm? Without being able to refer to a specific institution, the content of these duties remain unclear. And so deontologists find themselves in a seemingly intractable disagreement with each other. They either have to refer to a set of duties of an unknown nature and origin, or they have to accept that the pregnant woman does not have any kind of duty towards the fetus (in which case she may do with it as she pleases).

By contrast, virtue ethicists like Hursthouse and Annas would argue that there is a strong demand on a pregnant woman (as well as everyone else, for that matter) to take the pregnancy seriously. Doctors, nurses, and midwives will have various role-specific duties towards the pregnant woman and the fetus, but neither they nor the pregnant woman has a general (or non-role specific) duty towards the fetus. Instead, it is the virtues that make demands on them. As we've seen, Hursthouse (1991) argues that given the familiar facts about human reproduction and parenthood, it would be callous and light-minded to view the fetus merely as a lump of cells, as something that doesn't matter. Abortion is an evil, given that it involves cutting short a human life. But in some cases it might well be the lesser of two evils, for example, if the pregnancy itself would take a very high a toll on the mother (because she is very young, or in poor health, or if the pregnancy is a result of rape or incest). Opting for an abortion for such a reason would not be selfish, callous, light-minded, or grossly materialistic.

Finally, it is worth considering whether the virtue ethicist can respond to Kornegay's objection, namely that we cannot account for the moral difference between abortion and infanticide without presupposing that the moral status of the fetus is lower than that of an infant (such that we have a duty not to kill an infant, but not a duty not to kill a fetus). To examine this claim, compare the case of Anna, who opts for an abortion in the first trimester on the grounds that having another child will seriously affect her ability to be a good mother to her other children, with that of Iris, who opts for infanticide for the same reason. (Let us assume, for the sake of argument, that both abortion and infanticide are legally permitted.) Clearly, there is a moral difference between the two cases, but the question is: Can we explain the difference without making reference to moral status or personhood?

In one sense, Anna and Iris were both facing the same choice: either to kill the fetus/infant or to give it up for adoption. And so whether or not killing it can be justified seems to depend entirely on the moral status of the being in question. But thinking about the issue in this way obscures an important difference between the cases. If we consider the relevant biological and psychological facts about pregnancy, childbirth, and parenthood, as Hursthouse (1991, 235–236) recommends, then we will see that the option of "giving it up for adoption" means something very different. For Anna, it means enduring the physical and psychological hardship that comes with carrying on with the pregnancy, giving birth, and relinquishing the baby. It is by no means an easy solution to the problem of an unwanted pregnancy. We cannot describe "giving it up for adoption" as the kind of thing a minimally decent person would do in Anna's situation. Instead, given that an early abortion will allow Anna to avoid a considerable amount of hardship, choosing to carry on with the pregnancy in order to have the baby adopted would be a praiseworthy, even heroic, thing to do. The same is not true in Iris's situation. Clearly, infanticide will not allow Iris to avoid the pains of pregnancy and childbirth, and giving the baby up for adoption wouldn't involve much more than handing it over and signing appropriate paperwork.

In short, then, although virtue ethicists might disagree about the acceptability of abortion in Anna's case, they would agree that opting for infanticide is much worse than opting for an early abortion. A woman who carries a pregnancy to term and then opts for infanticide on the grounds that she cannot raise it, acts in a way that can only be described as cruel and inhumane. However, it is worth noting that virtue ethicists are not opposed to infanticide "in principle," that is, because it violates a moral command or a duty to the infant. Instead, they would accept that there could be exceptional cases in which ending the life of an infant is the only compassionate and humane thing to do.

In the remainder of this chapter we briefly consider the problem of moral narcissism (or self-centeredness). The problem is closely related to the egoism objection we discussed in Chapter 3, but it is relevant here because it captures another reason why one might feel uneasy about the way virtue ethics approaches the question about the morality of abortion, namely that it seems inappropriate for a pregnant woman who is wondering whether she should end the life of a fetus to consider whether *she* will come off as selfish, irresponsible, callous, or immature. Shouldn't her focus be on the rights or interests of the fetus?

7.5 The Problem of Moral Narcissism

Damian Cox (2006) argues that Aristotelian virtue ethics is vulnerable to what he calls the "charge of moral narcissism." A normative theory is supposed to help us decide how to act, particularly in difficult cases. But as soon as we try to use a qualified-agent account of right action in moral deliberation, we end up violating it. That is, we *cannot* act in the way required by the theory. Cox asks us to consider those situations in which being virtuous requires caring for another. Genuinely caring for another requires redirecting our attention to their needs. However, when we deliberate according to a virtue-ethical criterion of rightness, we would display a vicious degree of self-absorption or moral narcissism, since we would be asking questions such as, Will doing x adequately reflect the fact that I am a caring person? or: If I did x, would I come off as a virtuous person? What this shows, in his view, is that virtue ethics is self-defeating:

> Deliberating over the manifestation of your own virtue is not always compatible with manifesting that virtue. Indeed, deliberating about the manifestation of your own virtue in circumstances that call for exercise of the virtues of care exhibits a vice – the vice of moral narcissism – rather than a virtue.

> (Cox 2006, 511)

The problem, then, is that if the rightness of an action is grounded in judgments of virtue and virtuous agency rather than in features of the action itself, then it seems to follow that in deciding what to do, we should direct our attention inwards, towards our own motives and attitudes rather than to features of the action, such as whether it would involve breaking a promise or harming others. Yet thinking about our "own moral status as the only matter directly at stake [in a given situation] is moral narcissism; it is exactly *not* what would exhibit a caring attitude to [the other person]" (Cox 2006, 515).

John Hacker-Wright (2010, 218–219) responds to this objection by arguing that it is based on a misunderstanding. Cox assumes that when we deliberate we are thinking about the permissibility of our actions, and so he makes the mistake of assuming that Hursthouse uses "right action" in the deontic (or strong) sense of an action that is either morally obligatory (required by duty) or permissible (not contrary to duty). Seen thus, the virtue ethical standard for determining the permissibility of our actions is whether our actions would reflect well on our character. Put in simpler terms, whether I have a duty to do x will depend on whether I would come across as kind, honest, just (or the like) if I did x. This clearly invites the charge of moral narcissism. However, Hacker-Wright argues that Hursthouse avoids this problem because she uses "right action" in the weaker sense of an act that is good or commendable. In providing an account of right action, Hursthouse is not picking out that feature of an action that makes it permissible. Instead, she claims that an ideally virtuous agent is our benchmark for answering the question of whether someone is acting well as a human being. If our aim is not to discover the permissibility of a proposed action, then all we are left with is concern with what we do. One way in which this concern can manifest is by considering whether the act is just or caring, that is, the kind of thing a just or caring person would do.

This would not be narcissistic because it "would immediately lead to considerations about the impact of our actions on others" (Hacker-Wright 2010, 219).

Chapter Summary

- One of the oldest objections to virtue ethics is that it is unable to provide action guidance, given that it focuses on character rather than action and doesn't give us a set of moral rules or principles, or a decision procedure that can be applied to particular situations.
- Deontologists subscribe to the "strong codifiability thesis," that is, the view that the task of normative theory is to provide a set of universal moral rules that can be used as a decision procedure. D-rules usually take the following form: "In situation x, one should (or should not) do y."
- Virtue ethicists support a "weak codifiability thesis," the view that given the complexity of moral life, normative theory can only offer a set of rules that apply "for the most part." The v-rules don't include reference to a situation or to a specific action. They merely state that one should do what is kind, honest, just, etc., and not do what is cruel, dishonest, unjust, etc.
- Hursthouse takes the central question about the morality of abortion to be: "In having an abortion in these circumstances, would the agent be acting virtuously or viciously, or neither?" She argues that opting for an abortion is sometimes the right decision. An objection to a virtue-ethical approach to the morality of abortion is that this approach *presupposes* that terminating a pregnancy is permissible, that is, that the right not to be killed does not extend to the fetus.
- A more recent version of the action guidance objection to virtue ethics claims that it cannot account for the demands of morality: If we reject the d-rules and the associated notion of moral duty or obligation, then morality becomes an optional extra, something that is nice to do but not required of us.
- A second objection is that virtue ethics is vulnerable to the problem of moral narcissism: It directs our attention inwards, towards our own motives and attitudes, rather than to features of the action itself, such as whether it would involve breaking a promise or harming others.

In the following chapter, we will consider the role of rules and principles in moral thought and decision-making. The rejection of the strong codifiability thesis is a distinguishing feature of virtue ethics. It is also one of its most controversial features. One way to challenge the virtue ethicist's rejection of moral rules goes roughly as follows. The virtue ethicist claims that it would be wrong for Iris to kill her infant merely on the grounds that she doesn't want to raise it. If that is the case, then he must also accept that it would be wrong for anyone in Iris's situation to kill an infant for the same reason. In doing so, he has adopted at least one general moral d-rule: "Whenever one has given birth to a baby and does not want to raise it, one should not intentionally end its life." Arguably, then, a virtuous person – someone with practical wisdom – is someone who knows (or can figure out) a suitable set of d-rules. And if the ethicist accepts this, he is no longer a virtue ethicist but a deontologist: someone who thinks that virtue is important but that virtue (and other moral concepts, such as right action and practical wisdom) can be defined in terms of universal moral rules.

Notes

1 If it turns out that having an abortion is always (or almost always) a vicious thing to do, then we can ask the further question: Should it be legally prohibited?

2 It is important to keep in mind that a diagnosis of fetal abnormality is typically made in the later stages of pregnancy, at a time when parents have already committed to the pregnancy and started preparing for the baby's birth. If they opted for an abortion at this stage, it would be for a reason that is related to the diagnosis.

3 This is an important point. Many people assume that applied virtue ethicists cannot make an appeal to the professional and other role-specific duties of physicians, nurses, lawyers, and so on, but must rely exclusively on the virtuous character traits of the individuals occupying these roles. But this is a mistake. Rules, protocols, conventions and role-specific duties play an important part in any institution, and a virtuous person will take these seriously.

Further Reading

Annas, Julia. 2004. "Being Virtuous and Doing the Right Thing." *Proceedings and Addresses of the American Philosophical Association* 78(2): 61–75. doi:10.2307/3219725

Annas, Julia. 2015a. "Applying Virtue Ethics (Society of Applied Philosophy Annual Lecture 2014)." *Journal of Applied Philosophy* 32(1): 1–14. doi:10.1111/japp.12103

Annas, Julia. 2015b. "Virtue and Duty: Negotiating between Different Ethical Traditions." *The Journal of Value Inquiry* 49(4): 605–618. doi:10.1007/s10790-015-9520-y

Cox, Damian. 2006. "Agent-Based Theories of Right Action." *Ethical Theory and Moral Practice* 9(5): 505–515. doi:10.1007/s10677-006-9029-3

Hacker-Wright, John. 2010. "Virtue Ethics without Right Action: Anscombe, Foot, and Contemporary Virtue Ethics." *The Journal of Value Inquiry* 44(2): 209–224. doi:10.1007/s10790-010-9218-0

Hursthouse, Rosalind. 1991. "Virtue Theory and Abortion." *Philosophy and Public Affairs* 20(3): 223–246. www.jstor.org/stable/2265432

Kornegay, R. Jo. 2011. "Hursthouse's Virtue Ethics and Abortion: Abortion Ethics without Metaphysics?" *Ethical Theory and Moral Practice* 14(1): 51–71. doi:10.1007/s10677-010-9230-2

Louden, Robert B. 1984. "On Some Vices of Virtue Ethics." *American Philosophical Quarterly* 21(3): 227–236. www.jstor.org/stable/20014051

8   Virtue-ethical Particularism

According to the dominant tradition in Western moral philosophy, the ideal moral agent knows a set of action-guiding moral rules or principles, such as "Keep your promises" and "Help people in need if you can do so at little cost to yourself." This position is known as *moral generalism*. It is a meta-ethical position, and both deontologists and consequentialists subscribe to it in some form or another. In this view, knowledge of general principles, together with the ability to correctly apply them, is what makes it possible to judge whether, and explain why, a particular action is right or wrong.

Contemporary virtue ethicists like John McDowell, Christine Swanton, and Rosalind Hursthouse reject the "strong codifiability thesis," that is, the view that the task of normative theory is to provide a set of universal moral principles that can be used as a decision procedure. Instead, they support some version of *moral particularism*, roughly, the view that moral principles do not play a crucial role in the thought and actions of the ideal moral agent. As we have seen in Chapter 5, Aristotelian virtue ethicists emphasize the role of practical wisdom (*phronesis*) in moral thought and action. According to Aristotle, the *phronimos* – the practically wise man – doesn't rely on moral principles but instead exercises judgment in discerning the morally relevant features of particular situations. Practical wisdom is an intellectual virtue: a kind of perceptual capacity or situation-specific know-how that involves making good judgments about how to act and feel in any particular situation. But what exactly is practical wisdom? What kind of knowledge does the Aristotelian *phronimos* possess? What does he know, if not a set of rules or principles?

Although Aristotle is often described as a proponent of particularism, some writers challenge this interpretation by pointing out that principles do play an important role in his ethics, and hence, that he is committed to a form of generalism. This presents a significant challenge for contemporary Aristotelian virtue ethics. If practical wisdom is just knowledge of a set of sophisticated moral principles (together with the ability to apply these principles), then we will have to admit that virtue ethics is not a distinctive normative theory. It will just be a version of deontology, one that emphasizes virtue but ultimately relies on moral principles.

The main focus of this chapter is on two ways in which contemporary virtue ethicists have tried to distance themselves from generalism. The first, more radical, strategy is to argue that the virtuousness (e.g., kindness, justness, honesty) of an action is sometimes a reason *against* it. This is the strategy employed by Swanton, and it involves departing from Aristotle in important ways. The second is a strategy employed by Hursthouse, which is to defend a weaker form of particularism. Hursthouse admits that there are genuine moral principles but denies that knowledge of such principles is what allows the ideal moral agent to live and act well. Before looking at these two strategies, we consider important aspects of the current debate between generalists and particularists about the role of principles in normative theory.

8.1 Moral Generalism

Moral generalism can be defined as the view that "the very possibility of moral thought and judgment depends on the provision of a suitable supply of moral principles" (Dancy 2004, 7). Moral knowledge is knowledge of a set of action-guiding moral principles. The ideal moral agent is a person of principle, someone who has learnt, and knows how to apply, a sufficient range of principles. The task of normative theory is to identify these principles.

The strongest version of generalism holds that morality is a system of *absolute* principles, that is, principles that do not allow for exceptions. Possible examples include: "It is always wrong to intentionally kill an innocent person" and: "One should never break a promise." A principle is absolute if it claims that each and every action of a certain type is right (or wrong). If, for example, we know of an action that it involves intentionally killing an innocent person, we know enough to be able to conclude that it is wrong. Nothing else that we may possibly discover about the action, such as the fact that the person asked to be killed, or that the killing was done to prevent the deaths of millions of people, will change its moral status.

Absolutists view the ideal moral agent as someone who has learnt (or has figured out for themselves) a suitably broad range of absolute principles and is able to correctly apply them in particular situations. Applying a moral principle is not always a simple matter. For example, to correctly apply the prohibition against intentionally killing an innocent person, one has to know which beings are included in the category of *persons* (does it include, for example, some animals, fetuses, newborn infants, or human beings who are in a permanently vegetative state?), what it means to be *innocent*, and what it means to *intentionally* kill someone (does it include, for example, withdrawing life-sustaining treatment?). These questions are notoriously difficult to answer, but the important thing to note is that the knowledge needed to correctly apply an absolute principle is thought to be *non-moral* knowledge, the kind of knowledge that can be taught and that any reasonably intelligent being can possess.

An obvious difficulty for the view that morality is a system of absolute principles is that it is fairly easy to think of exceptions to most moral principles. Take, for example, the principle "It is always wrong to break a promise." It seems obvious that it is acceptable to break a promise, say, to meet a friend for lunch, if doing so will prevent a great harm from occurring. Somewhat more controversially, many people believe that it is justifiable to kill an innocent person if that person is suffering extreme pain or discomfort and repeatedly asks for their life to be ended. A frequent response to this problem is to refine the principle in such a way that it incorporates these exceptions; for example, "One should never break a promise except when doing so will prevent a great harm from occurring" or "It is always wrong to intentionally kill an innocent person against their wishes." And this is indeed what many deontologists try to do. The problem, however, is that for these principles to remain absolute, they will have to include every possible exception, with the result that they will eventually become so complicated that they will no longer be useful when it comes to providing action guidance (see Dancy 2004, 126).

A more popular form of generalism is what is sometimes referred to as Rossian generalism. In this view, morality consists of a (possibly infinite) number of *contributory* (or what W. D. Ross calls *prima facie*) principles that cannot be ranked in order of priority. Unlike an absolute principle, which identifies a set of actions that is always right (or wrong), a contributory principle provides us with a *reason* to act (or not to act) in a certain way. For example, the principle "Lying is wrong" gives us a reason not to tell a lie. But it doesn't follow that each and every action that involves telling a lie is wrong. Whether telling a lie is wrong in a particular situation will depend on whether there is a stronger reason in support of telling a lie, for example that it will protect someone from danger. If there is such a reason, telling a lie is right (permissible). In this sense, contributory principles allow for exceptions. However, the view that morality consists of a system of contributory principles is still a version of generalism because it holds that certain features of an action, such as its being a lie or the breaking of a promise, *always* count as reasons against it, whereas other features of an action, such as its helping someone in need or repaying a debt, *always* count as reasons in favor.

For Rossian generalists, moral decision-making is a somewhat more complicated matter than it is for the absolutist. The ideal Rossian moral agent knows a set of principles and how to apply them to particular cases, and this includes knowing how to handle situations in which two or more contributory principles conflict. Correctly resolving moral dilemmas requires good judgment and moral sensitivity, as well as paying attention to the relevant features of the particular situation. For example, where the conflict is between "Do not tell lies" and "Do not cause harm to others," the ideal moral agent is able to figure out which principle provides an overriding reason in support of a given action in the particular situation. Rossian generalists share with absolutists the view that moral principles play a crucial role in moral thought and judgment, and that the reasons identified by principles make an invariant contribution to the moral status of an action.

8.2 Moral Particularism

Jonathan Dancy is the leading proponent of moral particularism. He argues that there are no moral principles of the kind that generalists have in mind, but that "morality can get along perfectly well without principles" (Dancy 2004, 2). He defines particularism as the view that "the possibility of moral thought and judgement does not depend on the provision of a suitable supply of moral principles" (2004, 7). In defense of this thesis, he argues that any property of an action has *variable valence*, that is, it can count as a reason in favor of an action in one context, but in another context it may not be a reason at all or even be a reason against a particular action. He notes that examples of valence shifting are fairly common in non-moral contexts. For example, if I'm deciding whether to go somewhere the fact that nobody else will be there is sometimes a good reason for going there, but at other times a good reason for staying away. And the fact that a candidate wants the job is sometimes a good reason for giving it to her, but at other times a good reason for doing the opposite (Dancy 2004, 74). He refers to this phenomenon as the "holism of reasons": reasons for action are holistic (context-dependent) rather than general.

Dancy argues that the same is true of moral reasons. The property of producing pleasure generally counts in favor of an action. But it can also be a reason against, for example, when the pleasure in question is the pleasure that the sadist will get from torturing his victim. In such a case, the property of producing pleasure makes the action worse and hence counts as a reason against doing it (Dancy 1993, 56, 61). Similarly, he claims that reasons given in terms of virtue and vice concepts (v-reasons) have variable valence (2004, 123–125). He gives the following example.

It may be considerate to wipe the torturer's brow, but this fact hardly functions as a reason to wipe, or makes his sweat a reason for us to wipe it off. The torturer's other activities prevent what would ordinarily give us a reason from doing so here.

(2013, section 6)

Note that Dancy is not saying that the considerateness of the action is a reason in favor but one that is overridden by other stronger reasons against wiping a torturer's brow. Nor is he claiming that wiping the torturer's brow is not truly considerate. Instead, his claim is that the action is considerate, but that its being considerate does not count as a reason in favor of the action. Given the holism of reasons, Dancy argues, there is no good reason to believe that normative theorists will be able to discover a suitable supply of moral principles.

8.2.1 Objections to Dancy's Particularism

Moral particularism remains a very controversial doctrine and various objections have been leveled against it in recent years.[1] Here we briefly consider two objections made by Brad Hooker (2000; 2008). The first has to do with the value of predictability. Hooker argues that one of the great advantages of a shared commitment to moral principles is that it creates settled expectations about how others will behave. If we know of someone that they are committed to moral principles, we can reliably predict that they won't attack us, steal from us, or break their promises to us, and such predictions will allow us to make better choices and plans for the future. If we knew of someone that they are a particularist, however, we have no reason to trust them. Hooker uses the following example to illustrate this point:

> [Patty] asks you to help her get in her crop now in return for her promising to help you get yours in next month. Half her crop will spoil if you don't help her. This would drive her to bankruptcy. That is why she is willing to promise to help you later in return for your helping her now. Likewise, you must have help with your crop later if you are to avoid going bankrupt yourself. That is why she thinks you might be willing to accept the deal she proposes. Suppose you have no direct or indirect experience of Patty. Nor do you have time to ask others how trustworthy she is. All you have to go on is her self-description as a particularist.
>
> (2000, 17)

Hooker thinks it's obvious that you can't trust Patty. You cannot reliably predict that she will keep her promise because you know that she thinks promise-keeping is not always a reason in favor of an action. When the time comes to keep her promise, she might not attach any weight to the promise at all. Further, a society made up of particularists would not only be unpredictable but also a highly insecure place to live in. Hooker asks us to consider whether we would feel safe living in a society where people do not think that the fact that someone has not killed or threatened anyone and has not asked to be killed, always counts as a reason against killing that person. In Hooker's view, then, irrespective of whether it is *true*, we have good reason to reject particularism as *bad*.

Hooker's second objection is related to the first, and concerns the importance of moral principles in moral education. Parents don't teach their children that lying, cheating, or stealing is wrong in this particular situation. Rather, they teach them that certain kinds of action are wrong, that, as a general rule, they should not lie, steal, cheat, and hurt others. In due course, children will learn to refine these principles, and so might replace "Lying is always wrong" with something like "Lying is wrong, except when ..." The question, then, is how moral education would proceed in a society where everyone adheres to particularism? The particularist can accept that general principles can be taught to children as "rules of thumb." However, in their view, moral education and development is not a matter of refining these principles, but rather of learning to get by without them. The morally competent person is someone who has come to see that a moral principle is just a summary of judgments one made on previous occasions. But if this is the case, then the difficulty for particularists is to show how it is possible for us to learn from our experience. If moral properties have variable valence, then the fact that promise-keeping counted in favor of an action in one case (or even in a series of cases) gives us no reason to believe that it will count in favor of an action in another case (see Hooker 2000; 2008; Väyrynen 2008).

We will return to these objections later on in this chapter, when we consider whether virtue-ethical particularism is able to avoid them. But first, we will briefly discuss Aristotle's views on moral knowledge and moral principles.

8.3 Aristotle on Practical Wisdom and Moral Principles

Aristotle is widely regarded as the forefather of particularism. He emphasizes the complexity of moral life, the inadequacy of rules, and the importance of judgment in moral thought and decision-making. The ideal moral agent possesses practical wisdom, which Aristotle defines as "a true and reasoned state of capacity to act with regard to the things that are good or bad for man" (*The Nicomachean Ethics* 1140b5). Practical wisdom is the virtue that allows one to grasp the truth about morality, that is, to have practical knowledge (see Ridge and McKeever 2016, section 1).

In Book VI of *The Nicomachean Ethics*, Aristotle distinguishes practical knowledge from two more familiar forms of knowledge, namely, theoretical and productive knowledge. He defines *theoretical knowledge* as "scientific knowledge, combined with intuitive reason, of the things that are highest by nature" (*The Nicomachean Ethics* 1141b). Scientific knowledge is knowledge of what is universal, unchanging, and necessary. It is not open to deliberation because it is independent of human action. The task of the natural sciences, theology, and mathematics is to obtain theoretical knowledge, which includes knowledge of first principles, such as mathematical axioms and universal truths that serve as the foundations of the various sciences, and knowledge of propositions that can be logically deduced from these principles. Aristotle identifies three intellectual virtues that are needed for attaining theoretical knowledge: Intuitive understanding (*nous*), which is the virtue that allows one to grasp first principles; Science (*episteme*), which is the virtue that allows one to deduce necessary or invariable truths about a particular subject from universal truths; and Theoretical wisdom (*sophia*), which combines science and intuitive understanding, and aims at discovering truths about the general structure of reality.

Productive knowledge is concerned with the making or production of various sorts of things, including artifacts (such as tables, saddles, and buildings), and ends (such as a healthy patient, a grammatical sentence, a musical performance, and so on). The corresponding virtue is craftsmanship or skill (*technē*), which can roughly be defined as "the ability to make things as a result of knowing how to do so" (Battaly 2015, 47). Whereas a theoretically wise person has knowledge of the causes of things that obtain independently of human action, the virtue of craftsmanship produces contingent knowledge. There is no necessary truth about how to make a specific artifact. For example, the best way to make a chair depends on various factors, such as the materials and tools that are available, the desires and tastes of the carpenter and/or customer, the function or purpose of the particular chair, and so on. A skilled carpenter is someone who is able to figure out how to build a good chair, given particular constraints and circumstances.

The important question, then, is whether practical wisdom is more like theoretical wisdom (which requires knowledge of universal principles as well as the ability to deduce particular truths from these principles), or more like craftsmanship (which is a kind of know-how or skill aimed at producing things). As we've seen, moral generalists claim that moral knowledge is similar to theoretical knowledge. It involves knowledge of

universal moral principles together with the ability to apply these principles to particular situations to arrive at the truth about what should be
done. Aristotle disagrees, however. He argues that practical wisdom is very
similar to craftsmanship. Both are a kind of know-how or skill that
involves deliberation and choice and is directed at certain ends. To be sure,
the ends in question are very different. Whereas craftsmanship is concerned with the making or production of artifacts, practical wisdom is
concerned with action and is directed towards what is good. This distinction points to another important difference: whereas practical wisdom
requires a correct conception or understanding of what is good or bad for
human beings, craftsmanship is judged purely on the basis of the quality
of the work itself. A skilled craftsman will be able to produce excellent
weapons, but it requires practical wisdom to make good decisions about
how these weapons are to be used (or whether they should be manu-
factured at all).

An important respect in which practical wisdom is similar to craftsmanship is that it is not a matter of applying universal rules or principles
to a particular situation in order to arrive at the right action. A good
carpenter doesn't just follow a set of instructions. Instead, as we've seen,
he has the ability to figure out how to make a chair with the specific tools
and materials available to him on any given occasion. In much the same
way, someone with practical wisdom has the ability to see which actions
and emotions are appropriate in a particular situation. In both cases, the
skill in question is acquired through the help and guidance of a role model as
well as a good amount of experience and practice. And in both cases,
generalizations are of limited use. One might learn how to make a chair by
following instructions, but as one comes across new and challenging situations (e.g., a customer is unusually tall and needs a comfortable chair, or the
only wood available is very brittle, or the chair is supposed to match a
specific table), these instructions will no longer suffice. Aristotle thinks
the same is true of acting well. A rule like "Repay your debts" will be
useful in many situations, but of little help in unusual or difficult cases.
Practical wisdom, like craftsmanship (but unlike theoretical wisdom), does
not rely on knowledge of a set of universal principles. Aristotle writes:

> Since, then, the present inquiry does not aim at theoretical knowledge like
> the others (for we are inquiring not in order to know what virtue is, but in
> order to become good, since otherwise our inquiry would have been of no
> use), we must examine the nature of actions, namely how we ought to do
> them ... . But this must be agreed upon beforehand, that the whole
> account of matters of conduct must be given in outline and not precisely
> ...; matters concerned with conduct and questions of what is good for us

have no fixity, any more than matters of health. The general account being of this nature, the account of particular cases is yet more lacking in exactness; for they do not fall under any art or precept, but the agents themselves must in each case consider what is appropriate to the occasion, as happens also in the art of medicine or of navigation.

(*The Nicomachean Ethics* 1103b27–1104a9)

In this passage, Aristotle suggests that it is possible to distinguish between good and bad actions, in the same way that it is possible to distinguish appropriate and inappropriate courses of action in the field of medicine. But in both cases, what is right or appropriate can vary from one situation to another, which means that right reasons cannot be codified into a set of moral principles. In the same way that the art (or craft) of medicine is not a matter of applying general rules (like "Always give a feverish patient a pink pill"), practical wisdom is not a matter of applying general principles to particular situations.

8.4 A Challenge for Virtue Ethics

As we've seen, Aristotle claims that the ideal moral agent does not follow a set of moral rules or principles, but instead possesses a kind of perceptual capacity or practical judgment that allows him to see the morally relevant features of particular situations. However, some scholars argue that Aristotle was not a particularist, given that he accepts that there are general moral principles. To begin with, he acknowledges that there are at least a few absolute principles. He claims that acts of adultery, theft, and murder are *always* wrong, and he also admits that the emotions of spite, shamelessness, and envy are *always* inappropriate (*The Nicomachean Ethics* 1107a10–14). Further, Aristotle mentions a number of general rules that hold only "for the most part"; for example, that one should repay a debt instead of giving money to help a friend (*The Nicomachean Ethics* 1164b30). An important question is: In what sense do these rules hold only for the most part? From Aristotle's discussion, it is clear that he doesn't think the property of "repaying a debt" has variable valence. That is, he doesn't think the fact that an act is one of repaying a debt can ever count as a reason against it. So he wouldn't support Dancy's particularism. Instead, his position appears very similar to Rossian generalism, for he suggests that a reason in favor can be *outweighed* by a stronger reason against. Aristotle imagines a situation in which your father has been kidnapped, and you are faced with a choice between repaying a debt and ransoming your father. He claims that it is more important to ransom your father than to repay the debt: "generally the debt should be paid, but if the gift is exceedingly noble or exceedingly necessary, one should defer to these considerations" (*The Nicomachean Ethics* 1165a1–5). It appears, then, that Aristotle's general rules are very similar to what contemporary philosophers call contributory principles. They hold "for the most part" in the sense that they can be overridden by another general rule or principle.

Aristotle's acceptance of general principles has led some scholars to conclude that he wasn't a particularist. Karen Nielsen writes:

> It is true that Aristotle thinks the particular features of circumstances matter. But that is a far cry from dispensing with moral principles alto- gether. The fact that these principles hold "usually," and not "always," is no argument for their dispensability. For we can admit that ethical rules hold *hôs epi to polu* [for the most part] while insisting that our judgment in particular cases should be guided by them.
>
> (Nielsen 2015, 43; see also Irwin 2000)

Nielsen doesn't merely challenge the prevailing interpretation of Aristotle's moral thought. She also poses a significant challenge to virtue ethics more generally. If it turns out that practical wisdom is just knowledge of a set of general moral principles, together with the ability to apply them to parti- cular situations, then virtue ethics will no longer be a distinctive moral theory. It will just be a form of deontology, one that emphasizes the virtues but ultimately relies on principles.

Virtue ethicists might try to get out of this conundrum by claiming that Aristotle was simply mistaken in those few passages where he admits the existence of general moral principles. But this response is unlikely to get them very far, given that what Aristotle says in these passages seems entirely reasonable. Surely, we have to admit that certain kinds of action, like killing or torturing innocent people for fun, are always wrong, and also that some reasons, like "I owe her a debt," are always reasons in favor. Further, many contemporary virtue ethicists do appeal to general- izations of some sort. For example, Hursthouse responds to the objection that virtue ethics doesn't provide action guidance by stating that every virtue generates a prescription (e.g., "Do what is kind") and every vice generates a prohibition (e.g., "Do not do what is cruel") (1999, 36; 2011, 46). Does this mean that virtue ethicists are committed to generalism after all, whether they like it or not? Andrew Jordan thinks it does:

> [I]f we accept some form of virtue [ethics], then it is a short step to the thought that the virtuousness of an act in some regard (e.g. its kindness, generosity, or courageousness) is always a reason to do it. This, in turn, looks very close to the endorsement of a set of general principles that

ground reasons for action, and hence one on which moral thought and judgement would seem to depend.

(Jordan 2013, 249)

In the remainder of this chapter, we will discuss two forms of virtue-ethical particularism.

8.5 Virtue-ethical Particularism: A Radical Version

Christine Swanton defends a fairly radical form of particularism. Swanton distances herself from the view that there are no moral principles *at all*, but she claims, following Dancy, that moral reasons *characteristically* function holistically. She writes:

> We cannot claim that certain features *always* contribute positively (or negatively) to the overall virtuousness of an act, even if those kinds of feature characteristically contribute positively (or negatively).
>
> (Swanton 2003, 242)

Swanton argues that the same is true of reasons phrased in terms of virtues and vices (v-reasons). Although the kindness or justice of an action characteristically makes a positive contribution to its rightness, there are cases in which kindness or justice is the very thing that makes it wrong. Swanton gives the following two examples.

> We are at a conference where a stranger looks lonely. It turns out he is a person from overseas with a poor command of English, and cannot participate in the scintillating and sophisticated discussion on moral theory. Our agent Tim performs a kind act, namely, going to talk to the stranger. However, ... Tim is exceptionally keen to participate in the discussion, but leaves in order to talk to the stranger who could have made more effort to amuse himself in other ways and whose hangdog expression is expressive of a rather weak, spoilt approach to life. The conversation with the stranger is difficult and Tim does not enjoy it. Furthermore, Tim is always doing this kind of thing, sacrificing his interests in the performance of such kind acts. He has resolved to be more self-protective and strong, and encourage others to do their share of the burdensome tasks. But he consistently fails to abide by the resolution.
>
> (2003, 243–244)

It is important to notice that Swanton is not saying that Tim's action is not truly kind. Neither is she saying that the kindness of the action is outweighed by other, stronger reasons against talking to the stranger. Instead, she claims that in this context, "the kindness of the act contributes negatively to the overall virtuousness of the act" (2003, 244).

Swanton's second example concerns justice in the context of family life:

> I have been training my children not to be obsessive about justice or fairness, particularly in an intrafamily context and where the stakes are not high. I want them to be more caring, magnanimous, and generous. Despite my personal tendencies to be overly concerned with justice, I resolve to drive the lesson home at the next opportunity. An opportunity soon arises. A family tradition of "fair shares" requires that the person making the division has last choice. There is a cake to be cut. I allow my older son to cut the cake. I notice that he has cut carelessly, but in a state of unawareness takes the biggest piece... . My younger son, apparently unnoticing and uncaring, looks delightedly at the smaller piece that he has been left with... . I make my older son swap pieces, telling him that the division, and his action in going first, having cut, is unjust.
>
> (2003, 244)

Swanton claims that the mother's action is just, but that "[t]he justice of the intervention is in this context expressive of the obsessive, weak quality of [her] behaviour" (2003, 244). It is therefore a wrong-making feature of the action.

8.5.1 Predictability and Moral Education

As we've seen, Dancy's critics argue that if particularism is true, then we won't be able to predict how people will act in any given situation, which means that we won't be able to rely on them to keep their promises, tell the truth, and so on. Swanton's radical virtue-ethical particularism is vulnerable to the same objection. If we knew of someone that they believed that the kindness, honesty, or justness of an action is not always a reason in favor of doing it, and that its being selfish, dishonest, or unjust is not always a reason against doing it, then we won't be able to predict their behavior. Virtue-ethical particularism also encounters a version of the moral education objection: if the kindness, honesty, or justness of an action is sometimes a reason in favor and sometimes a reason against an action, there doesn't seem to be much point in teaching or encouraging children to acquire these virtues. Indeed, it seems questionable whether we can describe these traits as *virtues*, as good traits to have, if they can motivate one to act wrongly.

Swanton responds to these objections by noting that the particularist can accept that there are general principles of the form "Characteristically (or normally) thus and so," and that this makes it possible to predict whether a particular feature will have positive or negative valence. V-rules are good examples of such principles. The virtuousness of an act in a given respect (for example, its being just or kind) is *characteristically*, albeit not invariably, right-making. The fact that justice and kindness characteristically serve as a reason in favor is what allows us to identify these traits as virtues (Swanton 2003, 242–244). Swanton thereby supports a weak version of the codifiability thesis. In her view, morality is codifiable through the v-rules, and the v-rules hold only "for the most part" in the sense that the virtuousness of an action in a given respect can sometimes count as a reason against, and the viciousness of an action in a given respect can count as a reason in favor (see Swanton 2015b, 39–41).

This response removes some of the worry about predictability and moral education, but it still leaves us with the problem of correctly identifying exceptional cases. If I knew that honesty characteristically counts in favor of an action, then my guess that it is a right-making feature in a particular case will usually be spot on. However, I still have no way of predicting when and why honesty will not be a right-making feature. Swanton addresses this problem by appealing to Dancy's notion of a "default reason." Default reasons are reasons that are "set up to be reasons, in advance," that is, they are reasons in favor (or against) an action *unless* they have been "switched off if the circumstances so conspire" (Dancy 2004, 112–113). Swanton thinks virtue and vice terms are paradigm cases of default reasons. The kindness of an action can be cited as a reason in its favor unless we can point to a feature of the situation that serves to switch off its positive valence (Swanton 2011, 203–206; 2015b, 48–53). In the case of Tim's kindness to the stranger, two such features can be identified: the fact that the stranger could have made more of an effort to amuse himself, and the fact that Tim has previously resolved to be more self-protective and to encourage others to do their share of burdensome tasks.

The implication of this is that whether or not a particular feature counts as a reason in favor or against an action is often fairly stable and predictable, such that it makes moral education possible. We can teach children to be kind, just, and honest, and not to be cruel, unjust, and dishonest. But in due course they have to learn *why* the kindness, justness, or honesty of an action is a strong default reason in favor of performing it, such that they are able to justify their claim that the default status of kindness, justness, or honesty has been switched off in a particular case. Swanton (2011, 205) notes that some virtues, such as kindness and justice, supply default reasons that are strongly positive, meaning that it is extremely uncommon for the kindness or justness of an action to be a reason against doing it. Similarly, some vices supply default reasons that are strongly negative. For example, it will be extremely uncommon for the cruelty of an action to be a reason in favor. In the case of virtues like honesty and loyalty, however, the positive default status is weaker and less predictable. Loyalty doesn't count in favor of an action in cases involving unjust institutions or violent family members.

On Swanton's account, the ideally virtuous agent – the person with practical wisdom – has an understanding of what is required by the virtues and why it is required, such that he is able to identify those exceptional cases in which an action's being virtuous in a given respect doesn't count as a reason in favor. He also has an understanding of when and why the viciousness of an action counts against it, such that he is able to correctly identify exceptional cases in which the negative default status of a given vice has been switched off.

8.5.2 Moral Motivation

The above characterization of the ideal moral agent suggests a different objection to Swanton's particularism. On Swanton's account, the ideal moral agent is a purely rational being. He has a superior grasp of v-reasons, and can identify situations in which their default status has been switched off. However, as we've seen in Chapter 4, in addition to the intellectual aspect, the virtues also have an emotional aspect. A virtuous person is characterized by certain kinds of emotional responses, attitudes, and motives.

Rebecca Stangl (2008, 668–673) argues, in this regard, that Swanton's radical particularism presents us with an unattractive model of moral motivation. The virtues are not merely rules of thumb that can be abandoned when they don't apply. Someone who has the virtue of compassion will in fact be motivated to act compassionately in certain situations; they cannot simply "switch off" the feelings, attitudes, and motives that are characteristic of a compassionate person. According to the radical particularist, however, the fact that an act is compassionate is sometimes a reason against it. In such cases the agent will experience a peculiar kind of motivational disharmony: their compassion will motivate them to do what is wrong, so they will have to resist or overcome their compassionate feelings and attitudes in order to do what is right. It follows, then, that compassion is a dangerous disposition, for it can lead one by its very nature to perform a wrong action. A further implication of this is that moral education remains a problem for Swanton. Virtue ethicists emphasize the importance of encouraging people to acquire the virtues, but if it is true that virtue can lead one astray, then the wisdom of this policy is put into question. In short, acquiring the virtues would not be sufficient for moral thought and action (Stangl 2008, 670). We will return to this objection later on in the chapter. First, we consider Hursthouse's response to the generalist's challenge.

8.6 Virtue-ethical Particularism: A Weaker Version

Rosalind Hursthouse (2006c; 2011) supports a weaker form of moral particularism (or what she calls "anti-generalism" or "anti-codifiability"). She accepts that rules and principles play a role in moral thought and decision-making. As we've seen in Chapters 6 and 7, she argues that virtue ethics provides guidance in the form of the v-rules. When we are unsure what to do, we should try to do what is kind, generous, and courageous, and avoid doing what is selfish, inconsiderate, arrogant, and cowardly (Hursthouse 2011, 46). Hursthouse also thinks Aristotle is correct in claiming that there are a few absolute moral prohibitions as well as a large number of action-guiding principles that hold "for the most part" (contributory principles):

> Is it not plausible to say that the *phronimos* thinks of debts as the sorts of thing that are to be repaid, of benefits as the sorts of thing that are to be returned, and of friends as the sorts of people you put yourself out for? This is part of his virtue and one of the many ways in which he contrasts with the shameless and wicked, who think of debts as money for jam, of benefits as the harvest to be reaped from suckers, and of friends merely as people you know it is fun to be with.
>
> (Hursthouse 2011, 42)

By accepting that there are genuine moral rules and principles and that practical wisdom includes knowledge of such principles, Hursthouse distances herself from the more radical forms of particularism espoused by Dancy and Swanton. But she doesn't think this commits the Aristotelian to a form of generalism either. She argues it is a mistake to view the disagreement between Aristotelian virtue ethics and generalism as a disagreement about the mere *existence* of moral principles. Instead, what they disagree about is the role such principles play in moral life, more specifically, whether the ideal moral agent "has knowledge of a code by following which he is able to live and act well" (Hursthouse 2011, 39).

Hursthouse accepts that the *phronimos* has knowledge of rules and principles, but she denies that it is this knowledge that allows him to act well. Consider, first, the role of absolute principles. Hursthouse thinks the list of absolute principles will be very short, and she points out that they provide very little guidance in our everyday life: "If I want to know … how to act well, day to day, knowing that, say, theft, murder, and adultery cannot form part of a well-spent day still leaves me pretty much in the dark" (2011, 40; see also 1999, 57–58). With regard to the large number of contributory principles, Hursthouse thinks that they are the kind of things that anyone with a minimally decent upbringing – including the *phronimos* – knows. She refers to them as "mother's knee" rules, and she accepts that they provide quite a bit of guidance in our everyday lives (2011, 38). The important point, however, is that knowledge of these principles is not what allows the ideal moral agent to act well. To fully appreciate the nature of practical wisdom, we have to consider not only what distinguishes the ideal moral agent from the wicked, but also what distinguishes him from someone we might describe as a fairly decent person: good-hearted but inexperienced. That is, Hursthouse is interested in finding out what special knowledge the *phronimos* has, that allows him, unlike the rest of us, not only to avoid wrongdoing but to act in ways that are truly virtuous.

What about the v-rules? Does knowledge of the v-rules allow the *phronimos* to act well? And if so, isn't the Aristotelian virtue ethicist committed to a form of generalism after all? Hursthouse doesn't think so. She argues that there are important differences between the v-rules and the sort of principles that generalists have in mind. In their view, moral principles are similar to scientific principles. They are discovered by experts – normative theorists – and they are formulated in purely descriptive terms, such that any clever adolescent can understand and correctly apply them (Hursthouse 2011, 47). An example of such a principle can be found in Hooker's discussion of promise-keeping. Speaking, presumably, as an expert in normative theory, Hooker argues that "Keep your promises" is inadequate as a principle, because we don't have to keep an immoral promise, such as a promise to harm someone or to destroy others' property. We should therefore replace it with a more carefully formulated principle, namely: "[T]he fact that an act would involve keeping a morally permissible promise that was elicited from you without coercion or deception always counts morally in favour of your doing the act" (Hooker 2000, 10).

Hursthouse argues that the v-rules differ from the generalist's principles in that they are just "common moral knowledge." As such, they do not capture what is special about the *phronimos*'s knowledge. Any reasonably well-brought-up person knows that one should be kind and not cruel, that one should be courageous and not cowardly or reckless, and is able to apply such rules to some extent. What sets the *phronimos* apart from the reasonably well-brought-up person, Hursthouse argues, is not that he has expert knowledge of a set of sophisticated moral principles. Instead, what sets him apart is his superior grasp of the virtues and vices. The *phronimos* understands, for example, that "[i]t is not mean to spend no more on presents than you can afford," that "[i]t is not always cowardly to run away, and not always intemperate to eat a lot" (Hursthouse 2006c, 291). This understanding is made possible by his superior mastery of *concepts*:

> [T]he *phronimos* has a grasp of the important, the fine, and the necessary superior to that of most of us.... . He has a superior grasp of the right or correct as it occurs "to the right extent, towards the right people, for the right reason, etc." He also has a superior grasp of *eupraxia* – acting well – and *eudaimonia*. And he has a superior grasp of the virtues and vices.
>
> (Hursthouse 2011, 45)

Consider, for example, the v-rule, "Do what is courageous." Hursthouse argues that we cannot specify the conditions for the application of "courage" without referring to what is important or worthwhile, that is, without an understanding of what is good or bad in relation to *eudaimonia* or human flourishing (2011, 49). We might know that courage involves overcoming fear (of pain, failure, injury, or the like) for the sake of a worthy goal, but it takes practical wisdom to know which goals are worthy. And it is this kind of knowledge that is uncodifiable:

> There is nothing the *phronimos* could say that would fully articulate his (intellectual) perceptual capacity, because there is nothing that could be written down that could replace the training through which he has acquired it ... . There is no short cut to what the *phronimos* knows. Nothing but the acquisition of personal virtue will yield it.
>
> (Hursthouse 2011, 52–53)

Practical wisdom also allows the *phronimos* to correctly resolve difficult moral dilemmas. Hursthouse considers the example in which the requirements of kindness and honesty conflict. This sort of dilemma is often presented as forcing a choice between lying (which would be dishonest) and telling a hurtful truth (which would be unkind). Hursthouse thinks the *phronimos* will be able to correctly resolve the dilemma. In some cases, he will realize that it would not be dishonest to remain discreetly silent. In other cases he will realize that telling the hurtful truth is the kindest thing to do. Again, what allows the *phronimos* to correctly resolve moral dilemmas is his knowledge of what the virtues do and do not require, and what does and does not fall under a vice term, and this kind of knowledge is not codifiable (Hursthouse 2006c, 291).

The Aristotelian view of practical wisdom has important implications for moral education. In the generalist view, moral education involves learning a code or set of principles, which can be understood by both the virtuous and the non-virtuous. By contrast, *phronesis* is an intellectual virtue, which can only be acquired through experience. One cannot obtain a correct understanding of the virtues and vices by attending lectures or reading books but only through virtuous activity itself (Hursthouse 2011, 47–49).

8.6.1 The Problem of Motivation (Revisited)

As we've seen, Swanton distances herself from generalism by arguing that the v-rules supply reasons that have variable valence: although the kindness or justice of an action is characteristically a reason in favor, it can also be a reason against. In her view, the justness of the mother's act of interfering in the division of the cake, or the kindness of Tim's act of talking to the lonely stranger, makes the actions worse. One implication of Swanton's view is that a virtuous agent is sometimes led astray by virtue. This invites Stangl's objection, namely that the virtuous agent will sometimes experience motivational disharmony.

As noted above, Hursthouse supports a weaker version of particularism. She doesn't deny the existence of general moral principles, but she distances herself from generalism by arguing that the *phronimos*'s knowledge of these principles is not what allows him to act well. Importantly, Hursthouse doesn't think the reasons supplied by the v-rules have variable valence. In her view, the kindness or justness of an action is always a reason in favor.

The main challenge for the weak particularist is how to deal with examples that appear to show that v-reasons do have variable valence. Consider, again, Swanton's cake-cutting example. Can the weak particularist give a plausible explanation for why the mother's act of interfering in the division of cake is wrong (or, at least, less than fully virtuous), without admitting that the justness of the action makes it worse? The weak particularist has at least two responses available to her when dealing with this kind of case, and both responses allow her to avoid Stangl's objection about motivational disharmony.

The first is to argue that the mother's act of interfering is not what is called for by the virtue of justice. Aristotelian virtue ethicists claim that although the virtuousness (justness, kindness, honesty) of an action is always a reason in favor, generalizations about what is required by specific virtues do allow for exceptions. So, for example, courage generally requires facing the enemy, but not always, and honesty generally requires telling the truth, but not always (see Hursthouse 2006c, 292; Sherman 1999, 39). Similarly, although justice generally requires a fair or equal division of goods, the cake-cutting case is an exception. Whereas a naïve and inexperienced person might describe the mother's action as just, the *phronimos*, with his superior understanding of justice, will see that (and understand why) justice does not in fact call for interference in the division of cake. This response allows the weak particularist to avoid the problem of motivational disharmony: A virtuous mother, one who has practical wisdom, would not experience any kind of internal conflict because she will see that interfering would be petty and not just.

The second option is to view the situation as presenting a moral dilemma in which the demands of justice conflict with the demands of magnanimity or generosity. In this view, justice does indeed provide the mother with a reason to interfere, but this reason is outweighed by reasons of magnanimity. If she insists that the children swap their pieces of cake then she acts wrongly, but this is not because she is just. Rather, she acts wrongly because she fails to be magnanimous (see Stangl 2008, 672). A fully virtuous mother, one who has practical wisdom, would understand why magnanimity is more important than justice in this case. But would she experience the kind of motivational disharmony that Stangl is worried about? Stangl doesn't think so. She accepts that a virtuous mother would experience some inner conflict, given that she is faced with a choice between doing what is just and doing what is generous. She has a reason to do what is generous, and she has a reason to do what is just, but she cannot do both. So if she decides not to interfere, she is likely to feel a certain degree of regret or frustration. However, Stangl argues that the mother will experience a kind of inner harmony, for her motivation (to do what is magnanimous) will be in agreement with her values. She would be able to rest content with the knowledge that she did what was generous, and that generosity was more important than justice in this case. As Stangl points out, this solution is not available to the radical particularist, for whom "there are situations in which the fact that an action is virtuous in some respect is not only outweighed, but actually counts against performing the action" (2008, 673).

The weak particularist can use either of these responses to deal with examples that appear to show that v-reasons have variable valence. To defeat the weak particularist, radical particularists like Swanton will have to present an example where neither of these responses is satisfactory.[2]

Chapter Summary

- Moral generalism is the view that "the very possibility of moral thought and judgement depends on the provision of a suitable supply of moral principles" (Dancy 2004, 7). The ideal moral agent is a person of principle, someone who has learnt, and knows how to apply, a sufficient range of rules or principles. The task of normative theory is to identify these principles.

- Moral particularism is the view that "the possibility of moral thought and judgement does not depend on the provision of a suitable supply of moral principles" (Dancy 2004, 7).
- Aristotle is regarded as the forefather of particularism. In his view, practical wisdom is not a matter of applying general principles to particular situations. Instead, it is a situation-specific know-how that allows its possessor to perceive correctly which actions and emotions are appropriate in a particular situation, and it is made possible by an understanding of what is good or worthwhile.
- Many writers challenge this interpretation by pointing out that rules and principles do play an important role in Aristotle's ethics. This raises the further question of whether contemporary virtue ethicists are justified in rejecting generalism.
- Contemporary virtue ethicists try to distance themselves from generalism in two main ways. The first is to argue that the kindness, justness, or honesty of an action is sometimes a reason against it. This is the strategy employed by Christine Swanton, and it involves departing from Aristotle in important ways. By contrast, Rosalind Hursthouse follows Aristotle by defending a weaker form of particularism. She accepts that there are genuine moral principles but denies that knowledge of such principles is what allows the ideal moral agent to live and act well.

In this chapter we considered an important challenge to virtue ethics, which is to show that Aristotle was correct in rejecting the view that moral principles play a central role in moral thought and decision-making. In the following chapter we consider a very different, though equally serious challenge to virtue ethics, which is to show that virtues and vices do in fact exist and that it is possible for us to acquire practical wisdom and hence to become more virtuous.

Notes

1 For a discussion of some of these objections, see Lance et al. (2008); Tjiattas (2007); McKeever and Ridge (2006) and Crisp (2007).
2 A possible example is the familiar case of the Nazis who come knocking at the door, demanding to know whether there are Jews in the house. Clearly, if you're hiding a Jew in the cellar then telling the truth is not the right thing to do. In Swanton's view, the example demonstrates that honesty has variable valence. Telling the truth would be honest, but honesty has negative valence in this case. Against this, the weak particularist would have to convince us (a) that telling the truth is not an honest action in this case, or (b) that telling the truth is honest, and that you have a reason to tell the truth, but that benevolence gives you a much stronger reason to lie.

Further Reading

Dancy, Jonathan. 1993. *Moral Reasons*. Oxford: Blackwell.

Dancy, Jonathan. 2004. *Ethics without Principles* Oxford: Oxford University Press.

Dancy, Jonathan. 2013. "Moral Particularism." *The Stanford Encyclopedia of Philosophy.* https://plato.stanford.edu/archives/fall2013/entries/moral-particularism/

Hooker, Brad. 2000. "Moral Particularism: Wrong and Bad." In *Moral Particularism*, edited by Brad Hooker and Margaret Olivia Little, 1–22. Oxford: Oxford University Press.

Hooker, Brad. 2008. "Moral Particularism and the Real World." In *Challenging Moral Particularism*, edited by Mark Norris Lance, Matjaž Potrč, and Vojko Strahovnik, 12–30. New York: Routledge.

Hursthouse, Rosalind. 2006c. "Practical Wisdom: A Mundane Account." *Proceedings of the Aristotelian Society* 106(1): 285–309. doi:10.1111/j.1467-9264.2006.00149.x

Hursthouse, Rosalind. 2011. "What does the Aristotelian *Phronimos* Know?" In *Perfecting Virtue: New Essays on Kantian Ethics and Virtue Ethics*, edited by Lawrence Jost and Julian Wuerth, 38–57. Cambridge: Cambridge University Press.

Jordan, Andrew. 2013. "Reasons, Holism and Virtue Theory." *The Philosophical Quarterly* 63(251): 248–268. doi:10.1111/1467-9213.12015

Lance, Mark Norris, Matjaž Potrč, and Vojko Strahovnik, editors. 2008. *Challenging Moral Particularism*. New York: Routledge.

McKeever, Sean and Michael Ridge. 2006. *Principled Ethics: Generalism as a Regulative Ideal*. Oxford: Oxford University Press.

Nielsen, Karen Margrethe. 2015. "Aristotle on Principles in Ethics: Political Science as the Science of the Human Good." In *Bridging the Gap between Aristotle's Science and Ethics*, edited by Devin Henry and Karen Margrethe Nielsen, 29–48. Cambridge: Cambridge University Press.

Ridge, Michael, and Sean McKeever. 2016. "Moral Particularism and Moral Generalism." *The Stanford Encyclopedia of Philosophy.* https://plato.stanford.edu/archives/win2016/entries/moral-particularism-generalism/

Stangl, Rebecca. 2008. "A Dilemma for Particularist Virtue Ethics." *The Philosophical Quarterly* 58(233): 665–678. doi:10.1111/j.1467-9213.2007.537.x

Swanton, Christine. 2003. *Virtue Ethics: A Pluralistic View*. Oxford: Oxford University Press.

Swanton, Christine. 2011. "Virtue Ethics." In *The Continuum Companion to Ethics*, edited by Christian Miller, 190–214. London: Continuum International.

Swanton, Christine. 2015b. "A Particularist but Codifiable Virtue Ethics." In Vol. 5 of *Oxford Studies in Normative Ethics*, edited by Mark Timmons. Oxford: Oxford University Press.

Tjiattas, Mary. 2007. "Against Moral Particularism." *The Proceedings of the Twenty-First World Congress of Philosophy* 1: 19–24. doi:10.5840/wcp2120071270

Väyrynen, Pekka. 2008. "Usable Moral Principles." In *Challenging Moral Particularism*, edited by Mark Norris Lance, Matjaž Potrč, and Vojko Strahovnik, 75–106. New York: Routledge.

9 The Situationist Critique

Elizabeth Anscombe's paper, "Modern Moral Philosophy" (1958), is often credited for giving rise to the revival of virtue ethics. One of her main objections to modern moral philosophy (i.e. deontology and consequentialism) is that claims about what is morally obligatory or permissible, and about what we have a moral duty to do, simply make no sense in the absence of a divine lawgiver.[1] Instead, she calls for a return to an earlier tradition in moral philosophy, one that is focused on the virtues, that is, on character traits that people actually possess (or can come to possess) and that allow them to flourish or live well as human beings. And indeed, many people are attracted to virtue ethics by this very feature: instead of trying to ground morality in some abstract principle, such as the Categorical Imperative or the Principle of Utility, virtue ethics asks us to think about the traits of character that we admire in other people, and to consider how these traits contribute to the good of society and/or to the happiness of their possessors.

One of the most serious attacks on virtue ethics comes from a group of philosophers – known as "philosophical situationists" – who argue that studies in social psychology show that many of the core assumptions that virtue ethicists make about character are fundamentally mistaken. The most prominent philosophical situationists are Gilbert Harman (1999; 2000), John Doris (1998; 2002) and Maria Merritt (2000; 2009). Their critique of virtue ethics comes in two successive waves. The first can be summarized as follows. Virtue ethics assumes that people have character traits, where these are understood as *reliable* dispositions to act in certain ways. However, experiments performed by a group of psychological situationists suggest that this is not the case. Whether or not someone helps another is influenced more by situational factors, such as the presence of an authority figure, the number of people in the room, or whether or not they are in a hurry, than by traits of individuals. In other words, human behavior is best explained in terms of features of the situation they find themselves in rather than with reference to character traits. This seriously undermines the plausibility of virtue ethics. If it turns out that virtue ethics is based on a non-existent property, then it would not have the advantage over rival normative theories that attracted Anscombe and others to it in the first place. It would simply have replaced one fictional concept – "moral duty" – with another – "moral virtue."

The second, more recent wave of critique is focused on practical rationality, and questions whether it is possible for human beings to learn to become virtuous: Aristotelian virtue ethicists argue that practical wisdom is required for virtue, and that the process of acquiring virtue is an intelligent process over which we have some control. We learn to become more virtuous through active deliberation, by consciously reflecting on our past actions, and by paying attention to our role models and teachers, in particular, to the reasons they give for acting in certain ways. However, this model of moral thought and decision-making is not consistent with the findings of empirical studies, which show that our behavior is influenced by non-conscious cognitive processes that we cannot control. What this means is that attempts at deliberate self-improvement are unlikely to succeed (Merritt et al. 2010). Whereas the first wave of critique calls into question whether character traits exist, the second wave aims to show why the virtues don't – and cannot – exist.

We will discuss both waves of the situationist critique as well as some responses to each. The chapter begins with a brief discussion of relevant developments in social psychology, followed by a summary of some of the situationist experiments.

9.1 Personality and Character in Social Psychology

A common assumption is that human beings have personality traits. We often describe people as, for example, shy, friendly, outgoing, energetic, and so on. Personality traits involve mental states (thoughts, feelings, desires, and attitudes) that influence behavior in all sorts of ways. Shy people often feel self-conscious and so will tend to avoid speaking in public or drawing attention to themselves. People who are friendly and outgoing enjoy the company of others and so will tend to seek out occasions for socializing. We often invoke personality traits to explain someone's behavior (e.g., "She didn't speak up because she is shy") and to predict how they will behave in a given situation (e.g., "He probably won't speak up because he is shy"). When a shy person comes out and makes a brilliant speech at his wedding, we are surprised and might wonder about the explanation for this – did he practice for hours and hours? Did he take a tablet to help calm his nerves?

This view of personality is supported by an influential group of personality psychologists, who claim that personality is a collection of "global" (or "robust") traits, that is, traits that are (a) consistently manifested in a wide variety of trait-relevant situations and (b) temporally stable (see, e.g., Ross and Nisbett 2011). For example, someone who has shyness as a global trait will manifest it in different situations (when being called upon to make a speech, when socializing with strangers, when being asked intimate questions about their past, and so on) and in repeated instances of the same kind of situation (e.g., whenever they are called upon to make a speech, and so on).

Personality theorists view character traits (virtues and vices) as a subset of personality traits. Someone who has honesty as a global trait will consistently behave honestly in a wide range of trait-relevant situations (e.g., when taking exams, testifying in court, returning lost property, and so on) and in repeated instances of similar situations. This view of character traits is consistent with an Aristotelian theory of virtue, which, as we have seen, defines a virtue as a *reliable* disposition to act, feel, and reason in certain ways. A truly honest person will manifest honesty whenever this is called for, and he will do so despite the presence of incentives or temptations to do otherwise. What allows the virtuous person to reliably do what is right is that he has practical wisdom. This involves correctly identifying relevant features of the situation and responding with appropriate actions and feelings. Most importantly, however, practical wisdom involves an understanding of what is good or worthwhile, and as such shapes a person's feelings and desires.

If the Aristotelian theory of virtue is accurate, we would expect the virtues to be more reliable or stable than other personality traits. Personality traits, unlike virtues, do not involve any kind of commitment or sense of what is worthwhile. We might find it a bit puzzling that someone is too shy to make a speech but is perfectly happy singing in front of a large audience, but it doesn't lead us to question whether they are *truly* shy. By contrast, a certain degree of reliability is required for virtue. Consider, for example, how we might react if we discovered that our child's school teacher, someone we had reason to believe was kind to children, was a regular spectator at dog fighting events on weekends. Would we still trust her with the care of our children? Or would we just conclude that she is kind to children and cruel to dogs, in much the same way that someone might be shy when making a speech but confident when singing to an audience? Aristotelians would argue that the school teacher does not have kindness as a virtue, for it turns out that she lacks the basic commitment that lies at the heart of kindness. A person who is truly kind will manifest kindness in different trait-relevant situations (e.g. when dealing with children at school, when taking care of animals, when talking to a grieving friend, and so on) and will do so in a fairly consistent manner. In short, then,

Aristotelians would agree with personality psychologists that character traits are robust in the sense that they are cross-situationally consistent and temporally stable (see Doris 2002, 18–20; Merritt 2000, 365–366).

During the 1960s and 1970s, a group of situationists in social psychology (sometimes referred to as "psychological situationists") launched a critique of theories that view personality as a set of robust traits. Walter Mischel, a leading figure in the situationist movement, reviewed a large quantity of the relevant empirical research and came to the conclusion that personality traits are not robust, and that the situations we find ourselves in have a far greater impact on our behavior than any traits we may be thought to possess:

> With the possible exception of intelligence, highly generalized behavioral consistencies have not been demonstrated, and the concept of personality traits as broad response predispositions is thus untenable.
>
> (Mischel 1968, 146)

Although many of the behavioral studies are focused on personality traits more generally, quite a few of them looked at specific virtues (mainly compassion and honesty), and the results of these studies are very similar. It appears that robust character traits, like robust personality traits more generally, simply do not exist. If we want to predict how someone will behave in a particular situation, we are better off looking at aspects of the situation rather than at features of the individual herself. In what follows, the four studies most often discussed in the philosophical literature on situationism are summarized.[2]

9.2 The Situationist Experiments

9.2.1 The Milgram Obedience Experiments

Beginning in the early 1960s, Stanley Milgram conducted a series of "obedience experiments" at Yale University. He was interested in discovering how seemingly decent and compassionate people could nevertheless become involved in the atrocities carried out in Nazi Germany. Milgram invited people to participate in what they were told was a study of punishment and learning. In reality, however, he wanted to study people's willingness to obey an authority figure who instructed them to perform acts that conflicted with their moral commitments. Upon arrival, they were assigned the role of "teacher." The "learner," who was actually a confederate (i.e., an actor working with the experimenter), was seated in a different room, strapped to what appeared to be electrical probes, and asked a series of questions. Whenever the learner gave a wrong answer the teacher was expected to administer what he was told were "painful but ... not dangerous" electrical shocks. He was also made to believe that the shocks increased in intensity, beginning at 15 volts (labelled "Slight Shock") to 300 volts (labelled "Extreme Intensity Shock") and ending with a massive 450-volt shock (labelled "XXX"). The learner responded with increasingly vehement protests. (This was all an act, for the shocks were not real.) Whenever a teacher was reluctant to continue, an experimenter in a lab coat firmly but politely responded with a series of scripted prompts, such as "The experiment requires that you continue" and "It is absolutely essential that you continue." The experiment ended when the teacher refused to continue after three scripted prompts (Milgram 1974).

Before running the experiment, Milgram surveyed a number of behavioral experts and laypeople, and asked them to predict how participants would react. They predicted that no more than 1 or 2 percent of the subjects would continue to shock the learner all the way to the end, and 100 percent of the respondents said that they themselves would defy the experimenter (see Milgram 1974, 27–31). The actual results were quite different. Twenty-six of the forty participants (65 percent) were "obedient," continuing to shock the learner all the way up to the end of the scale. The remaining fourteen were "disobedient," but they only defied the experimenter somewhere between 300 volts and the maximum 450 volts. Milgram summarizes "the most fundamental lesson" of the study as follows.

> [O]rdinary people, simply doing their jobs, and without particular hostility on their part, can become agents in a terrible destructive process. Moreover, even when the destructive effects of their work become patently clear, and they are asked to carry out actions incompatible with fundamental standards of morality, relatively few people have the resources needed to resist authority.
>
> (1974, 6)

9.2.2 The Good Samaritan Study

John Darley and Daniel Batson (1973) invited students at the Princeton Theological Seminary to participate in a study of religious education. Participants filled out a questionnaire to determine whether they related to religion as a means to salvation, an end in itself, or a quest for meaning, and were then asked to prepare a talk either on job prospects for seminarians or on the parable of the Good Samaritan. When they left the building, they were told either that they were running late, were a little early, or were right on time. On their way to give their talk they encountered a distressed person (actually a confederate) slumped over in a doorway, coughing and groaning. The question for Darley and Batson was: Would they act like the Good Samaritan and help the distressed person, or would they continue on their way? The experimenters were interested in discovering the effect of three factors on the subjects' helping behavior: their views on religion, the subject of their talk, and their degree of hurry. Surprisingly, it was found that the first two factors, which related to the participants' beliefs and values, made very little difference. There was some correlation between the subject of their talk and helping behavior, but not as much as they expected: 53 percent of those who read the parable of the Good Samaritan helped, while 29 percent of those who talked about job prospects did the same. And although Darley and Batson expected participants who saw religion as an end in itself to be more likely to help, they found no correlation between the participants' views on religion and their helping behavior. The main factor that affected helping behavior was the degree of hurry. Only 10 percent of subjects who were in a hurry stopped to help, compared to 63 percent of those who were a little early and 45 percent of those who were right on time.

The experimenters concluded that personality variables (such as thoughts, feelings, attitudes, and beliefs) are not useful in predicting whether a person will help or not. Neither does consciously thinking about moral values, in this case helping norms, have a significant effect on people's behavior. Instead, the decision whether to help is made instantly, and it is "likely to be situationally controlled" (Darley and Batson 1973, 107–108).

9.2.3 Isen and Levin's Mood Studies

Alice Isen and Paula Levin (1972) conducted an experiment designed to study the effect of mood on helping behavior. Subjects made a call from a public pay phone, and then encountered a confederate who had dropped a folder full of papers in their path. The experimenters varied the mood of one group of callers by arranging for them to find a dime in the coin return slot; for the other group, the slot was empty. They were interested in whether the subjects with an elevated mood would be more likely to help than the group who did not find a coin.

One would expect that some people (those who are kind, compassionate, and generous) would make an effort to help regardless of mood, whereas others (those who are focused on achieving their own goals) would not help, again, irrespective of whether they found a dime in the coin slot. But once again, the results were surprising. Of the 16 subjects who found a coin, 14 (87.5 percent) stopped to help. By contrast, only 1 of the 25 (4 percent) who did not find a coin helped the confederate. A seemingly small and insignificant situational factor – whether or not one's mood was slightly elevated by an instance of good fortune – made all the difference. In another version of the experiment, Isen and Levin varied some subjects' mood by giving them cookies. Again, they found that subjects with elevated mood were much more likely to help. As Doris (2002, 30) points out, what is surprising about these findings is not that mood influences behavior – we have known this all along. Rather, the interesting observation is just how insignificant the stimuli that affect mood – and with it, behavior – can be. It seems that trivial and morally irrelevant situational factors, factors that we might not even be aware of, have more of an effect on our behavior than aspects of our character or personality.[3]

9.2.4 Hartshorne and May's Honesty Studies

Hugh Hartshorne and Mark May (1928) performed a study to examine whether the disposition to behave honestly (or dishonestly) is cross-situationally consistent. They observed how thousands of school children behaved in various specific "honesty-relevant" situations. These included a stealing situation (the child finds money that has been left on a table in an empty classroom and has an opportunity to take it without being seen), a cheating situation (the child has to mark their own test sheet and has an opportunity to amend their answers), and a lying situation (another child is going to get in trouble and the child can prevent this by making a false statement).

Hartshorne and May found that there was a very low correlation between any two of the behavioral measures. Children who cheated on the test were not more likely to steal the money or to lie than children who did not cheat on the test. Very few of the subjects turned out to be cross-situationally honest. The experiment was repeated a few times with the same group of children, and this showed that there was a good deal of temporal stability within a given honesty-relevant situation. Children who cheated in a spelling test on one occasion were much more likely to cheat in future spelling tests. Hartshorne and May summarize their results as follows:

> [N]either deceit not its opposite, "honesty," are unified character traits, but rather specific functions of life situations. Most children will deceive in certain situations and not in others. Lying, cheating, and stealing as measured by the test situations used in these studies are only very loosely related. Even cheating in the classroom is rather highly specific, for a child may cheat on an arithmetic test and not on a spelling test.

(1928, 411)

A review of the relevant literature suggests that these results are consistent with the findings of other (including more recent) studies of cross-situational consistency (see Ross and Nisbett 2011).

9.3 The Situationist Critique I: The Existence of Character Traits

Psychological situationists think the only conclusion we can draw from these and countless other studies in social psychology is that our ordinary intuitions about character (and personality more generally) are mistaken. Although we quite commonly make statements such as, "Jim will tell the truth because he is honest," and "Jane helped out because she is kind," our assumptions about character are deeply misguided. Human behavior does not flow from character. Instead, it is influenced by features of the situation of which we may not even be aware. Doris states the central situationist claim as follows:

> Behavioural variation across a population owes more to situational differences than dispositional differences among persons. Individual dispositional differences are not as strongly behaviourally individuating as we might have supposed.
>
> (Doris 1998, 507)

Situationism is an "error theory" (Merritt 2000, 373), that is, it claims that although we believe in the existence of certain entities, in this case robust character traits, these entities do not actually exist. This naturally raises the questions: How did we come to be so mistaken? and: Why do we believe in the existence of character traits despite the lack of evidence? Situationists answer this question by pointing towards various kinds of biases and errors that we are prone to. The most prominent among these is the "fundamental attribution error," which is the tendency to attribute other people's behavior to internal or dispositional factors rather than to external or situational factors, while explaining our own behavior in terms of situational causes rather than internal characteristics (especially if our behavior has negative results) (see Harman 1999, 315–328). So, for example, if Mary fails to do her homework I might think it is because she is lazy or disorganized, whereas if I fail to do my homework I am more likely to explain it in terms of situational factors – perhaps, as the case may be, the neighbors had a noisy party or my grandmother visited unexpectedly. Psychologists have all sorts of explanations for why we are prone to this error. One such explanation is that when we observe other people, our focus is on them rather than their situation. This makes us more likely to attribute their behavior to their character or personality, while remaining unaware of the situational forces at play. For example, we see a colleague repeatedly arriving late for meetings, and think it must be because she is disorganized, disrespectful, inconsiderate, or the like. By contrast, when we observe ourselves we are much more aware of the situational forces acting upon us, and so will be more likely to (correctly) explain our behavior with reference to these forces. Another explanation for our tendency to ascribe people's behavior to character traits is known as the "just-world phenomenon": We want to believe that the world is just, that people get what they deserve. When we see someone suffer we like to think it is the result of some character flaw or poor decision-making on their part. The thought that their suffering is due to situational factors beyond their control makes us uneasy, for it reminds us that we are vulnerable in similar ways.[4]

The important question for our purposes is: What are the implications of situationism for virtue ethics? As Gopal Sreenivasan (2013, 290) notes, psychological situationists don't make any philosophical claims. The "situationist critique" refers instead to the argument made by philosophical situationists, in particular Harman (1999; 2000), Doris (1998; 2002) and Merritt (2000), namely that experiments in social psychology call into question the plausibility of virtue ethics as a normative theory. Their basic argument can be summarized as follows. Aristotelian virtue ethics tells us to become virtuous and act virtuously. Virtues are understood as robust dispositional traits, that is, traits that dispose us to act in similar ways in a variety of situations and in repeated instances of those situations. But empirical research shows that most people do not possess robust character traits, and that behavior is best explained by situational influences. So if most people don't have the virtues, then it is very unlikely that we can ever become virtuous or act virtuously. It follows that Aristotelian virtue ethics is deeply flawed.[5]

Although philosophical situationists agree that the results of empirical studies spell trouble for virtue ethics, they have different views about the implications of the situationist critique.

9.3.1 Gilbert Harman: Trait Eliminativism

Harman (2000) claims that there is no empirical reason to believe that character traits exist or have anything to do with producing behavior. Indeed, he thinks it is questionable whether people differ in character traits. While there are certainly differences in the way people behave, these differences are the result of differences in the situations they find themselves in. What the Milgram experiments show is that almost anyone would inflict suffering on an innocent person when placed in a certain kind of situation. This suggests that the best explanation for why most of us do not go about inflicting suffering on others in the course of our daily lives is not that we are compassionate people. It has more to do with the situations we find ourselves in.

Harman thinks our habit of attributing behavior to character traits has several harmful or undesirable consequences, all of which can be avoided by simply doing away with talk of character traits altogether. Explaining people's behavior in terms of vice can have an adverse effect on inter-personal relationships. To illustrate this point, Harman uses the example of the man whose friend fails to greet him. The man attributes this to poor character, when in fact, his friend has poor eyesight and just didn't see him. Harman thinks that by avoiding vice attributions and gaining greater appreciation of the role of situational factors, we will become more toler-ant and understanding of each other, and thereby avoid the interpersonal conflict that often results from our readiness to attribute bad behavior to bad character traits (1999, 328).

Another undesirable effect of virtue and vice attributions concerns the problem of moral luck. Harman considers Thomas Nagel's (1991, 28–29) example of two truck drivers, both of whom failed to have the brakes of their trucks checked. In one case, a child runs out in front of the first truck driver, who fails to stop in time, resulting in the child's death. In the other case, no such child is encountered and the second truck driver arrives at his destina-tion without incident. Nagel notes that we tend to think of the first truck driver as negligent or irresponsible, whereas the second is not blamed to the same extent. And yet both, having failed to check their brakes, are equally blameworthy. Our judgments are not only inconsistent but unfair to the unfortunate truck driver. Harman thinks the inconsistency in our judgments is the result of the fundamental attribution error: "This bad thing has happened and we attribute it to the bad character of the agent in the fore-ground" (1999, 328). As we have seen, one of the reasons we are prone to the fundamental attribution error is that we want to believe the world is just. But in the case of the truck drivers, it leads us to behave in a way that is unjust: we blame one truck driver and not the other, even though they deserve the same treatment. Again, Harman thinks we can avoid many of these problems by giving up talk of character traits and instead paying closer attention to the kinds of situation that encourage good or desirable behavior.

9.3.2 John Doris: Local Traits

Doris (1998; 2002) defends a slightly more modest position. He agrees with Harman that studies in social psychology do not support ascriptions of character traits that are robust or global. But he thinks there is empirical support for the existence of what he calls "local" or situation-specific traits. Consider, for example, the claim that Nelson Mandela was a generous person. To support this claim one might list the various ways in which he behaved generously: while in prison he planted a vegetable garden and shared the produce with fellow inmates, he forgave those who wronged him, he saw the good in people, and he gave freely of his time and resources to help the poor. Mandela appears to have had generosity as a stable or reliable trait. He was committed to the good of others, and he was wise – he knew what the good of others consisted in, and he knew how to bring it about. However, in his biography of Mandela, Richard Stengel makes a rather puzzling claim, namely that Mandela was not generous to waiters. Stengel recounts an incident where he dined with Mandela. The waiter provided excellent service, the bill came to well over a thousand rand, and yet Mandela left "a few tiny pieces of change" as a tip to the waiter. Stengel claims to have witnessed Mandela behaving in such a manner on multiple occasions (Stengel 2010, 7).

Assuming that Stengel's account is accurate, how are we to make sense of it? After all, Mandela cared about the good of others, and he was wise, so how could he possibly have been miserly to waiters? An Aristotelian will try to find an explanation for this uncharacteristic lapse in generosity – perhaps Mandela, having spent so much time in prison, was unaware of tipping conventions and remained unaware because no-one would dare criticize him. Doris, by contrast, would say that this kind of fragmentation or inconsistency is fairly typical. As we've seen, Hartshorne and May's honesty study (1928) suggests that although people don't have global honesty, they do have local traits such as "spelling test honesty." Similarly, Doris thinks that although courage as a global trait doesn't exist, some people have "battlefield physical courage," "storms physical courage," or "heights physical courage." He therefore urges us to develop a more fine-grained vocabulary, and to replace robust traits with local traits. Hence, instead of claiming that Mandela was generous, we should be more specific and say, as Stengel (2010, 7) does, that Mandela was generous with his children but stingy with waiters.

Doris's distinction between local and global traits helps to explain why our predictions of how someone will behave are often fairly accurate. For example, I rely on my husband to pick up our children from school every day. I don't have to send reminders or phone home to see whether they arrived there on any given day. So he has what Doris might call "pick up children from school reliability," and my knowing this about him allows me to predict his behavior. But the distinction also allows us to see why our predictions are sometimes wrong. The fact that I can rely on my husband to pick the children up from school might lead me to believe that I can also rely on him to mow the lawns and take out the trash. But this could well be a mistake, one that comes from confusing a local trait ("pick up children from school reliability") with a global trait (reliability *tout court*). Over time, I might learn that my husband has "pick up the children reliability" and "mow the lawns reliability," but, alas, not "take out the trash reliability."

Doris agrees with Harman that we should redirect our attention in light of the situationist findings. Instead of trying to acquire character traits that will "determine our behavior in ways substantially independent of circumstance," a project that is doomed to fail, he thinks we will do better by paying attention to features of the situation that influence our behavior (2002, 146). To illustrate the danger of relying on the robustness of our own virtue, Doris uses the example of the man who is invited for dinner by a colleague with whom he has had a long flirtation. His spouse is out of town and so he knows he will be tempted to be unfaithful. But he is not worried, because he is committed to his spouse and he sees himself as a trustworthy person, and so, foolishly, he accepts the invitation. According to Doris, the man is making a mistake in thinking that he could trust himself to be faithful in any situation. If he understood that situational pressures can affect our behavior, he would have declined the invitation, thereby avoiding a risky situation (Doris 2002, 147). Note that Doris does not deny that people have values or commitments or that there are important differences between people in what they value. What he denies is that these values or commitments have a significant effect on how people behave in particular situations. A more reliable way to achieve the things we value (such as a happy marriage or a successful career) is to manipulate situational features rather than trying to develop certain character traits.

9.4 Responses and Reactions

9.4.1 The Rarity Response

The most common response to the situationist critique is that the experiments merely confirm what Aristotelian virtue ethicists have been saying all along, namely that virtue is rare and difficult to achieve. Although it is certainly regrettable that so few people can be described as genuinely virtuous, this does not present a challenge to virtue ethics, given that virtue ethics is a normative theory, a theory about how we ought to live. As such, it is not committed to the descriptive claim that many people actually possess the virtues. The claim that we ought to strive to become more virtuous is entirely consistent with admitting that true virtue is rare. Christian Miller (2014a; 2014b) calls this the "rarity response."[6]

Aristotle makes a distinction between four kinds of people: the virtuous, the continent, the incontinent, and the vicious.[7] With regard to their attitudes and behavior towards the suffering of others, we should expect people to fall into one of the following categories:

a   those who have compassion as a global virtue and will act compassionately whenever it is appropriate to do so;
b   those who don't really care about the suffering of others, but who usually manage to act compassionately because they know it is right;
c   those who don't really care about the suffering of others, and who often fail to act compassionately, even though they know it is right;
d   those who have indifference as a global vice, and who will always fail to act compassionately because they simply don't care about the suffering of others.

Aristotle clearly thinks of virtue as a robust trait – he describes it as a "firm and unchangeable" state (*The Nicomachean Ethics* 1105b1). But he also says that most people do not possess full virtue: "it is no easy task to be good ... goodness is both rare and laudable and noble" (*The Nicomachean Ethics* 1109a24–29). The situationist experiments confirm this: very few people possess compassion as a virtue. They also confirm Aristotle's claim that most people are either continent (they usually succeed in acting well) or incontinent (they usually fail to act well). Whether or not they manage to act well on any given occasion will very much depend on features of the situation: the amount of pressure they are under, and the rewards and temptations in play. In other words, their behavior will lack both temporal stability and cross-situational consistency. Aristotle writes, for example, that:

> [The many] do not by nature obey the sense of shame, but only fear, and do not abstain from bad acts because of their baseness but through fear of punishment; living by passion they pursue their own pleasures and the means to them, and avoid the opposite pains and have not even a conception of what is noble and truly pleasant, since they have never tasted it.
> (*The Nicomachean Ethics* 1179b11–16)

Aristotle here suggests that most people – the non-virtuous – don't have knowledge of what is truly good and so are not committed to it. Instead, they pursue pleasure and avoid wrongdoing only because they fear punishment. Arguably, then, Aristotle would agree that much of the stability in people's behavior is achieved through the imposition of rewards and penalties, that is, by manipulating situational features.

Further, Aristotle thinks that the process of acquiring virtue is a gradual one that takes time and experience. The implication of this is that someone might behave courageously in certain situations (say, when sitting an exam), but not in other situations (when their physical safety is under threat), simply because they have not had much opportunity to learn how to behave courageously in these situations. Someone can possess a virtue without possessing it fully or perfectly, and this seems to be confirmed by Hartshorne and May's honesty studies: some children have learnt to be honest when taking a test, but have not yet grasped that taking money that doesn't belong to you is dishonest. In short, then, the situationist experiments demonstrate what virtue ethicists have known to be true all along, which is that very few people are genuinely virtuous. The virtue ethicist's central normative claim, namely that we should try to become more virtuous, remains unchallenged.

As it stands, however, the rarity response has a serious shortcoming. Situationists make two important points about human behavior:

a   Very few people possess the virtues as robust traits.
b   Situational features have a much larger effect on people's behavior than features of individuals.

The rarity response deals with the first claim, by rightly pointing out that it does not undermine the normative claim that people should try to become more virtuous. But it ignores the second, more damaging claim. What is at issue is not merely whether people possess the virtues but whether they possess robust character traits at all. That is, empirical research appears to show that people's behavior is influenced more by situational features than by any of the values, commitments, or ideals they might have. Whether or not we act compassionately has little to do with whether we actually care about the suffering of others and more to do with whether there is an authority figure telling us what to do. If this is true, then it is questionable whether we are the kind of beings that can come to possess virtue at all. Jesse Prinz makes the point as follows.

> It would be perfectly reasonable to say that virtue is rare if most people were driven by character traits that were not virtuous. But situationist psychology purports to show that people are not ordinarily driven by character traits at all.... . If situationists are right about human psychology, the acquisition of virtuous traits is not merely the acquisition of nobler versions of the minds we currently possess, but rather the acquisition of

minds of an entirely different kind... . There is absolutely no reason to think that moral education could give us new mental machinery.

(2009, 125)

9.4.2 The Behaviorist Response

While the claim that virtue is rare forms an important part of many responses to the situationist critique, it is often accompanied by two further arguments, which aim to show that people do have character traits. The first is known as the behaviorist response. In this view, the situationist critique is based on a crude behaviorist model of character, that is, it views character as a set of dispositions to act in certain ways while ignoring internal dispositional factors.[8] Experimenters tend to divide participants into two groups: Group 1 includes everyone who helped (or administered shocks, lied, stole, etc.), and Group 2 includes everyone who did not help (or administer shocks, etc.) in a given situation. But by lumping together all the participants who administered shocks (in the Milgram experiments) or failed to help (in the Good Samaritan and mood experiments) situationists ignore important differences in their inner states. As Swanton notes:

> [C]haracter is determined by such factors as dispositions of emotion and feeling, what the agent is disposed to recognize as reasons for action, the agent's ends, the agent's wisdom, and the agent's strength of purpose and other strengths, all of which are "internal" dispositional factors not reducible to patterns of behavior.
>
> (2011, 200)

The implication of this is that we cannot evaluate a person's character purely on the basis of their behavior. We also have to consider their inner states – their beliefs, attitudes, emotions, and reasoning. Situationists make the mistake of only paying attention to people's behavior and drawing conclusions about their character (or lack thereof) from these observations. The experimenters in the Good Samaritan study did not record participants' internal reactions to the distressed confederate at all. Had they done so, they might have found that some of them either: did not notice him, noticed him but didn't think he needed help, noticed that he needed help but were indifferent, noticed that he needed help but thought it was more important to be on time for their talk, noticed that he needed help but thought it was more important to be on time but then felt terribly guilty afterwards, and so on. These kinds of differences in the participants' internal reactions would reveal important differences in their characters. To be sure, none of these reactions are consistent with compassion as a virtue, but some come much closer to it than others.

There is reason to believe that something like this is true in the case of the Milgram experiments. Situationists take the fact that most participants repeatedly pressed the button to administer shocks as evidence in support of their claim that these participants did not possess compassion as a virtue. However, when we consider their inner states, a very different picture emerges. Although we don't exactly know what the participants were thinking or feeling, Milgram notes that some of them appeared to remain calm throughout the experiment, whereas others "heaved sighs of relief, mopped their brows, rubbed their eyes, or nervously fumbled cigarettes" (Milgram 1963, 376). The fact that there appeared to be considerable variation in the inner states of these participants reveals significant differences in character. Participants who remained calm throughout certainly appeared to be indifferent to the suffering of others (unless they realized that the learner was just acting). But participants who showed signs of "intense strain and anguish" exhibited at least a degree of compassion. Swanton (2011, 200) admits that the tendency to *act* benevolently is not as robust as one would hope. But she thinks it is a mistake to conclude that none of the obedient participants possessed compassion.

9.4.3 Moral Dilemmas and Temptation

The second, closely related response to the claim that the situationist experiments show that character traits do not exist, is to point out that in many of these experiments, the participants were caught in a moral dilemma. They had to make a choice between responding to the demands of different virtues. In the honesty studies, for example, children were given a choice between telling the truth and being loyal to a friend (who would get in trouble if they told the truth). And in the Milgram studies, participants faced a choice between obedience to the experimenter and the demands of compassion.

The fact that participants were caught in a moral dilemma allows for a different explanation of their behavior. In the Milgram experiments, the best explanation for why so many of the participants continued to shock the learner is not that they lacked compassion. As noted earlier, the fact that many of them were distressed shows that they were not indifferent to the learner's suffering. Given this, a more plausible reason why they nevertheless continued to administer shocks is that they had respect for authority and a desire to honor their commitments. Of course, they should have given more weight to the demands of compassion than to the demands of obedience, but the important point to note here is that their behavior can be explained with reference to their character traits, that is, their beliefs, values, and attitudes. We don't have to conclude that situational factors played a predominant role in determining how they behaved.[9]

In some of the experiments, the participants, though not exactly facing a moral dilemma, were tempted by other goods. Participants in the honesty studies were tempted to act dishonestly by money lying around unattended and getting better marks for a test. A plausible explanation for why some participants consistently took the money is that they cared more about money than about honesty. And we can explain why some of them consistently cheated in spelling tests but not in math tests by noting that they cared more about doing well in spelling than in math, and so they would have been tempted to cheat in the former but not in the latter. Virtue ethicists have always claimed that whether or not non-virtuous people behave continently or incontinently depends on the kind of temptations they face. For some of us, resisting the desire to take money when we can get away with it will be more difficult than, say, resisting the temptation to cheat in a spelling test. So while it is true that the participants did not display honesty as a global virtue, the results do not rule out an explanation of their behavior that makes reference to their character traits (or, to be more precise, their character flaws).

In response, situationists argue that similar explanations are not available in many of the other experiments. Mark Alfano (2013, 36–37) points out that the participants in Isen and Levin's mood studies were not tempted or pressured at all: the only factor that influenced their behavior was whether or not they found a dime or were given a cookie. He argues that although it is possible for virtue ethics to find a place for temptations and competing demands in its moral psychology, situational factors like mood elevators and depressors pose a more difficult challenge. These factors do not present people with bad reasons, rather, they don't present them with reasons at all. And yet, these "non-reasons" can have a significant influence on people's behavior, even while they remain entirely unaware of them. Alfano therefore takes what he calls situational non-reasons to be the heart of the situationist challenge: "The idea is not that people easily succumb to temptation, but that *non-temptations* play a surprisingly large role in moral conduct" (Alfano 2013, 44).

9.4.4 Minimizing the Effect of Mood

John Sabini and Maury Silver (2005) offer a reply to the situationist critique that focuses specifically on the effect of mood on behavior. They accept that the dime study (and others like it) show that minor manipulations can affect people's moods and behavior. But they don't think these have as serious an effect on behavior as situationists claim. Whether or not someone will help pick up some dropped papers might well depend on mood, but they point out that picking up dropped papers is such an unimportant matter that we really can't base conclusions about character on it. Further, they note that good moods tend to broaden attention, whereas bad moods narrow it. So being in a bad mood might well mean that one fails to notice "the petty trials and tribulations of those around us" (2005, 540). Such a failing is excusable, given that helping someone pick up papers is so insignificant, and shouldn't affect our evaluation of someone's character. But from our everyday experience, we can be fairly confident that small changes in mood do not affect people's behavior where more serious matters are concerned, such as whether they pick their children up from school, tell the truth in a job interview, or risk their lives to save someone from a burning building.

Psychological situationists are not convinced by this response. Prinz (2009) argues that mood has a significant effect on people's behavior. Isen and Levin's studies show that small changes in mood do affect moral behavior, and if we consider the many ways in which emotions are swayed, for example by weather, diet, sound, smells, and sleep, it becomes difficult to deny that situational influences have a major effect on people's behavior. Various other studies show that mood can have a powerful effect on our behavior and judgment.[10]

Given the wealth of evidence, psychological situationists conclude that our behavior is influenced by countless situational features, and that this makes it difficult, if not impossible, for us to acquire the virtues. In light of this, philosophical situationists like Doris and Harman argue that we should reject virtue ethics and do away with talk of (global) character traits altogether. But there are two other reactions to the empirical research that deserve some attention. The first is Alfano's view, namely that we should reject virtue ethics but continue to use virtue language. The second is a view supported by Christian Miller and Lorraine Besser-Jones, which is to hold on to virtue ethics but to look for better ways of acquiring virtue.

9.4.5 Factitious Virtue

Alfano accepts that the situationist experiments show that most people do not have global character traits, and that this spells trouble for virtue ethics. As he puts is, "Since virtue ethics presupposes the explanatory and predictive power of the virtues, it rests on a foundation of sand" (2013, 82). Further, he agrees that in order to improve people's behavior, we should manipulate situational factors rather than encouraging them to acquire the virtues (as robust traits). But he thinks that one way to manipulate situational factors is through what he calls "virtue labelling." When someone is told that they are honest, they are more likely to act in ways that are consistent with honesty. This is because it encourages them to think of themselves as honest and to believe that others expect them to behave honestly, and people want to live up to their own self-conceptions and the expectations of others. In this way, he claims, "[t]rait attributions of the right sort function as self-fulfilling prophecies" (Alfano 2013, 83).

Alfano cites various studies in social psychology that support this thesis. He is careful to point out that only the right sort of virtue attributions will have the desired effect. They have to be stated *publicly*, so that the person will come to believe that others expect him to behave virtuously. They also have to be *plausible* for the person to take it seriously. For example, a study by Kraut (1973) found that people who were labelled generous after donating to a charity were more likely to donate to another charity two weeks later than people who were not labelled generous. Alfano also notes that telling people that they are vicious makes it more likely that they will act accordingly, and so we had better avoid vice labelling. This doesn't mean that people who are labelled virtuous actually come to possess the virtue in question (although Alfano leaves open the possibility that this might happen). Rather, virtue labelling results in "factitious virtue," a kind of artificial or simulated virtue. Unlike Aristotelian virtue, factitious virtue is temporally unstable, for it requires constant social reinforcement. And whereas Aristotelian virtue involves being motivated by the right reasons, the factitiously virtuous agent is motivated by the desire to maintain their self-image and to satisfy others' expectations.

This suggests a possible reason why we do (and should continue to) attribute virtue in spite of the lack of evidence for its existence: it is one way in which we can encourage people to behave in socially desirable ways. In this sense, the virtues are useful fictions.

9.4.6 Working Harder to Acquire Virtue

Miller (2013; 2014b) and Besser-Jones (2008; 2014) accept that most people do not possess traditional virtues or vices. However, they don't think this is sufficient reason for rejecting virtue ethics altogether. Whether or not virtue ethics is a plausible normative theory will depend on whether it is possible for us to acquire the virtues. Research in psychology shows that some of the strategies we rely on are ineffective or inadequate. In addition to learning how to resist temptation, we also have to learn how to regulate the influence of various subtle and often subconscious factors, such as mood enhancers and inhibitors (see Miller 2014b, 22). Miller and Besser-Jones think there are a few strategies that appear promising.

The first involves the use of models of virtuous character and action (Miller 2014b, 24). Virtue ethicists often emphasize the importance of role models in moral education. We use stories of real and fictional role models to teach children how to be virtuous, and encourage them to consider what a kind or brave person would do in their situation. Miller (2014b, 24–25) points out that empirical research supports the idea that role modelling is an effective strategy for improving behavior and character. For example, a study by Holloway et al. (1977) found that subjects who were exposed to a news report about a benevolent person were more cooperative than other subjects. Spivey and Prentice-Dunn (1990) similarly found that subjects who saw a role model donate money were themselves more likely to do so at a later time.

Another strategy suggested by Miller (2014b, 25–27) is to increase awareness of the psychological processes that affect moral behavior. The idea is that once we become aware of their presence, we will have a chance to counterbalance or correct them. For example, had they been made aware that morally irrelevant factors, such as being in a hurry, can influence behavior, the participants in the Good Samaritan study might have been more likely to offer help. Miller thinks a similar point can be made with regards to our judgments of others. If people were made aware of the biases and errors that affect their judgments of others, they might become more careful when making such judgments (and hopefully get it right more often).

Besser-Jones (2014) recommends a strategy that draws on a branch of empirical psychology known as "self-regulation theory," which is concerned with questions about how people can best achieve their goals. Studies done by self-regulation theorists show that we can become more efficient in our pursuit of general goals by forming more concrete plans or "implementation intentions." For example, someone who wants to lose weight is more likely to be successful if they form a very specific plan about what, how much, and when to eat, rather than just having a general intention to eat less. Similarly, we are more likely to acquire a particular virtue by forming specific and more concrete plans about how to do this. Instead of having a general intention to become more caring and benevolent, we should think of specific ways in which we can achieve this, for example, offering to help an elderly neighbor with her shopping, or taking more care to listen to people's complaints. The idea is not only that a specific or concrete plan is easier to achieve than a more general one, but that conscious reflection or reasoning allows one to regulate one's own behavior.

9.5 The Situationist Critique 2: Practical Rationality

To recap, the first wave of the situationist critique focuses on the question of whether virtues and vices, and character traits more generally, exist. Situationist philosophers argue that empirical research shows that behavior does not flow from character, and that we should improve our behavior by paying more attention to the situational factors that affect it. Against this, virtue ethicists argue that although very few of us possess virtues as robust traits, it is possible for us to learn to become more virtuous. The way to do this is through a deliberate process of moral education and development, which includes doing things like seeking guidance and inspiration from virtuous role models, and forming more concrete plans and goals.

These strategies for improving our character all rely on the claim that moral behavior is (or at least can be) the outcome of rational thinking. This is consistent with the Aristotelian view that rationality plays a crucial role in moral development. Moral decision-making is a result of reasoning, and a virtuous person is someone who reasons well (see Chapter 5). More recently, philosophical situationists (Merritt, Doris, and Harman) have joined forces and extended their critique to practical rationality. They argue that our behavior is not the outcome of deliberate and conscious reasoning. Rationality is fragmented, involving both conscious and non-conscious processes. These processes can come into conflict, and we are often unaware of the influence of non-conscious processes on our behavior. The implication of this is that we cannot have the kind of coherent character that virtue ethics sees as the ideal. Despite our belief that human beings, unlike animals, are capable of rational thought and decision-making, the evidence shows that we cannot attain practical wisdom (Merritt et al. 2010).

As we've seen, situationists claim that the Milgram experiments show that people's behavior is affected by situational factors. Some virtue ethicists accept this, but hold out hope that we can learn to resist these factors by making use of our capacity for rational deliberation. Situationists think this hope is in vain. A closer look at the Milgram experiments shows that practical reasoning does not play an important role in moral decision-making at all. Obedient subjects displayed a form of "moral dissociation," that is, they endorsed a social norm (in this case, that it is wrong to inflict suffering on an innocent person against his will) and yet their behavior violated this norm. Early on in the experiment, when asked to shock the learner, the subjects' reasoning might have been: "I ought to obey the experimenter because it is good to contribute to society by participating in scientific research." However, at the point where the learner shouts out in agony and demands to be let out, it should have been obvious to any rational being that they should stop, and that the learner had withdrawn his consent. The reasoning required is pretty straightforward: "I should stop because it is wrong to inflict suffering on an innocent victim against his will." And yet, most of the subjects failed in this regard. Merritt, Doris, and Harman accept the point made by virtue ethicists, namely, that the fact that many of the obedient subjects felt terrible about what they were doing shows that they didn't altogether lack compassion. But this only highlights the extent of their moral dissociation. The obedient subjects continued to violate a social norm that they themselves were committed to, and did so despite the fact that it was causing them immense agony. This amounts to a spectacular failure of practical reasoning (Merritt et al. 2010, 363ff).

The question, then, is how to explain moral dissociation – what prevents the smooth transition from a moral commitment to a choice of action in line with this commitment? Various explanations can be put forward, including things like temptation, distraction, being fooled or misled, and errors in judgment. But Merritt et al. (2010, 371) think the most likely explanation is that "many important cognitive and motivational processes proceed without intentional direction," that is, they are beyond the reach of practical rationality. In support of this view they draw on dual process theory in psychology, which holds that the mind's workings consist of both conscious and non-conscious processes. We devote attention to, and can therefore control, conscious processes. By contrast, non-conscious processes are automatic and operate below the level of consciousness. This means that they are often not available for introspection, even when we are encouraged to think about them. Consider, for example, the well-known phenomenon of the "bystander effect": the greater the number of bystanders at the scene of an emergency, the less likely each individual is to offer help. One study found that when asked whether the number of bystanders affected their own behavior, subjects persistently denied that it did, and continued to do so even when presented with evidence of the bystander effect (Latané and Darley 1970; Merritt et al. 2010, 373).

According to dual process theorists, conscious and non-conscious processes are often in conflict. In many instances behavior is influenced by non-conscious processes that, were they available for critical reflection, the agent would not endorse as acceptable reasons for action. This means that our best laid plans, including our plans to act virtuously, are often undermined by non-conscious processes. In an experiment involving racial stereotypes it was found that non-black subjects who were subliminally primed with a picture of a black male face showed more hostility in response to a computer failure than subjects who were primed with a white male face. This suggests that there was some racial prejudice at work. More alarmingly, the study also found that subjects were often unaware of their own prejudice. Subjects filled out a questionnaire designed to measure racial attitudes, and those who scored low on self-reported measures for racist attitudes were just as likely to express hostility after being primed than the ones who scored high (Bargh et al. 1996, 239; Merritt et al. 2010, 374–375).

These studies (and many others like them) pose a significant challenge for the Aristotelian model of practical rationality. Aristotelians accept that automatic processes play a role in moral decision-making. On many occasions we don't have time to deliberate, and so we rely on perceptions and judgments that have been shaped through habituation. But Aristotelians assume that these automatic cognitive processes are available for critical reflection, so that a person who finds that her automatic responses are in conflict with her consciously held moral commitments is first of all able to recognize this, and then to take steps to rectify this. Consider, for instance, Rosalind Hursthouse's discussion of the role of non-rational responses in moral behavior (1999, 114–119). She uses the example of the person who, as a result of bad moral training in childhood, holds racist attitudes. Hursthouse notes that racism expresses itself in emotion, which makes it incredibly hard, perhaps even impossible, to eliminate. The mere realization that one's emotional reactions are wicked is not sufficient for getting rid of them. Nevertheless, Hursthouse claims that "we know that some re-training is possible" and so "anyone decent must be anxiously seeking ways to control [racist emotions], refusing to give up hope" (1999, 116). By continuing to strive to undo the effects of a bad moral upbringing, we hope to become "better people, more charitable and just than we are at present" (1999, 117). She accepts, however, that someone who had racism inculcated in them as a child may remain morally inferior, despite their greatest efforts (Hursthouse 1999, 116).

Although Hursthouse's claims about the possibility of moral self-improvement are fairly modest, situationists seem to think they are too optimistic:

> [T]he cognitive processes apparently at work in classic experimental observations of moral dissociation do not bear much resemblance to philosophical models of reflective deliberation or practical reasoning, processes that are expected to be governed, to a considerable extent, by the actor's evaluative commitments. Instead, the determinative cognitive processes occur unreflectively and automatically, cued by morally arbitrary situational factors. In this sense, we suggest, many of the processes implicated in moral functioning – or dysfunctioning – are likely to be largely unaffected by individuals' personal, reflectively endorsed values.
>
> (Merritt et al. 2010, 387)

The implication of this is that we cannot alleviate moral dissociation – and thereby become more virtuous – through any strategy of deliberate self-improvement, such as the ones suggested by Miller and Besser-Jones. Our best hope, it seems, is to put ourselves in situations that are likely to automatically activate the desired aspects of moral cognition. Merritt (2000; 2009) suggests that the behavioral consistency that many people achieve is not a manifestation of the stability of their character, but rather the stability of their environment, in particular, the expectations that others have of them. People are more careful and critical in their thinking and less vulnerable to cognitive biases when they believe they will have to justify their decisions to others. At an organizational level, what this suggests is that we should not rely on people's strength of character or on the power of their practical rationality. Instead, we should have clear rules and guidelines and make sure that we hold people accountable.

9.6 An Empirically Grounded Virtue Theory

A few virtue theorists have responded to the situationist challenge by developing a philosophical theory of virtue that is informed by research in social psychology. Daniel Russell (2009), Nancy Snow (2010; 2014; 2015), and Denise Vigani (2016) are the most prominent among them. All three have taken on the task of defending a broadly Aristotelian conception of virtue that is grounded in empirical research. For the sake of brevity we will focus on Snow's work, in particular her book *Virtue as Social Intelligence* (2010). Snow argues that research in empirical psychology supports three central claims made by virtue ethicists:

a   there are global personality traits;
b   character traits, as traditionally conceived, are a subset of such traits; and
c   it is possible for us to acquire the virtues.

Snow begins by considering empirical research performed by two social-cognitivist psychologists, Walter Mischel and Yuichi Shoda (1995). Mischel and Shoda have developed a theory of personality as a cognitive-affective processing system (CAPS). The components of the CAPS system, called "cognitive-affective units," include variables such as beliefs, desires, feelings, expectations, goals, and values. These variables can be activated by external or situational features as well as by internal stimuli (e.g., thinking, reasoning, and imagining). So, for example, seeing or imagining a person in distress can make one feel sad, cause one to believe that one should help, and set in motion plans to offer help. Taken together, these thoughts, feelings, plans and desires constitute a compassionate response to the real or imagined distress of another. And the repeated activation of these variables can result in a CAPS trait, that is, a personality trait or disposition that is relatively stable. Michel and Shoda suspected that the reason why situationists could not find evidence of robust traits is that they described situations in purely objective terms, without considering the subject's interpretation of the situation. According to the CAPS model, situational features activate cognitive-affective units (or what virtue ethicists refer to as "inner states"), which in turn motivate action. We are therefore more likely to find evidence of behavioral consistency – and hence, of CAPS traits, if the situations are redefined in terms of the meanings they have for subjects.

The team of psychologists led by Mischel and Shoda conducted a few experiments to investigate whether CAPS traits exist. Snow (2010, 21–25) discusses a study in which eighty-four children were observed during a six-week summer camp. Researchers interviewed the children in order to identify the psychological situations that were important to these children, and selected the following interpersonal situations:

a   positive contact between peers;
b   negative contact between peers (e.g. teasing, provocation, and threatening);
c   praising by adults;
d   warning by adults; and
e   punishing by adults.

One of their hypotheses was that subjects would exhibit stable situation-behavior profiles. And indeed, their findings supported this hypothesis. For example, one child was consistently aggressive across different types of interpersonal situations, showing low verbal aggression when teased by a peer, higher verbal aggression when warned by an adult, and very high verbal aggression when punished by an adult. The researchers found that the profiles of a significant proportion of the children were very stable, such that they could accurately predict how they would behave in other situations (Shoda et al. 1994, 680–682).

Snow thinks these findings support the existence of CAPS traits. Character traits (virtues and vices) are a subset of CAPS traits. Like CAPS traits, virtuous dispositions are "relatively stable configurations of characteristic types of thoughts, motivations, and affective reactions, standing 'on call' and ready to be activated in response to the appropriate stimuli" (Snow 2010, 31). Snow then goes on to argue that psychological research on stereotyping shows that it is possible – though difficult – for us to cultivate the virtues and inhibit vices through a process of self-regulation. Social psychologists use the term "stereotype" to refer to a thought that can be adopted about specific types of individuals or certain ways of doing things, and stereotyping often becomes a habit that occurs outside an agent's conscious awareness. However, research on stereotype modification shows that it is possible for us to prevent, interrupt, or inhibit these processes, even when the situation favors a prejudiced response. Devine and Monteith (1999, 351ff) give the following example of how stereotype modification works: Paula (a white person), is looking for a grocery item in a shop. She is tired, hungry and frustrated. She then has a stereotypical response: she assumes that a black woman is an employee rather than a fellow shopper, and asks her where the sought-after item is shelved. Paula realizes her mistake and the discrepancy between her internalized standards and her response causes her to feel guilty and to reflect on her mistake. This makes it less likely that she will have a stereotypical response on future occasions. Devine and Monteith (1999) claim that relevant literature on stereotype modification shows it is possible to control stereotyping. They compare the process of stereotype inhibition to that of breaking a bad habit. People can break a habit if they decide to do so, remember the resolution, and repeatedly try to stop the behavior. Snow thinks that if it is possible to break bad habits and inhibit stereotypic responses through self-regulation, then the same will be true about character traits. We can acquire the virtues by habitually performing virtuous actions, where these are conceived as rational actions that are directed at achieving relevant goals. A mature agent who has a virtue-relevant goal, such as being a good parent, can become virtuous by repeatedly and deliberately acting in ways that advance this goal (Snow 2010, 39–62).

As we have seen, situationists claim that our consciously formed plans to act virtuously are often undermined by non-conscious, automatic processes. The implication of this is that we cannot become more virtuous through any strategy of deliberate self-improvement (Merritt et al. 2010). Snow (2015) responds to this in a more recent article. She accepts that non-conscious mental processes play an important role in human behavior, but argues that they do not seriously undermine our conscious and deliberate efforts to act virtuously. She draws attention to various studies in psychology which she thinks supports the view held by virtue ethicists like Julia Annas (2011) and Daniel Russell (2009), namely that virtue is like a practical skill: although both the acquisition and exercise of virtue relies on non-conscious processes, it is an intelligent disposition that is deliberately cultivated.

As we've seen in Chapter 5, Annas argues that acquiring virtue is like learning a practical skill, such as playing the piano or speaking Italian, in so far as the learner must be motivated to learn. He must pay attention to what his teacher does and says, and try to understand her reasons for doing things in a certain way. In this sense acquiring virtue is not comparable to developing a good habit, which often occurs as a result of copying a role model or following her instructions. Instead, acquiring virtue involves conscious thought and reasoning. Someone can learn kindness in one context, for example, by helping his mother give out food to hungry children in the neighborhood. But to acquire the virtue for himself, he has to figure out what being kind would mean for him, given his personality and circumstances. He cannot simply copy the things his mother does. So although virtue is cultivated through habituation, it is an intelligent process. At the same time, however, Annas thinks that the exercise of virtue does not always require conscious deliberation. A learner might well have to think about things like whether it is appropriate to help, how to help without hurting someone's pride, or what kind of help is required, in much the same way that someone who is still learning to speak Italian has to think about the grammatical structure of a sentence before he tries to order a meal during a visit to Italy. But a more experienced person, someone who has acquired a level of moral expertise, doesn't have to consciously deliberate about such matters. Her act of benevolence will be immediate but also intelligent. And this is shown, in part, by the fact that if asked for an explanation of why she acted in a given way, she is able to give one (see Annas 2011, chapter 3).

Snow argues that empirical studies of moral education support Annas's account of virtue acquisition, thereby allowing her to avoid the situationist critique of practical rationality. Snow's main point in this regard is that although non-conscious, automatic processes do play a role in moral decision-making, these processes are shaped by deliberate and intelligent thought, and are usually not in conflict with conscious processes. Instead, they play an important role in allowing an agent to achieve his goals. Snow (2015, 303) draws attention to research on goal-dependent automaticity, which shows that skilled behaviors, such as driving a car, "typically operate autonomously, with little need of conscious control or significant attentional resources" (Narvaez and Lapsley 2005, 145). Snow thinks the same can be said of virtuous action as a form of skilled behavior. A virtuous person (or moral expert) will often act without first having to think about the reasons for acting. Further, psychological research on expertise shows that an expert's knowledge is richer and better organized, such that they are able to correctly perceive or interpret a situation and respond appropriately. As a result, their decision-making often occurs quickly and automatically, whereas novices tend to be slower and more deliberate when making decisions (Narvaez and Lapsley 2005, 151; Snow 2015, 305–306).

Chapter Summary

- *Situationism* is the view that behavioral variation across a population owes more to situational differences than dispositional differences among persons.
- The *situationist critique* refers to the argument made by philosophical situationists, in particular Harman, Doris, and Merritt, namely that research in empirical psychology calls into question the plausibility of virtue ethics as a normative theory.
- The situationist critique comes in two waves. The first concerns the existence of character traits, and can be summarized as follows: Virtue ethics tells us to acquire the virtues. Virtues are understood as robust dispositional traits, that is, traits that lead us to act in similar ways in a variety of situations and in repeated instances of such situations. But empirical research shows that most people do not possess robust character traits, and that behavior is best explained by situational influences. So if most people don't have the virtues, then we cannot become the kind of beings that virtue ethics tells us to become. It follows that virtue ethics is deeply flawed.
- In response, some virtue ethicists argue that: (a) The situationist experiments merely confirm what Aristotelian virtue ethicists have been saying all along, namely, that virtue is rare and difficult to achieve. (b) The situationist critique is based in a crude behaviorist model of character. It views character as a set of dispositions to act in certain ways while ignoring internal dispositional factors. If we consider the inner states of participants, we will find important differences in character. (c) Many of them were either tempted or caught in a moral dilemma, which means that we can explain their behavior in terms of character traits. (d) Very few people possess the virtues, but this only means we should find better (empirically grounded) strategies for acquiring virtue.
- The second wave of the situationist critique focuses on practical rationality: human behavior is not the outcome of conscious and rational thought. Rationality is fragmented, involving both conscious and non-conscious processes, and these often come into conflict. The implication of this is that we cannot have the kind of coherent character that virtue ethics sees as the ideal.
- Snow responds to the situationist critique by developing a theory of virtue that is informed by research in social psychology. She argues that global character traits do exist, that the virtues are intelligent dispositions, and that it is possible for us to cultivate virtue.

Notes

1 See Chapters 1 and 6.
2 For more detailed and comprehensive discussion of these experiments, see Doris (2002, chapter 3) and Alfano (2013, chapter 2).
3 As Doris (2002, 30 n. 4) notes, researchers have had difficulty replicating the results of the Isen and Levin study, but situationists point out that various other studies show that mood or affect influences behavior.
4 For an excellent summary of various attribution errors and biases that explain our intuitions about traits, see Alfano (2013: 54–60).
5 It is worth noting that not all theories of virtue are vulnerable to the situationist critique. Julia Driver's consequentialist account of virtue avoids the objection because it does not make any claims about psychology at all. On Driver's view, a virtue is a trait that systematically produces good results, and she argues that virtue does not have a necessary connection with good psychological states (2001: xxi). While many people find this account implausible, it turns out that it might have a distinct advantage over rival accounts of virtue.
6 Proponents of the rarity response include see DePaul (2000); Athanassoulis (2000); Sreenivasan (2002); Miller (2003); Kamtekar (2004); Annas (2005); Kristjánsson (2008)
7 As we've seen in Chapter 4, the virtuous do what is right for the right reasons and with the right attitude and emotions. The continent (or strong-willed) usually do what is right for the right reasons, but they don't have the right attitude or emotions. The incontinent (or weak-willed) usually don't do what is right, even though they know what is right, because their desires and emotions lead them astray. The vicious don't know what is right, don't do what is right, and don't care about the right things.
8 See Swanton (2003, 30–33); Swanton (2011, 199–202); Kamtekar (2004); Kristjánsson (2008).
9 For discussion of this response, see Swanton (2003); Miller (2003); Kamtekar (2004); Sreenivasan (2002; 2013).
10 For example, suicide rates in Scandinavian countries have been shown to correlate with seasonal changes in temperature (Holopainen et al. 2013). A series of studies by Simone Schnall et al. (2008) found that feelings of disgust can shape our moral judgments, even when they are unrelated to the action being judged. Participants were asked to evaluate the wrongness of various actions, such as eating one's dead dog, finding a wallet and not returning it, and putting false information in one's CV, and their answers varied depending on whether they were seated at a clean desk. Participants seated at a dirty desk gave significantly higher wrongness ratings for the same actions than those seated at a clean desk.

Further Reading

Alfano, Mark. 2013. *Character as Moral Fiction*. Cambridge: Cambridge University Press.
Annas, Julia. 2005. "Comments on John Doris's *Lack of Character*." *Philosophy and Phenomenological Research* 71(3): 636–642. doi:10.1111/j.1933-1592.2005.tb00476.x
Besser-Jones, Lorraine. 2014. *Eudaimonic Ethics: The Philosophy and Psychology of Living Well*. New York: Routledge.
Darley, John M., and Daniel C. Batson. 1973. "'From Jerusalem to Jericho': A Study of Situational and Dispositional Variables in Helping Behavior." *Journal of Personality and Social Psychology* 27(1): 100–108. doi:10.1037/h0034449
Doris, John M. 1998. "Persons, Situations, and Virtue Ethics." *Noûs* 32(4): 504–530. doi:10.1111/0029-4624.00136
Doris, John M. 2002. *Lack of Character: Personality and Moral Behavior*. Cambridge: Cambridge University Press.

Harman, Gilbert. 1999. "Moral Philosophy Meets Social Psychology: Virtue Ethics and the Fundamental Attribution Error." *Proceedings of the Aristotelian Society* 99: 315–331.

Harman, Gilbert. 2000. "The Nonexistence of Character Traits." *Proceedings of the Aristotelian Society* 100(1): 223–226. doi:10.1111/j.0066-7372.2003.00013.x

Hartshorne, Hugh and Mark A. May. 1928. *Studies in the Nature of Character. Vol. 1: Studies in Deceit.* New York: Macmillan.

Isen, Alice M. and Paula F. Levin. 1972. "Effect of Feeling Good on Helping: Cookies and Kindness." *Journal of Personality and Social Psychology* 21(3): 384–388. doi:10.1037/h0032317

Kamtekar, Rachana. 2004. "Situationism and Virtue Ethics on the Content of Our Character." *Ethics* 114(3): 458–491. doi:10.1086/381696

Merritt, Maria. 2000. "Virtue Ethics and Situationist Personality Psychology." *Ethical Theory and Moral Practice* 3(4): 365–383. doi:10.1023/A:1009926720584

Merritt, Maria. 2009. "Aristotelian Virtue and the Interpersonal Aspect of Ethical Character." *Journal of Moral Philosophy* 6(1): 23–49. doi:10.1163/174552409X365919

Merritt, Maria W., John M. Doris, and Gilbert Harman. 2010. "Character." In *The Moral Psychology Handbook*, edited by John M. Doris and the Moral Psychology Research Group, 355–401. Oxford: Oxford University Press.

Milgram, Stanley. 1963. "Behavioral Study of Obedience." *Journal of Abnormal and Social Psychology* 67(4): 371–378. doi:10.1037/h0040525

Milgram, Stanley. 1974. *Obedience to Authority: An Experimental View.* New York: Harper & Row.

Miller, Christian. 2013. *Moral Character: An Empirical Theory.* New York: Oxford University Press.

Prinz, Jesse. 2009. "The Normative Challenge: Cultural Psychology Provides the Real Threat to Virtue Ethics." *The Journal of Ethics* 13(2–3): 117–144. doi:10.1007/s10892-009-9053-3

Russell, Daniel C. 2009. *Practical Intelligence and the Virtues.* Oxford: Oxford University Press.

Snow, Nancy E. 2010. *Virtue as Social Intelligence: An Empirically Grounded Theory.* New York: Routledge.

Snow, Nancy E., editor. 2014. *Cultivating Virtue: Perspectives from Philosophy, Theology, and Psychology.* Oxford: Oxford University Press.

Sreenivasan, G. 2013. "The Situationist Critique of Virtue Ethics." In *The Cambridge Companion to Virtue Ethics*, edited by Daniel C. Russell, 290–314. Cambridge: Cambridge University Press.

10 Virtue and Environmental Ethics

Our focus in this book has been on questions in normative ethics that are of particular interest to virtue theorists, including: What is virtue? Is there a link between virtue and happiness? Can virtue ethics provide a satisfactory account of right action? Does virtue ethics provide action guidance? and: Is it possible to be or become virtuous? In recent years there has been a growing interest in applying virtue ethics to some of the moral problems that arise in the spheres of medicine, business, sport, the military, and so on. Our focus in this chapter is on environmental virtue ethics as an example of applied virtue ethics.[1] However, it is important to note, from the outset, that environmental ethics differs from other areas in applied ethics. Moral philosophy has traditionally been concerned, almost exclusively, with human beings and their relationships with each other. Environmental ethics, by contrast, seeks to extend our sphere of moral concern to animals and the environment. This requires not merely applying a particular normative theory, but revising it in often quite significant ways. In the case of environmental virtue ethics, we have to begin by reconsidering some of the central questions in normative ethics.

The first of these is: What is virtue? (or, more specifically: What is environmental virtue?). Whereas applied virtue ethicists working in other spheres can simply select, from the list of traditional virtues, the ones that appear to be most important in the relevant context, the environmental virtue ethicist's task is much more complicated. Many of the traditional virtues – for example, honesty, generosity, kindness, and justice – don't seem relevant, at least not in their standard forms. The first task is therefore to identify traits that are *environmental* virtues. This leads to the further question, namely, What makes a trait an environmental virtue? Aristotelian virtue ethicists define virtue as a trait needed for human flourishing, but this view strikes many people as inappropriately anthropocentric when dealing with questions about animals and the environment. Shouldn't environmental virtue be defined in terms of the good of the environment? We will discuss these questions in Sections 10.2 and 10.3.

In Sections 10.4 and 10.5, we will consider a further challenge to environmental virtue ethics, which is to show that virtue ethics provides a better approach to environmental problems than alternative normative theories. This requires revisiting some of the questions explored in earlier chapters regarding the link between virtue and right action, and the role of moral duties and consequences. There are various reasons why environmentalists are attracted to the language of virtue. One such reason is that it focuses our attention on our habits, attitudes, and ways of life. Many of our destructive behaviors, such as driving unnecessarily large and powerful vehicles, consuming more resources than we need, and using disposable items, are a manifestation of character defects – arrogance, greed, laziness, and selfishness. Preventing wholesale environmental catastrophe requires, at least in part, that we change our habits, attitudes, and ways of life. Applied ethics often focuses on moral dilemmas, but very few of us will ever face a weighty environmental dilemma, such as whether to burn down a forest to develop a palm oil plantation, or allow destructive mining projects to boost economic growth. Instead, we face a host of smaller issues on a daily basis, such as whether to use another plastic bag, drive to work, or eat another steak. Acting well in this regard is not a matter of correctly solving moral dilemmas, but of acquiring good habits. Another reason why virtue language is often more suitable in this context is that it allows for degrees, unlike deontic language, which encourages us to think of actions as either right (permissible) or wrong (impermissible). We might never be perfectly virtuous, but we can certainly do better, for example by using fewer plastic bags, driving to work less often, and consuming less meat. Although many environmental ethicists acknowledge the importance of cultivating virtues, as we will see, they disagree about whether virtue ethics provides the best framework for thinking about our relationship with animals and the environment.

In the final section, we will briefly revisit the situationist critique, which takes a particularly serious form in the case of environmental virtue ethics: if our behavior is the result of situational factors rather than character traits, then it seems foolish to encourage people to acquire environmental virtues as a means of protecting the environment.

10.1 What Is Environmental Virtue Ethics?

Environmental ethics is concerned with questions about the moral value and status of the environment, where "environment" is used broadly to include natural, agricultural, and urban ecosystems, as well as the individuals (both human and nonhuman) that populate and constitute those ecosystems. It attempts to understand the human relationship with the environment, and determine the norms that should govern our relationship with it. Environmental ethicists share a commitment to what Rosalind Hursthouse (2007, 155) calls "the green belief," that is, the belief we have brought about, and are continuing to bring about, large-scale ecological disasters and that a fairly radical change in the way we engage with nature is needed. *Environmental virtue ethics* approaches ethical questions about the environment through the lens of virtue ethics, rather than consequentialism or deontology.

One of the figures who inspired the interest in environmental virtue is Thomas Hill. He asks us to consider the following case:

> A wealthy eccentric bought a house in a neighborhood I know. The house was surrounded by a beautiful display of grass, plants, and flowers, and it was shaded by a huge old avocado tree. But the grass required cutting, the flowers needed tending, and the man wanted more sun. So he cut the whole lot down and covered the yard with asphalt. After all it was his property and he was not fond of plants.
>
> (Hill 1983, 211)

Hill claims that the traditional focus on right and wrong action fails to account for our moral discomfort in cases involving the destruction of the environment. Thinking in terms of rights is not very useful, because trees are not generally believed to have rights, whereas the man has the right to cut down a tree on his property. And neither does a consideration of the consequences of the act really help to account for our moral discomfort. Instead, the important question in this case concerns the character of the agent:

> Let us turn for a while from the effort to find reasons why certain *acts* destructive of natural environments are morally wrong to the ancient task of articulating our ideals of human excellence. Rather than argue directly with destroyers of the environment who say, "Show me why what I am doing is *immoral*," I want to ask, "What sort of person would want to do what they propose?" … [E]ven if there is no convincing way to show that the destructive acts are wrong (independently of human and animal use and enjoyment), we may find that the willingness to indulge in them reflects the absence of human traits that we admire and regard morally important.
>
> (Hill 1983, 215)

Hill goes on to argue that a person who would do things like cover his garden with asphalt, strip-mine a wooded mountain, or level an irreplaceable redwood tree, would have to be insensitive, arrogant, and lacking in proper humility. A fitting response to the wonders of nature is to feel humble and to reflect on "the comparative insignificance of our daily concerns and even of our species" (Hill 1983, 219).

While Hill argues that *some* questions in environmental ethics are best handled by thinking in terms of virtue, he doesn't think virtue should play a central role in normative theory. Hill supports a Kantian view of what makes an action right, which is why he claims that although the man's destructive actions display bad character, they are not necessarily wrong or immoral (contrary to duty). By contrast, the Aristotelian virtue ethicist would argue that if it is the kind of action that only a vicious person would perform, then it is wrong (see Chapter 6). One issue that concerns philosophers working in this field, then, is the question about the proper role of virtue in environmental ethics. Should we think about environmental problems in terms of virtue ethics rather than deontology or utilitarianism? Or should a discussion of environmental virtues merely supplement discussions of environmental problems in terms of rights, duties, or utility?

Before considering these questions, it is useful to make a distinction between environmental virtue *ethics* and environmental virtue *theory*. The term "environmental virtue ethics" is often used very broadly to refer to the general project of exploring the nature and role of environmental virtue (see Sandler 2005, 1–2). The problem with this usage is that not all writers who are interested in environmental virtue are committed to virtue ethics as a normative theory. Many consequentialists and deontologists (including, as we've seen, Kantians like Hill) share an interest in environmental virtue, but they don't think it should play a central role in environmental ethics. For this reason, and in line with the widely used distinction between "virtue theory" and "virtue ethics,"[2] it is preferable to use the term "environmental virtue theory" to refer to the broader project of thinking about the nature and role of environmental virtue, while reserving "environmental virtue ethics" for the view that virtue ethics provides a better approach to environmental issues than other normative theories.

10.2 Which Traits Are Environmental Virtues?

An obvious strategy when making up a list of virtues is to think about the traits we admire in the people we know, and then to subject this list to critical scrutiny. This exercise is likely to produce a list that would include standard virtues such as honesty, kindness, courage, fairness, generosity, and moderation. However, this strategy is not very useful for identifying environmental virtues, for the simple reason that so few people possess such virtues. People we consider to be "nature lovers" often turn out, on reflection, not to be all that virtuous. Think, for example, of the many keen gardeners who cultivate beautiful gardens and lawns, but who are completely oblivious to the environmental impact of the choices they make.

Various strategies have been used to try to identify environmental virtues. One strategy is the *environmental exemplar approach*, which involves reflecting on the lives and writings of the handful of people who are recognized as environmental role models. Philip Cafaro (2005b: 31–44) uses this approach, and focuses on the lives of Henry David Thoreau, Aldo Leopold, and Rachel Carson. Cafaro argues that although these three role models express their virtue in very different ways, they share certain traits that are characteristic of environmental excellence. These traits include the rejection of a purely economic view of nature, a commitment to science as well as an appreciation of its limits, non-anthropocentrism (i.e., an extension of moral considerability beyond human beings), an appreciation of the wild and support for wilderness protection, and a belief in the goodness of life (Cafaro 2005b, 37–39).

A different strategy, which is sometimes used in conjunction with the first, is *extensionism*. This involves arguing by extension from traits that are already recognized as virtues in the interpersonal sphere. For example, compassion is widely recognized as a virtue when it comes to responding to the suffering of other human beings, and since there is no morally relevant difference between the suffering of human and nonhuman animals, it is argued that compassion is also the appropriate response to the suffering of nonhuman animals. Geoffrey Frasz uses this approach to defend benevolence as a central environmental virtue. Benevolence involves a genuine concern for the welfare of others, and includes more specific virtues such as "compassion, kindness, friendship and gratitude" (Frasz 2005, 121). Environmental benevolence, then, is the virtue that motivates people to rescue or protect particular animals, such as whales trapped in ice or maltreated zoo animals, but also to protect vulnerable species, ecosystems, and biogeographical zones. Frasz also argues, somewhat more controversially, that we should cultivate friendship with the land, just as we should cultivate friendship with other people (2005, 121–134).

Although the exemplarist and extensionist approaches are useful in getting us to think about environmental virtue, they don't include a strategy for resolving disagreement about which character traits are environmental virtues. One source of disagreement concerns the role that human well-being should play in defining environmental virtue. For example, Frasz and Jennifer Welchman both use an extensionist approach, but whereas Frasz defends a non-anthropocentric ethic, Welchman supports what she calls "an enlightened anthropocentrism." She writes:

> The dispositions in which I am interested are those that typically dispose us voluntarily to act as stewards of the natural world in our species' long-run interests in the preservation of natural beauty, biodiversity, renewable and non-renewable resources, and so forth.
>
> (Welchman 1999, 414)

In Welchman's view, virtues of environmental stewardship, such as diligence, trustworthiness, justice, loyalty, and honesty, are dispositions to appreciate the various ways environments function as public goods. An environmentally virtuous person is someone who is disposed to preserve resources, biodiversity, and natural beauty from a concern for the long-term best interests of human beings. By contrast, Frasz emphasizes the virtues of environmental benevolence, which include generosity, compassion, and friendship, because it involves a concern for the happiness, well-being or interests of both human and nonhuman beings for their own sakes. He thinks that what is required for environmental virtue is that we expand our sphere of concern to all nonhuman beings (and not only to those species that are enough like us to evoke empathy in us) (Frasz 2005, 125–132).

A possible objection to Welchman's enlightened anthropocentrism is that there are rare species and isolated ecosystems whose loss is unlikely to affect the welfare of human beings, including future generations. Consider, for example, the *Powelliphanta*, a genus of large carnivorous land snails found in remote parts of New Zealand. Most species of *Powelliphanta* are under serious threat or in danger of extinction, mainly due to habitat destruction by human activity. But it would be close to impossible to garner support for conservation efforts by appealing to human interests. *Powelliphanta* are nocturnal creatures and live buried under leaf mold and logs, so people are extremely unlikely to encounter them or to miss them were they to become extinct. They are not a tourist attraction, and don't have the potential to benefit human beings in any other way. Nevertheless, many people find it obvious that they ought to be protected. Welchman's response to this kind of objection is simply to affirm her enlightened anthropocentrism:

> If species or entities about which virtually no one cares, has cared, or are ever likely to care can be saved from extinction only by demanding enormous sacrifices of things for which many people have cared, do care, and will continue to care, then we can and perhaps must permit their destruction. As a rule, uncertainty about our understanding of the natural systems involved favors preservation. However, in those instances where both our certainty and the costs are very high, I cannot see why we must accept the costs.
>
> (Welchman 1999, 421)

Hursthouse uses the extensionist approach to argue that many of our environmental practices can be assessed by appealing to, and re-interpreting, familiar "old" virtues such as benevolence, prudence, practical wisdom, and compassion, as well as familiar vices, such as greed, self-indulgence, cruelty, and short-sightedness. Following Hill, she also emphasizes the importance of proper humility as the virtue opposed to the vice of arrogance. She writes:

> We should, indeed, must, recognize and, in recognizing, perforce, abandon our undue assumption of dignity, authority, power, and knowledge – our arrogance in short – in relation to nature... . [O]ur rationality, whether in its own right, or as the mark of our having been made in the image of God, gives us no especial authority. We do not have "dominion" over nature; it is not true, as Aristotle claimed, that plants exist for the sake of animals and all other animals exist for the sake of human beings.
>
> (Hursthouse 2007, 157–158)

Hursthouse thinks we can make significant ethical progress by reinterpreting and reconfiguring the old virtues and vices in the context of our relations with nature. However, she doesn't think the extensionist approach goes far enough, for it leaves out virtues that are explicitly concerned with our relations with nature. One such virtue is a disposition to be rightly disposed with respect to wonder. Wonder is a familiar emotion, which involves a form of delight, aesthetic appreciation, and a sense of gratitude to nature for its beauty and abundance. As a *virtue*, it involves a disposition to feel wonder at the right objects, for the right reasons, in the right manner, on the right occasions, and to act accordingly:

> If we think and feel, not that nature is wondrous but that Disneyland or the Royal Family of Windsor is, that the other animals are not, but we are, that the seas are not but swimming pools on the twentieth floor of luxury hotels are, and act accordingly, then we will act wrongly.
>
> (Hursthouse 2007, 162)

A few environmentalists, most notably Carson (1965), emphasize the importance of cultivating a sense of wonder, and it is not unusual for conservationists to appeal to this sense – rather than to compassion, benevolence, or the public good – to garner support for efforts to protect the endangered species. In the case of *Powelliphanta* snails, for example, conservationists tend to emphasize facts about these creatures that are likely to inspire wonder, such as the fact that they can grow to the size of a man's fist, and that they suck up earthworms like strings of spaghetti.[3]

Hursthouse identifies another virtue specifically concerned with our relations with nature, namely, respect for nature. This is a complex disposition, arising from training in childhood, which involves perceiving, feeling, thinking, and acting in relation to nature in particular ways (Hursthouse 2007, 162–167). We will discuss this virtue in Section 10.5, when we consider how a virtue ethical view of respect for nature differs from a deontological view.

10.3 What Makes a Trait an Environmental Virtue?

As Ronald Sandler points out, many of the disagreements about which character traits are environmental virtues stem from different accounts of what makes a trait a virtue (2007, 9–37). Welchman appears to use a consequentialist account of virtue, which holds that environmental virtues are traits that reliably produce good consequences, namely, the preservation of nature and natural resources. Welchman's reason for tying environmental virtue to human interests is that she doesn't think people will be motivated to preserve and protect nature from non-anthropocentric motives.

Aristotelian virtue ethicists think it is a mistake to define virtue purely in terms of consequences. In their view, virtues are admirable traits or human excellences, and thus involve good or excellent inner states, including good motives, feelings, reasons, and attitudes. However, Sandler (2007), among others, argues that Aristotelian virtue ethics is unacceptably anthropocentric, for it claims that what makes a trait a virtue is that it is necessary for human beings to live well or be truly happy (see Chapter 3). Sandler doesn't dispute the claim that there is a link between environmental virtue and human happiness; clearly, the ability to appreciate and respect nature makes it possible for people to find enjoyment, comfort, and satisfaction from their relationship with nature (Sandler 2007, 2). However, he rejects the view that what makes a trait an *environmental* virtue is that it contributes to the happiness of human beings. He notes that our rational and psychological capacities enable us to value things in themselves, independently of whether doing so promotes our own good. If living things have a good of their own that justifies concern for them for their own sake, then some character traits are virtues at least in part because they promote the good of these beings (Sandler 2007, 27).

Sandler argues in favor of a pluralistic account of environmental virtue, and in this regard he follows Christine Swanton. As we've seen in Chapter 2, Swanton distinguishes four grounds of virtue, namely, status, bonds, value, and flourishing, and this suggests that there could be four distinctive types of environmental virtue.[4] Sandler focuses on flourishing-based virtues, but he distinguishes between virtues that are based on human flourishing, and virtues that are based on the flourishing of nonhuman beings and entities. Examples of the first kind include:

a   virtues of sustainability (e.g., temperance, frugality, and humility): dispositions that promote the integrity of ecosystems so that they can produce the goods necessary for human health;
b   virtues of communion with nature (e.g., wonder, aesthetic sensibility, and attentiveness): dispositions that allow people to enjoy nature; and
c   virtues of environmental stewardship (e.g., loyalty, justice, and diligence) and environmental activism (e.g., cooperativeness, perseverance, and commitment): dispositions conducive to maintaining opportunities for those goods and benefits (Sandler 2007, 39–61).

Examples of environmental virtues that involve responding well to the good of nonhuman beings include dispositions of care, considerateness, and compassion (Sandler 2007, 63–83; see also Swanton 2003, 34–48).

Cafaro (2005a), writing specifically about environmental vice, similarly argues that although many environmental virtues do promote human flourishing, it is a mistake to define environmental virtue solely in terms of human flourishing. He accepts Aristotle's claim that traits such as gluttony, arrogance, greed, and apathy are harmful both to the individuals who possess these vices and to those around them, and he thinks environmentalists need to emphasize these harms in order to motivate people to curb their vices. However, he argues that Aristotle failed to recognize another legitimate sphere of moral concern: the wider circle of nonhuman nature. Harm to nonhuman entities is bad in itself, and so a trait that produces such harm is a vice, irrespective of its effect on humans. Yet Cafaro also points out that human flourishing and nature's flourishing are closely connected. In the case of gluttony, for example, overconsumption of food is detrimental to the health and flourishing of the gluttonous person, and it also has significant environmental costs, given that it fuels a more intensive agriculture, which leads to increased habitat loss and pollution of rivers and streams. And unhealthy ecosystems in turn lead to direct human harms, including mental, physical and spiritual harms:

> Gluttony reminds us that the vices, although often selfish, harm both ourselves and others…. . [I]n the end, it becomes difficult to separate harms to self and harms to others, harms to people and harms to nature. Our flourishing is tied up with the flourishing of others.
>
> (Cafaro 2005a, 142)

Although there are interesting philosophical points of disagreement among virtue ethicists, one shouldn't overestimate the significance of these disagreements when it comes to applying virtue ethics to practical moral problems. In what follows, we will consider how virtue ethics differs from utilitarianism in approaching problems in environmental ethics.

10.4 Virtue Ethics and Utilitarianism: Trophy Hunting

Utilitarianism is the most popular version of consequentialism, and claims that an action is right if and only if it maximizes utility (which is variously defined as happiness, pleasure, or preference satisfaction). Jeremy Bentham, the father of utilitarianism, argues that the interests of all sentient beings (i.e., beings capable of experiencing pleasure and pain) should be given equal consideration in assessing an action as right or wrong:

> Other animals ... stand degraded into the class of *things* ... . The French have already discovered that the blackness of the skin is no reason why a human being should be abandoned without redress to the caprice of a tormentor. It may come one day to be recognized, that the number of the legs, the villosity of the skin, or the termination of the *os sacrum*, are reasons equally insufficient for abandoning a sensitive being to the same fate. What else is it that should trace the insuperable line? Is it the faculty of reason, or perhaps, the faculty for discourse? ... [T]he question is not, Can they *reason*? nor, Can they *talk*? but, Can they *suffer*?
>
> (Bentham 1876, 310–311)

Nevertheless, Bentham and his followers have tended to focus primarily on the consequences for human beings, while excluding or neglecting the interests of other sentient beings. In his influential book *Animal Liberation* (1990) Peter Singer argues in favor of an expanded version of utilitarianism, one that includes the interests of all sentient beings in its consideration of "the greatest good for the greatest number." He argues that by privileging the interests of human beings, we are guilty of a kind of prejudice (i.e., speciesism) that is as arbitrary and unjustified as sexism and racism. We give special consideration to human beings, while lumping together the great apes and oysters as mere "animals," despite the fact that the apes have more in common with humans than they do with oysters. Singer regards the animal liberation movement as comparable to the liberation movements of women and people of color.

Although Singer's expanded utilitarianism allows for the consideration of the interests of other animals, many of its critics argue that it doesn't go far enough. Consider, for example, the practice of trophy hunting, a recreational activity that involves selectively hunting wild game. Hunters often keep a part of the animal as a trophy or souvenir to represent the success of the hunt. Trophy hunting remains legal in many countries, but an increasing number of people oppose the practice on moral grounds. Some opponents appeal to an expanded version of utilitarianism, arguing that the pain that animals suffer is not justified by the enjoyment that the hunters experience. PETA (People for the Ethical Treatment of Animals) draws attention to the fact that many animals endure prolonged, painful deaths when they are injured but not killed by hunters, and that hunting can disrupt migration and hibernation patterns. For wolves and other animals that mate for life and live in close-knit family units, hunting can devastate entire communities (PETA 2016).

A frequent objection to utilitarianism is that in calculating costs and benefits, one must include the interests of all parties, and not only the interests of the hunter and the individual animals that are hunted. And once we do this, the utilitarian calculation can support the conclusion that trophy hunting is sometimes right. Supporters of the practice argue that money raised from the sale of hunting permits goes towards conservation efforts and that it benefits local communities (although the truth of both these claims is contested). Some conservationists argue that trophy hunting gives governments economic incentives to leave safari blocks as wilderness, and that it motivates private landowners to reintroduce endangered species onto their lands (see Lindsey et al. 2006). In this view, the suffering endured by some animals is justifiable given the benefits to humans and other animals.

Another objection to utilitarianism is that it doesn't take character seriously. Despite the possible advantages of allowing trophy hunting, what lies at the heart of many people's disapproval of the practice is that it is a display or manifestation of vice: cruelty, arrogance, ruthlessness, irresponsibility, and cowardice.[5] A few writers have tried to challenge the negative perception of the character of trophy hunters, pointing out that many of them love the wilderness and are concerned that the money they pay for a hunting permit be put to good use. Yet it is difficult to look past the fact that what motivates trophy hunters is not the possible benefit to the environment or to local communities, but the pleasure they get from killing a wild animal and taking home part of its body as a trophy. If they truly cared about the wilderness we'd expect to see them act quite differently. They might go on safari, take a few photographs, and donate money to conservation efforts.

The utilitarian might agree with this character assessment, but when it comes to evaluating the practice of trophy hunting, the hunter's character can only play a very small part. The main question for utilitarians is whether allowing the practice maximizes overall utility. Along with benefits to local communities and preservation of endangered species, the hunter's enjoyment will be considered as one of the positive outcomes of trophy hunting, and these benefits will have to be weighed against the harm caused to individual animals and species. Practices that cause harm to nonhuman animals could therefore be justified on the grounds that they are a source of great pleasure and satisfaction to humans. Many environmental ethicists reject utilitarianism for this reason. A fundamental problem with utilitarianism is that it attributes intrinsic value to the experience of pleasure rather than to the beings that have these experiences. A related problem is that non-sentient things, things that do not have experiences, such as plants, rivers, mountains, and ecosystems, can only be valued instrumentally.

The question, then, is whether virtue ethics provides a better approach to issues in environmental ethics than standard forms of utilitarianism. As we've seen in Chapter 6, virtue ethics specifies right and wrong action in terms of the virtues and vices. According to the dominant, Aristotelian, view, an action is right if and only if it is what a virtuous person would do in the circumstances, and a virtuous person would do what is kind, honest, generous, just, etc. (see Hursthouse 1999, Chapter 1). A significant difference between the two accounts is that utilitarianism is monistic in the sense that it judges actions solely in terms of consequences, whereas virtue ethics is pluralistic in the sense that it recognizes that there are many different virtues. Some of these (e.g., benevolence, compassion, generosity, etc.) are concerned with the good of others, but others (e.g., honesty, fairness, justice, loyalty, etc.) are not, at least not directly or primarily. Another difference is that virtue ethics takes inner states (motives, attitudes, reasons, and feelings) as relevant when evaluating a person's actions. In the case of trophy hunting, then, the virtue ethicist would argue that it is an act of cruelty, arrogance, and disrespect, and therefore wrong. The enjoyment that the hunter experiences does not count as a reason in favor of the practice – indeed, the fact that he enjoys killing an animal only supports the claim that he is a cruel person. Further, the virtue ethicist might argue that the possible benefit to the environment and local communities cannot serve to justify his actions, given that the hunter is not motivated by a concern for animals and the environment.

A possible objection to virtue ethics is that it is too personal in its evaluation of trophy hunting. By narrowly focusing on the character and actions of individuals, the virtue ethicist excludes from consideration a number of important matters that are relevant when assessing the practice of trophy hunting, such as the possible benefits to local communities and endangered species. Indeed, it is unclear whether virtue ethics can say anything about trophy hunting as an organized practice, given that many different people are involved, each with their own set of motives, reasons, and character traits. Consider the following cases:

> *Case 1:* The owner of a game farm wants to protect endangered animals on his farm, and sells hunting permits to obtain the necessary funds. When accompanying a trophy hunter, he always makes sure that only old or sick animals, who will no longer breed, are killed. The hunter remains unaware of this, and thoroughly enjoys the experience.
>
> *Case 2:* The owner of a game farm has established a lucrative business in trophy hunting, which allows him and his family to live a lavish lifestyle. He specifically breeds animals for this purpose, keeps them confined in small enclosures throughout their lives, and releases them just before the trophy hunter arrives. The hunter remains unaware of this, and thoroughly enjoys the experience.

From a virtue-ethical perspective, the actions of the two trophy hunters are equally bad (cruel, selfish, arrogant, etc.), for all they care about is the thrill of hunting and displaying a trophy. Both of them act wrongly. Some people will find this conclusion counterintuitive, and might argue that killing an animal raised in captivity is clearly worse than killing one that is old and sickly and will no longer breed, regardless of whether the hunters are aware of what they are doing. Further, and irrespective of whether one agrees with the assessment of the actions of the two trophy hunters, one might point out that there are important differences in the way the practice of trophy hunting is set up, and a utilitarian calculation clearly brings this out. In Case 1, very little harm is done to the hunted animals, but there is a significant benefit to endangered species. In Case 2, however, the animals are likely to endure suffering throughout their lives, and very few people benefit from the practice. The objection to virtue ethics, then, is that it doesn't allow for the possibility that some forms of trophy hunting ought to be encouraged, since it evaluates the practice in terms of the character of the hunter, which is invariably deemed vicious.

In response, a virtue ethicist could draw attention to the distinction between *acting from virtue* and *acting virtuously*. Acting from virtue involves being well-motivated and possessing (and displaying) good character traits, whereas acting virtuously involves doing what a virtuous person would do (Hursthouse) or hitting the target of virtue (Swanton), which doesn't require good motivation (see Chapter 6). Trophy hunters clearly do not act from virtue, and it is debatable whether they ever succeed in acting virtuously. However, we can account for the difference between the two cases by focusing on the actions of the game farmers, and we can do so without knowing anything about their character or what actually motivates them. In Case 2, the owner (and anyone who allows, facilitates, or encourages the practice of trophy hunting) does what a vicious (cruel, selfish, materialistic) person would do, and hence acts wrongly.

Assessing the actions of the game farmer in Case 1 is somewhat more complicated. His actions are not wrong, for they are not characteristic of someone who is selfish and cruel. But they are not characteristic of a virtuous person either. Even though the animals that are hunted are old and past their reproductive years, arranging for them to be killed by a trophy hunter cannot be described as benevolent or respectful. The fact that the owner puts the money to good use doesn't make up for the fact that the hunted animals are being harmed. However, a virtue ethicist would acknowledge that there is a sense in which the farmer does as well as he can in the circumstances. Arguably, he finds himself in what Hursthouse (1999, 71–77) calls a tragic dilemma. He is torn between protecting two groups of animals, but, through no fault of his own (let us suppose), he cannot protect both. If selling hunting permits is the only way in which he can raise enough funds to protect endangered species, then doing so could well be the right decision. And if he is virtuous, then he will make sure that harm to individual animals is minimized. But his actions still do not deserve a tick of approval as right or virtuous actions. Instead, it must be with great regret and pain that he allows the animal to be killed. Further, virtue ethics allows us to distinguish between instances of trophy hunting that cannot be justified and probably shouldn't be permitted, and instances that can be permitted under the understanding that it is the best we can do for now. But it can never be a practice that a good person (or a good society) can embrace or promote and regard with pride.

10.5 Virtue Ethics and Deontology: Respect for Nature

Many environmental ethicists reject utilitarianism in favor of a deontological approach to environmental issues. Deontologists claim that the rightness of an action is independent of its consequences and instead depends on whether the action is in accordance with a moral rule, such as "Do not intentionally kill an innocent person," "Respect the rights of others," and "Do not treat others merely as means to an end." These rules are typically justified by appealing to the intrinsic value of those to whom they apply, and for a long time, the consensus among deontologists was that only human beings have intrinsic worth. This kind of anthropocentrism encounters obvious difficulties when it comes to explaining what is wrong with the cruel treatment of nonhuman animals. Kant suggests, for example, that inflicting gratuitous suffering on animals is wrong because it might encourage people to become desensitized to cruelty towards humans (Kant 1997, 212–213).

Extending deontology to include animals and the environment requires that we recognize that they have intrinsic value. Tom Regan (1983), a prominent animal rights advocate, argues that some animals do have intrinsic value, which generates a right to be treated with respect as well as a duty on our part not to treat them as mere means to our ends. In his view, practices such as trophy hunting and animal experimentation are wrong because they violate the right of animals to be treated with respect. The implication is that the possible benefits to humans or other animals cannot be used to justify practices that are harmful to animals.

An important task for deontologists is to determine which beings have intrinsic value and hence a right to respectful treatment. According to Regan, all animals who are the "subject-of-a-life" have intrinsic value. Being the subject-of-a-life involves having sense-perceptions, desires, beliefs, motives, memory, a sense of the future, and a psychological identity over time. Such a being has the capacity to feel pleasure and pain, and its life can go well or badly for it (Regan 1983, 243). Some ethicists argue that Regan's subject-of-a-life criterion excludes too many life-forms from moral consideration. In Regan's view, beings that are not the subject-of-a-life, such as plants and micro-organisms, can only have instrumental worth, and hence may be used as mere means to our ends.

Paul Taylor (1981; 2011) puts forward an alternative position, which he refers to as *biocentrism* (as opposed to anthropocentrism) and that extends inherent value to all living things. Taylor argues that all individual living things, including animals, plants, and micro-organisms, have *equal* intrinsic worth and hence are entitled to be treated with respect. Human beings are not inherently superior to other species but are members of "Earth's community of life," along with all other species (Taylor 2011, 44). He argues that each living thing has a good or well-being of its own that can be enhanced or damaged, and the intrinsic worth of living things generates a *prima facie* (or contributory) duty on our part to preserve or promote their good as an end in itself. According to Taylor, biocentrism is an attitude of respect for nature, whereby one attempts to live one's life in a way that respects the welfare and inherent worth of all living creatures.

As mentioned earlier, Hursthouse herself identifies respect for nature (or, as she prefers to call it, the virtue of being rightly oriented to nature) as a central virtue in our dealings with nature (2007, 162–167).

This raises the question: How does a deontological account of environmental virtue differ from a virtue-ethical account? As we've seen, virtue ethicists think that virtue plays a fundamental role in moral decision-making. They define right action in terms of virtue rather than an adherence to moral rules. As Sandler explains:

> A substantive account of the virtues and the virtuous person informs what actions one ought or ought not to perform. In the context of environmental ethics this would imply that reflections on the content of the virtues and studying the character traits and behavior of environmentally virtuous people are what ultimately inform how we ought to behave regarding the environment.
>
> (2005, 7)

By contrast, deontologists regard virtue as a disposition to do the right thing, that is, to act in accordance with duty. In this view, the starting point for an environmental ethic is to formulate rules and principles of right action, and then to define environmental virtues as dispositions to act accordingly. Many contemporary deontologists accept that virtue – in particular, practical wisdom and sensitivity – plays an important role in moral decision-making. We need wisdom and sensitivity to determine which rules are relevant in a particular situation, to decide which course of action would be in accordance with those rules, and to resolve moral dilemmas by adjudicating between the demands of competing rules. In this view, the role of virtue is important, but it remains secondary and subservient to the role of duty (see Chapter 8).

Hursthouse (2007, 163–167) argues that a deontological view of respect for nature as based in the notion of "inherent worth" runs into significant difficulties. To begin with, Taylor limits his ascription of inherent worth to individual living things, which they have by virtue of their membership in the Earth's Community of Life. Non-living things, such as the planets, the seas, the ozone layer, spiders' webs, and ammonites, have only instrumental worth. One could, perhaps, try to avoid this problem by including non-living things as having inherent worth, but the notion then becomes so broad as to be of very little practical use. Furthermore, the deontologist will have to ground inherent worth in a feature, or set of features, that all living and non-living beings share, which is almost certainly an impossible task. What makes something valuable and worth protecting, it seems, is a unique set of features and relationships, rather than some characteristic it shares with all other things.

Another problem appears when we ask whether or not inherent worth admits of degrees. The idea that all living things (plants, flies, cockroaches, rats, rabbits, elephants, human beings, etc.) have equal worth is just not very plausible, and neither is it very practical. Surely, the life of a chimpanzee has more inherent worth than the life of a cockroach. However, if we allow that inherent worth admits of degrees, we would then be tempted to claim that human beings have the highest degree of inherent worth. At this point, Hursthouse notes, a view that "promised to be a radical reformation of our old understanding of ourselves in relation to other animals loses most of its revisionary character" (2007, 164). We are once again left with an anthropocentric ethic.

Hursthouse thinks we can avoid all these problems by giving an account of respect for nature in virtue-ethical terms, that is, without introducing the controversial notion of inherent worth as a foundational premise. Instead of seeing respect for nature as an attitude we adopt when we recognize that all living beings share a common feature, such as being a member of the Earth's Community of Life, Hursthouse argues that it is best understood as a virtue. The virtue being rightly oriented to nature involves accepting a whole range of reasons for action (and omission) in particular contexts, and having the appropriate emotional responses to both living and non-living things.

Hursthouse further argues that thinking about respect for nature as a duty is not very helpful. Deontologists commonly agree that something's possession of inherent worth generates a moral duty on the part of moral agents to protect or at least refrain from damaging it. Accordingly, Taylor thinks of respect for nature as an attitude one can adopt, perhaps after reading a philosophical book and being convinced of the claim that all living things have inherent worth by virtue of being members of the Earth's Community of Life, and that we therefore have a duty to treat nature with respect. However, when we look at Taylor's description of what is involved in adopting this attitude (and doing one's duty) it becomes clear that what he describes is a radical change in *character*:

> Really coming to see oneself as sharing "a common bond" with all living things would involve a radical change in one's emotions and perceptions, one's whole way of perceiving and responding to the world, of one's reasons for action and thereby actions.
>
> (Hursthouse 2007, 163)

If we think of respect for nature as a virtue, it becomes clear that it is a complex disposition that can only be acquired through moral habituation or training, beginning in childhood, and continuing through self-improvement. To succeed in treating living things with respect, we need to possess practical wisdom, and to understand what is involved in treating a specific being with respect, we need to develop certain perceptual capacities and emotional sensitivities. Hursthouse's point, then, is that the duty to respect nature doesn't do any real work: it doesn't motivate us, it doesn't help us to decide what to do, and it doesn't foster in us the right kinds of emotion and perception:

> From the perspective of virtue ethics, Taylor's introduction of the contentious notion of inherent worth is superfluous. "Regarding a living thing as having inherent worth" amounts to nothing more (though nothing less) in his account than regarding facts about whether a proposed course of action will benefit or harm a living thing as providing non-instrumental reasons for or against it, and it is his rich and insightful identification of this range of reasons which is significant. For, once they are identified, we can readily see how they might be used to inculcate a character trait – the virtue of "respect for nature", or ... "being rightly oriented to nature."
> (Hursthouse 2007, 164)

Some critics of environmental virtue ethics have argued that the focus on human virtue and, in the case of eudaimonism, human happiness or flourishing, makes this approach objectionably anthropocentric. Holmes Rolston (2005), a prominent environmental ethicist, claims that the focus on human excellence and human flourishing distracts us from the intrinsic value of natural entities. He argues that virtue is not the source of natural value – nature has value in itself, independent of its relationship to humans. Rolston accepts that virtue plays an important role in environmental ethics, but he warns against casting it in a fundamental role. Much like Taylor, Rolston thinks virtue is to be understood as a response to the independent value or inherent worth of natural entities, rather than as a trait needed for human flourishing. He is concerned that environmental virtue ethics will tend to focus on *human virtues* at the expense of intrinsic *values in nature*. He writes:

> To be truly virtuous one must respect values in nature for their own sake and not as a tributary to human flourishing. But if indeed intrinsic value in nature has become primary to the ethic, to call such an ethic a (human) environmental virtue ethics is no longer an adequately descriptive title. The virtue ethic is only a "start-up ethic," which can only get us halfway there. The better name would be an environmental value/virtue ethic.
> (Rolston 2005, 70)

In response to this objection, Hursthouse argues that eudaimonism should not be understood as claiming "that *eudaimonia* or human flourishing is the 'top value', ranked above any other in an improperly human chauvinistic way" (2007, 169). As human beings, we are inevitably faced with the question of how we are to live well as human beings. But it doesn't follow from this that *eudaimonia* is a foundational value, in the same way that dignity and utility play foundational roles in deontology and utilitarianism respectively. Instead, she writes, "if anything counts as the 'top value' in virtue ethics, it is acting virtuously" (Hursthouse 2007, 169). As we've seen in Chapter 3, some virtue ethicists share Rolston's concern that Aristotelian virtue ethics makes too strong a connection between virtue and human happiness. This is one of the main reasons why Swanton (2003) and Sandler (2007) prefer a pluralistic account, which defines virtue as a disposition to respond well to the demands of the world.

10.6 The Situationist Critique of Environmental Virtue Ethics

As we've seen in the previous chapter, one critique of virtue ethics is that it presupposes the existence of character traits, when in fact studies in psychology show that our behavior is influenced more by situational factors than by internal states. Environmental virtue ethics is vulnerable to the same objection. Drawing on studies that focus specifically on environmental behaviors, T. J. Kasperbauer (2014) argues that environmental virtues are not as robust as we might hope.

One of the experiments that Kasperbauer uses to support this claim is what he terms the "Smiley Faces" experiment conducted by Wesley Schultz et al. (2007). The researchers collected energy consumption rates from 290 households and used these to calculate a baseline consumption rate in the neighborhood. They then informed each household how their consumption rate compared with the baseline, and continued to monitor their consumption to see whether the information had any effect on their behavior. What the researchers found was that the people who were informed that their usage was above-average tended to decrease their consumption, whereas the people who were told their usage was below-average tended to increase their consumption. The study therefore demonstrates that most people have a strong tendency to conform to social norms, and this gives us reason to doubt whether many of the households in the below-average group manifested environmental virtue, given that they increased their usage after becoming aware of their status. But the findings also support the situationist's claim that our behavior is affected more by trivial situational factors than by character traits. To see how, it is necessary to note a further variable included in the experiment. The information flyer given to some of the below average users included a smiley face, and the one given to some of the above average users included a frowny face. The researchers found that below average users who received a smiley face along with the information went on to sustain rather than increase their level of consumption, whereas above average users who received a frowny face along with the information reduced their usage even more than the ones who only received the information. What this shows, according to Kasperbauer (2014, 477), is that our environmental behavior is a result of situational factors, including trivial social feedback such as smiley and frowny faces, rather than character traits.

Jason Kawall (2018, 667–668) replies to this objection by giving a version of the rarity response, discussed in Chapter 9. He reminds us that most people are not yet raised to be environmentally virtuous, and so we shouldn't be surprised to find that environmental virtues are even rarer than interpersonal virtues. If many people's behavior is so easily influenced by trivial situational factors, then all this shows is that they are not environmentally virtuous, and not that environmental virtue doesn't affect behavior. That is, the studies cited by Kasperbauer do not give us reason to doubt that people who are genuinely environmentally virtuous would reliably act well in this regard.

But this response is unlikely to satisfy Kasperbauer. He thinks the situationist critique takes a particularly serious form in the case of environmental virtue ethics, given its particular aims. As noted at the beginning of this chapter, environmental ethicists share a commitment to the view that we need to make a radical change to the way we engage with animals and the environment. It therefore seems that practical aims – preventing further destruction of species and habitats and staving off large-scale ecological disaster – have to take priority over more theoretical concerns. Hence Kasperbauer cites Sandler (2007, 107–108) as stating that an adequate environmental ethics "must be efficacious in promoting solutions to real world environmental problems. It must help bring about, not merely justify, environmentally sustainable practices, policies, and lifestyles." Kasperbauer (2014, 472) takes this to mean that "environmental ethics must produce behavioral change capable of providing adequate protection for the environment." Accordingly, a condition of adequacy for environmental virtue ethics, in his view, is that it "must promote environmental virtues that have real effects on the environment" (2014, 473).

Seen thus, environmental virtue ethics faces a serious problem: if it is true that most people do not (and perhaps never will) possess robust environmental virtues, then relying on the virtues in order to bring about this change would be foolish. Consider, for example, the practice of intensive animal farming. A virtue ethicist would judge it as cruel, or at least as lacking in compassion, given the suffering that these animals are forced to endure. By making people aware of this suffering, that is, by appealing to their compassion, we might well influence some of them to stop eating meat that was produced in this way, but it is likely that we will be far more successful in bringing about the desired change by manipulating situational factors. One proposal is to encourage the large-scale production of synthetic meat, which consumers will prefer to real meat if it is less expensive. Although it might be true that a virtuous person would choose synthetic over real meat for reasons of compassion rather than self-interest, this hardly seems relevant if our aim is to reduce animal suffering.

To see how the virtue ethicist can respond to Kasperbauer we need to return to a question discussed at the beginning of this book: What is the purpose of normative theory? As noted in Chapter 1, normative ethics aims to provide a systematic and coherent account of the values, norms, ideals, and standards that we appeal to when making moral judgments. In addition to its theoretical aims, it seems reasonable to include a more practical aim, which is to allow us to make better moral judgments and thereby to improve our practices, policies, and lifestyles. The same can be said of environmental virtue ethics: it should provide a systematic and coherent account of environmental values (etc.) and allow us to improve our actions, policies, and lifestyles with respect to animals and the environment. However, it is a mistake to suggest, as Kasperbauer does, that environmental virtue ethics must rely on the virtues or the virtuous actions of individuals to bring about these changes.

Virtue ethicists are concerned with the question, How should we live? and it responds by saying: We should live and act virtuously. It allows us to judge a particular practice, such as intensive animal farming, as wrong on the grounds that it is cruel or lacking in compassion, rather than on the grounds that it violates a moral duty or fails to bring about good consequences. The advice it gives to individuals in this regard is that participating in the practices (which includes consuming meat that has been produced in this way) cannot form part of what it means to live and act virtuously as a human being. However, it doesn't follow that the virtue ethicist's only strategy for reducing the consumption of factory-farmed meat in a given population is to rely on the compassion of individual consumers. Instead, an environmental virtue ethicist can propose any of a number of other strategies, such as regulating the meat industry, outlawing cruel practices, and encouraging synthetic meat production. That is, we need not wait for individuals to become environmentally virtuous.

Chapter Summary

- *Environmental ethics* is the discipline in philosophy that is concerned with questions about the moral value and status of the environment, including natural ecosystems, agricultural ecosystems, urban ecosystems, and the individuals (both human and nonhuman) that populate and constitute those ecosystems.

- *Environmental virtue theory* is a field of inquiry that is focused on questions about the nature and role of environmental virtue.
- Strategies for identifying environmental virtue include the *environmental exemplar approach*, which involves reflecting on the lives and writings of the handful of people who are recognized as environmental role models, and the *extensionist approach*, which involves arguing by extension from traits that are already recognized as virtues in the interpersonal sphere.
- *Environmental virtue ethicists* believe that virtue ethics provides a better approach to problems in environmental ethics than its two rivals, utilitarianism and deontology.
- The situationist critique of environmental virtue ethics holds that we do not possess robust environmental virtues, and that our behavior is influenced more by situational factors than by character traits. The implication of this is that we cannot rely on the virtues of individuals to combat the many problems facing animals and the environment.

Notes

1   For an overview of recent developments in applied virtue ethics, see Axtell and Olson (2012).
2   As explained in Chapter 1, virtue theory is a field of inquiry focused on questions about virtue and character more generally. Virtue ethics, by contrast, is a normative theory that competes with deontology and consequentialism.
3   The New Zealand Department of Conservation (2016).
4   A possible example of a status-based environmental virtue is the (nameless) virtue of recognizing and responding appropriately to the status of an individual animal, such as its being the alpha male in a pack of wolves. Bond-based environmental virtues, in turn, involve responding well to bonds between individual animals (such as their being a mating pair), bonds between animals and a given territory or habitat, as well as bonds between humans and animals. Many environmental virtues involve responding well to valuable things or states of affairs, such as rock formations, sunsets, mountains, and so on, and responding well could involve protecting, maintaining, and appreciating the inherent value of natural entities. Another important set of environmental virtues are flourishing-based virtues, such as benevolence and compassion.
5   This view is supported by a study in psychology, which found that people who hunt for sport demonstrate attitudes consistent with narcissism (an egotistical admiration of one's own attributes, coupled with a lack of compassion), Machiavellianism (being deceitful, cunning and manipulative) and psychopathy (impulsivity and a lack of remorse or empathy) (Kavanagh et al. 2013).

Further Reading

Cafaro, Philip. 2005b. "Thoreau, Leopold, and Carson: Toward an Environmental Virtue Ethics." In *Environmental Virtue Ethics*, edited by Ronald L. Sandler and Philip Cafaro, 31–45. Lanham, MD: Rowman & Littlefield.

Frasz, Geoffrey. 2005. "Benevolence as an Environmental Virtue." In *Environmental Virtue Ethics*, edited by Ronald L. Sandler and Philip Cafaro, 121–134. Lanham, MD: Rowman & Littlefield.

Hill Jr., Thomas E. 1983. "Ideals of Human Excellence and Preserving Natural Environments." *Environmental Ethics* 5(3): 211–224. doi:10.5840/enviroethics19835327

Hursthouse, Rosalind. 2006a. "Applying Virtue Ethics to Our Treatment of the Other Animals." In *The Practice of Virtue: Classic and Contemporary Readings in Virtue Ethics*, edited by Jennifer Welchman, 136–155. Indianapolis, IN: Hackett.

Hursthouse, Rosalind. 2007. "Environmental Virtue Ethics." In *Working Virtue: Virtue Ethics and Contemporary Moral Problems*, edited by Rebecca L. Walker and Philip J. Ivanhoe, 155–171. Oxford: Oxford University Press.

Kawall, Jason. 2018. "Environmental Virtue Ethics." *The Oxford Handbook of Virtue*, edited by Nancy Snow. Oxford: Oxford University Press.

Rolston III, Holmes. 2005. "Environmental Virtue Ethics: Half the Truth but Dangerous as a Whole." In *Environmental Virtue Ethics*, edited by Ronald L. Sandler and Philip Cafaro, 61–78. Lanham, MD: Rowman & Littlefield.

Sandler, Ronald. 2007. *Character and Environment: A Virtue-Oriented Approach to Environmental Virtue Ethics*. New York: Columbia University Press.

Bibliography

Adams, Robert Merrihew. 2015. "Comments on *Intelligent Virtue*: Moral Education, Aspiration, and Altruism." *The Journal of Value Inquiry* 49(1): 289–295. doi:10.1007/s10790-014-9477-2

Alfano, Mark. 2013. *Character as Moral Fiction*. Cambridge: Cambridge University Press.

Alfano, Mark, editor. 2015. *Current Controversies in Virtue Theory*. New York: Routledge.

Anderson, Elizabeth. 2008. "Emotions in Kant's Later Moral Philosophy: Honour and the Phenomenology of Moral Value." In *Kant's Ethics of Virtue*, edited by Monika Betzler, 123–145. Berlin: Walter de Gruyter.

Annas, Julia. 1993. *The Morality of Happiness*. New York: Oxford University Press.

Annas, Julia. 2004. "Being Virtuous and Doing the Right Thing." *Proceedings and Addresses of the American Philosophical Association* 78(2): 61–75. doi:10.2307/3219725

Annas, Julia. 2005. "Comments on John Doris's *Lack of Character*." *Philosophy and Phenomenological Research* 71(3): 636–642. doi:10.1111/j.1933-1592.2005.tb00476.x

Annas, Julia. 2006. "Virtue Ethics." In *The Oxford Handbook of Ethical Theory*, edited by David Copp, 515–536. New York: Oxford University Press.

Annas, Julia. 2008. "Virtue Ethics and the Charge of Egoism." In *Morality and Self-Interest*, edited by Paul Bloomfield, 205–221. New York: Oxford University Press.

Annas, Julia. 2011. *Intelligent Virtue*. Oxford: Oxford University Press.

Annas, Julia. 2015a. "Applying Virtue Ethics (Society of Applied Philosophy Annual Lecture 2014)." *Journal of Applied Philosophy* 32(1): 1–14. doi:10.1111/japp.12103

Annas, Julia. 2015b. "Virtue and Duty: Negotiating between Different Ethical Traditions." *The Journal of Value Inquiry* 49(4): 605–618. doi:10.1007/s10790-015-9520-y

Anscombe, G. E. M. 1958. "Modern Moral Philosophy." *Philosophy* 33(124): 1–19. doi:10.1017/S0031819100037943

Aristotle. 2009. *The Nicomachean Ethics*. Translated by David Ross, revised by Lesley Brown. Oxford: Oxford University Press.

Athanassoulis, Nafsika. 2000. "A Response to Harman: Virtue Ethics and Character Traits." *Proceedings of the Aristotelian Society* 100(1): 215–221. doi:10.1111/j.0066-7372.2003.00012.x

Athanassoulis, Nafsika. 2013. *Virtue Ethics*. London: Bloomsbury.

Axtell, Guy and Philip Olson. 2012. "Recent Work in Applied Virtue Ethics." *American Philosophical Quarterly* 49(3): 182–203. www.jstor.org/stable/23213479

Badhwar, Neera K. 1996. "The Limited Unity of Virtue." *Noûs* 30(3): 306–329. doi:10.2307/2216272

Badhwar, Neera K. 2014. *Well-Being: Happiness in a Worthwhile Life.* Oxford: Oxford University Press.

Bakhurst, David. 2005. "Particularism and Moral Education." *Philosophical Explorations* 8(3): 265–279. doi:10.1080/13869790500219596

Bargh, John A., Mark Chen, and Lara Burrows. 1996. "Automaticity of Social Behavior: Direct Effects of Trait Construct and Stereotype Activation on Action." *Journal of Personality and Social Psychology* 71(2): 230–244. doi:10.1037/0022-3514.71.2doi:230

Baril, Anne. 2013. "The Role of Welfare in Eudaimonism." *The Southern Journal of Philosophy* 51(4): 511–535. doi:10.1111/sjp.12042

Battaly, Heather. 2014. "Intellectual Virtues." In *The Handbook of Virtue Ethics*, edited by Stan van Hooft, Nafsika Athanassoulis, Jason Kawall, Justin Oakley, Nicole Saunders, and Liezl van Zyl, 177–187. Abingdon and New York: Routledge.

Battaly, Heather. 2015. *Virtue.* Cambridge: Polity Press.

Bennett, Christopher. 2010. *What Is This Thing Called Ethics?* Abingdon: Routledge.

Bentham, Jeremy. 1876. *An Introduction to the Principles of Morals and Legislation.* Oxford: Clarendon Press.

Besser-Jones, Lorraine. 2008. "Social Psychology, Moral Character, and Moral Fallibility." *Philosophy and Phenomenological Research* 76(2): 310–332. doi:10.1111/j.1933-1592.2007.00134.x

Besser-Jones, Lorraine. 2014. *Eudaimonic Ethics: The Philosophy and Psychology of Living Well.* New York: Routledge.

Besser-Jones, Lorraine and Michael Slote, editors. 2015. *The Routledge Companion to Virtue Ethics.* New York: Routledge.

Birondo, Noell and S. Stewart Braun, editors. 2017. *Virtue's Reasons: New Essays on Virtue, Character, and Reasons.* New York: Routledge.

Brady, Michael S. 2004. "Against Agent-Based Virtue Ethics." *Philosophical Papers* 33(1): 1–10. doi:10.1080/05568640409485132

Cafaro, Philip. 2005a. "Gluttony, Arrogance, Greed, and Apathy: An Exploration of Environmental Vice." In *Environmental Virtue Ethics*, edited by Ronald L. Sandler and Philip Cafaro, 135–158. Lanham, MD: Rowman & Littlefield.

Cafaro, Philip. 2005b. "Thoreau, Leopold, and Carson: Toward an Environmental Virtue Ethics." In *Environmental Virtue Ethics*, edited by Ronald L. Sandler and Philip Cafaro, 31–45. Lanham, MD: Rowman & Littlefield.

Carson, Rachel. 1965. *The Sense of Wonder.* New York: Harper Collins.

Cooper, John M. 1975. *Reason and Human Good in Aristotle.* Cambridge, MA: Harvard University Press.

Cox, Damian. 2006. "Agent-Based Theories of Right Action." *Ethical Theory and Moral Practice* 9(5): 505–515. doi:10.1007/s10677-006-9029-3

Crisp, Roger. 2000. "Particularizing Particularism." In *Moral Particularism*, edited by Brad Hooker and Margaret Olivia Little, 23–47. Oxford: Oxford University Press.

Crisp, Roger. 2007. "Ethics without Reasons?" *Journal of Moral Philosophy* 4(1): 40–49. doi:10.1177/1740468106072782

Cureton, Adam, and Thomas Hill. 2014. "Kant on Virtue and the Virtues." In *Cultivating Virtue: Perspectives from Philosophy, Theology, and Psychology*, edited by Nancy E. Snow, 87–110. Oxford: Oxford University Press.

Dancy, Jonathan. 1993. *Moral Reasons.* Oxford: Blackwell.

Dancy, Jonathan. 2004. *Ethics without Principles.* Oxford: Oxford University Press.

Dancy, Jonathan. 2013. "Moral Particularism." In *The Stanford Encyclopedia of Philosophy.* https://plato.stanford.edu/archives/fall2013/entries/moral-particularism/

Darley, John M. and Daniel C. Batson. 1973. "'From Jerusalem to Jericho': A Study of Situational and Dispositional Variables in Helping Behavior." *Journal of Personality and Social Psychology* 27(1): 100–108. doi:10.1037/h0034449

Das, Ramon. 2003. "Virtue Ethics and Right Action." *Australasian Journal of Philosophy* 81(3): 324–339. doi:10.1080/713659702

DePaul, Michael. 2000. "Character Traits, Virtues, and Vices: Are there None?" *The Proceedings of the Twentieth World Congress of Philosophy* 9: 141–157.

Devine, Patricia G. and Margo J. Monteith. 1999. "Automaticity and Control in Stereotyping." In *Dual-process Theories in Social Psychology*, edited by Shelly Chiaken and Yaacov Trope, 339–360. New York: Guilford Press.

Doris, John M. 1998. "Persons, Situations, and Virtue Ethics." *Noûs* 32(4): 504–530. doi:10.1111/0029-4624.00136

Doris, John M. 2002. *Lack of Character: Personality and Moral Behavior.* Cambridge: Cambridge University Press.

Doviak, Daniel. 2011. "A New Form of Agent-Based Virtue Ethics." *Ethical Theory and Moral Practice* 14(3): 259–272. doi:10.1007/s10677-10010-9240-0

Driver, Julia. 1996. "The Virtues and Human Nature." In *How Should One Live? Essays on the Virtues*, edited by Roger Crisp, 111–129. Oxford: Oxford University Press.

Driver, Julia. 2001. *Uneasy Virtue.* Cambridge: Cambridge University Press.

Driver, Julia. 2015. "The Consequentialist Critique of Virtue Ethics." In *The Routledge Companion to Virtue Ethics*, edited by Lorraine Besser-Jones and Michael Slote, 321–329. New York: Routledge.

Driver, Julia. 2016. "Minimal Virtue." *The Monist* 99(2): 97–111. doi:10.1093/monist/onv032.

Foot, Philippa. 1978a. "Euthanasia." In *Virtues and Vices and Other Essays in Moral Philosophy*, by Philippa Foot, 33–61. Oxford: Blackwell.

Foot, Philippa. 1978b. "Virtues and Vices." In *Virtues and Vices and Other Essays in Moral Philosophy*, by Philippa Foot, 1–18. Oxford: Blackwell.

Foot, Philippa. 2001 *Natural Goodness.* Oxford: Oxford University Press.

Frasz, Geoffrey. 2005. "Benevolence as an Environmental Virtue." In *Environmental Virtue Ethics*, edited by Ronald L. Sandler and Philip Cafaro, 121–134. Lanham, MD: Rowman & Littlefield.

Frazer, Michael L. and Michael Slote. 2015. "Sentimentalist Virtue Ethics." In *The Routledge Companion to Virtue Ethics*, edited by Lorraine Besser-Jones and Michael Slote, 197–208. New York: Routledge.

Gelfand, Scott. 2000. "Hypothetical Agent-Based Virtue Ethics." *Southwest Philosophy Review* 17(1): 85–94. doi:10.5840/swphilreview200017111

Hacker-Wright, John. 2010. "Virtue Ethics without Right Action: Anscombe, Foot, and Contemporary Virtue Ethics." *Journal of Value Inquiry* 44(2): 209–224. doi:10.1007/s10790-010-9218-0

Harman, Gilbert. 1999. "Moral Philosophy Meets Social Psychology: Virtue Ethics and the Fundamental Attribution Error." *Proceedings of the Aristotelian Society* 99: 315–331.

Harman, Gilbert. 2000. "The Nonexistence of Character Traits." *Proceedings of the Aristotelian Society* 100(1): 223–226. doi:10.1111/j.0066-7372.2003.00013.x

Harman, Gilbert. 2001. "Virtue Ethics without Character Traits." In *Fact and Value: Essays on Ethics and Metaphysics for Judith Jarvis Thomson*, edited by Alex Byrne, Robert Stalnaker, and Ralph Wedgwood, 117–127. Cambridge, MA: MIT Press.

Hartshorne, Hugh and Mark A. May. 1928. *Studies in the Nature of Character, Vol. 1: Studies in Deceit*. New York: Macmillan.

Herman, Barbara. 1981. "On the Value of Acting from the Motive of Duty." *The Philosophical Review* 90(3): 359–382. doi:10.2307/2184978

Hill Jr., Thomas E. 1983. "Ideals of Human Excellence and Preserving Natural Environments." *Environmental Ethics* 5(3): 211–224. doi:10.5840/enviroethics19835327

Hill, Thomas E. 2008. "Kantian Virtue and 'Virtue Ethics'." In *Kant's Ethics of Virtue*, edited by Monika Betzler, 29–59. Berlin: Walter de Gruyter.

Holloway, Stephen, Lyle Tucker, and Harvey A. Hornstein. 1977. "The Effects of Social and Nonsocial Information on Interpersonal Behavior of Males: The News Makes News." *Journal of Personality and Social Psychology* 35(7): 514–522. doi:10.1037/0022-3514.35.7doi:514

Holopainen, Jari, Samuli Helama, Charlotte Björkenstam, and Timo Partonen. 2013. "Variation and Seasonal Patterns of Suicide Mortality in Finland and Sweden since the 1750s." *Environmental Health and Preventive Medicine* 18(6): 494–501. doi:10.1007/s12199-013-0348-4

Hooker, Brad. 2000. "Moral Particularism: Wrong and Bad." In *Moral Particularism*, edited by Brad Hooker and Margaret Olivia Little, 1–22. Oxford: Oxford University Press.

Hooker, Brad. 2008. "Moral Particularism and the Real World." In *Challenging Moral Particularism*, edited by Mark Norris Lance, Matjaž Potrč, and Vojko Strahovnik, 12–30. New York: Routledge.

Hume, David. 1978. *A Treatise of Human Nature*. 2nd ed. Edited by L. A. Selby-Bigge with text revised and variant readings by P. H. Nidditch. Oxford: Oxford University Press.

Hurka, Thomas. 2001. *Virtue, Vice, and Value*. Oxford: Oxford University Press.

Hursthouse, Rosalind. 1991. "Virtue Theory and Abortion." *Philosophy and Public Affairs* 20(3): 223–246. www.jstor.org/stable/2265432

Hursthouse, Rosalind. 1999. *On Virtue Ethics*. Oxford: Oxford University Press.

Hursthouse, Rosalind. 2006a. "Applying Virtue Ethics to Our Treatment of the Other Animals." In *The Practice of Virtue: Classic and Contemporary Readings in Virtue Ethics*, edited by Jennifer Welchman, 136–155. Indianapolis, IN: Hackett.

Hursthouse, Rosalind. 2006b. "Are Virtues the Proper Starting Point for Morality?" In *Contemporary Debates in Moral Theory*, edited by James Dreier, 99–112. Malden, MA: Blackwell.

Hursthouse, Rosalind. 2006c. "Practical Wisdom: A Mundane Account." *Proceedings of the Aristotelian Society* 106(1): 285–309. doi:10.1111/j.1467-9264.2006.00149.x

Hursthouse, Rosalind. 2007. "Environmental Virtue Ethics." *Working Virtue: Virtue Ethics and Contemporary Moral Problems*, edited by Rebecca L. Walker and Philip J. Ivanhoe, 155–171. Oxford: Oxford University Press.

Hursthouse, Rosalind. 2011. "What Does the Aristotelian *Phronimos* Know?" In *Perfecting Virtue: New Essays on Kantian Ethics and Virtue Ethics*, edited by Lawrence Jost and Julian Wuerth, 38–57. Cambridge: Cambridge University Press.

Hursthouse, Rosalind and Glen Pettigrove. 2016. "Virtue Ethics." In *The Stanford Encyclopedia of Philosophy*. https://plato.stanford.edu/archives/win2016/entries/ethics-virtue/

Irwin, T. H. 2000. "Ethics as an Inexact Science: Aristotle's Ambitions for Moral Theory." In *Moral Particularism*, edited by Brad Hooker and Margaret Olivia Little, 100–129. Oxford: Oxford University Press.

Isen, Alice M. and Paula F. Levin. 1972. "Effect of Feeling Good on Helping: Cookies and Kindness." *Journal of Personality and Social Psychology* 21(3): 384–388. doi:10.1037/h0032317

Jacobson, Daniel. 2002. "An Unresolved Problem for Slote's Agent-Based Virtue Ethics." *Philosophical Studies* 111(1): 53–67. doi:10.1023/A:1021239412351

Johnson, Robert N. 2003. "Virtue and Right." *Ethics* 113(4): 810–834. doi:10.1086/373952

Johnson, Robert N. 2008. "Was Kant a Virtue Ethicist?" In *Kant's Ethics of Virtue*, edited by Monika Betzler, 61–75. Berlin: Walter de Gruyter.

Johnson, Robert and Adam Cureton. 2017. "Kant's Moral Philosophy." In *The Stanford Encyclopedia of Philosophy*. https://plato.stanford.edu/archives/spr2017/entries/kant-moral/

Jordan, Andrew. 2013. "Reasons, Holism and Virtue Theory." *The Philosophical Quarterly* 63(251): 248–268. doi:10.1111/1467-9213.12015

Kamtekar, Rachana. 2004. "Situationism and Virtue Ethics on the Content of Our Character." *Ethics* 114(3): 458–491. doi:10.1086/381696

Kant, Immanuel. 1996. *The Metaphysics of Morals*. Edited and translated by Mary Gregor. Cambridge: Cambridge University Press.

Kant, Immanuel. 1997. "Of Duties to Animals and Spirits." In *Lectures on Ethics*, translated by Peter Heath, edited by Peter Heath and J. B. Schneewind, 212–213. Cambridge: Cambridge University Press.

Kant, Immanuel. 2011. *Groundwork of the Metaphysics of Morals*. Edited and translated by Mary Gregor and Jens Timmermann. Cambridge: Cambridge University Press.

Kasperbauer, T. J. 2014. "Behaviorally Inadequate: A Situationist Critique of Environmental Virtues." *Environmental Ethics* 36(4): 471–487. doi:10.5840/enviroethics201436449

Kavanagh, Phillip S., Tania D. Signal, and Nik Taylor. 2013. "The Dark Triad and Animal Cruelty: Dark personalities, Dark Attitudes, and Dark Behaviors." *Personality and Individual Differences* 55(6): 666–670. doi:10.1016/j.paid.2013. 05. 01doi:9

Kawall, Jason. 2002. "Virtue Theory and Ideal Observers." *Philosophical Studies* 109 (3): 197–222. doi:10.1023/A:1019673427556

Kawall, Jason. 2009. "Virtue Theory, Ideal Observers, and the Supererogatory." *Philosophical Studies* 146(2): 179–196. doi:10.1007/s11098-008-9250-0

Kawall, Jason. 2014. "Qualified Agent and Agent-Based Virtue Ethics and the Problems of Right Action." In *The Handbook of Virtue Ethics*, edited by Stan van Hooft, Nafsika Athanassoulis, Jason Kawall, Justin Oakley, Nicole Saunders, and Liezl van Zyl, 130–140. Abingdon and New York: Routledge.

Kawall, Jason. 2018. "Environmental Virtue Ethics." In *The Oxford Handbook of Virtue*. Edited by Nancy E. Snow, 659–679. New York: Oxford University Press.

Kornegay, R. Jo. 2011. "Hursthouse's Virtue Ethics and Abortion: Abortion Ethics without Metaphysics?" *Ethical Theory and Moral Practice* 14(1): 51–71. doi:10.1007/s10677-010-9230-2

Korsgaard, Christine. 1996. "From Duty and for the Sake of the Noble: Kant and Aristotle on Morally Good Action." In *Aristotle, Kant, and the Stoics: Rethinking*

Happiness and Duty, edited by Stephen Engstrom and Jennifer Whiting, 203–236. Cambridge: Cambridge University Press.

Kraut, Richard. 2016. "Aristotle's Ethics." In *The Stanford Encyclopedia of Philosophy*. https://plato.stanford.edu/archives/spr2016/entries/aristotle-ethics/

Kraut, Robert E. 1973. "Effects of Social Labeling on Giving to Charity." *Journal of Experimental Psychology* 9(6): 551–562. doi:10.1016/0022-1031(73)90037-1

Kristjánsson, Kristján. 2008. "An Aristotelian Critique of Situationism." *Philosophy* 83(1): 55–76. doi:10.1017/S0031819108000302

Kupfer, Joseph. 2003. "The Moral Perspective of Humility." *Pacific Philosophical Quarterly* 84(3): 249–269. doi:10.1111/1468-0114.00172

Lance, Mark Norris, Matjaž Potrč, and Vojko Strahovnik, editors. 2008. *Challenging Moral Particularism*. New York: Routledge.

Latané, Bibb and John M. Darley. 1970. *The Unresponsive Bystander: Why Doesn't He Help?* New York: Appleton-Century Crofts.

LeBar, Mark. 2013. *The Value of Living Well*. Oxford: Oxford University Press.

Lindsey, P. A., R. Alexander, L. G. Frank, A. Mathieson, and S. S. Romañach. 2006. "Potential of Trophy Hunting to Create Incentives for Wildlife Conservation in Africa where Alternative Wildlife-Based Land Uses May Not Be Viable." *Animal Conservation* 9(3): 283–291. doi:10.1111/j.1469-1795.2006.00034.x

Louden, Robert B. 1984. "On Some Vices of Virtue Ethics." *American Philosophical Quarterly* 21(3): 227–236. www.jstor.org/stable/20014051

Louden, Robert B. 1986. "Kant's Virtue Ethics." *Philosophy* 61(238): 473–489. doi:10.1017/S0031819100061246.

MacIntyre, Alasdair. 1984. *After Virtue: A Study in Moral Theory*. 2nd ed. Notre Dame, IN: University of Notre Dame Press.

Mackie, J. L. 1990. *Ethics: Inventing Right and Wrong*. London: Penguin Books.

Macklin, Ruth. 1992. "Which Way Down the Slippery Slope? Nazi Medical Killing and Euthanasia Today." In *When Medicine Went Mad: Bioethics and the Holocaust*, edited by Arthur L. Caplan, 173–200. New York: Springer.

Major, John. 2013. "Nelson Mandela's Magic Lay in the Sheer Force of His Character." *The Telegraph*, December 6. www.telegraph.co.uk/news/worldnews/nelson-mandela/10500739/Nelson-Mandelas-magic-lay-in-thesheer-force-of-his-character.html

McDowell, John. 1979. "Virtue and Reason." *The Monist* 62(3): 331–350. doi:10.5840/monist197962319

McKeever, Sean and Michael Ridge. 2006. *Principled Ethics: Generalism as a Regulative Ideal*. Oxford: Oxford University Press.

Merritt, Maria. 2000. "Virtue Ethics and Situationist Personality Psychology." *Ethical Theory and Moral Practice* 3(4): 365–383. doi:10.1023/A:1009926720584

Merritt, Maria. 2009. "Aristotelian Virtue and the Interpersonal Aspect of Ethical Character." *Journal of Moral Philosophy* 6(1): 23–49. doi:10.1163/174552409X365919

Merritt, Maria W., John M. Doris, and Gilbert Harman. 2010. "Character." In *The Moral Psychology Handbook*, edited by John M. Doris and the Moral Psychology Research Group, 355–401. Oxford: Oxford University Press.

Milgram, Stanley. 1963. "Behavioral Study of Obedience." *Journal of Abnormal and Social Psychology* 67(4): 371–378. doi:10.1037/h0040525

Milgram, Stanley. 1974. *Obedience to Authority: An Experimental View*. New York: Harper & Row.

Mill, John Stuart. 1998. "Utilitarianism." In *John Stuart Mill: On Liberty and Other Essays*, edited by John Gray, 129–201. Oxford: Oxford University Press.

Miller, Christian. 2003. "Social Psychology and Virtue Ethics." *The Journal of Ethics* 7(4): 365–392.

Miller, Christian. 2010. "Character Traits, Social Psychology, and Impediments to Helping Behavior." *Journal of Ethics and Social Philosophy* 5(1): 1–36.

Miller, Christian. 2013. *Moral Character: An Empirical Theory*. New York: Oxford University Press.

Miller, Christian. 2014a. "The Problem of Character." In *The Handbook of Virtue Ethics*, edited by Stan van Hooft, Nafsika Athanassoulis, Jason Kawall, Justin Oakley, Nicole Saunders, and Liezl van Zyl, 418–429. Abingdon and New York: Routledge.

Miller, Christian. 2014b. "The Real Challenge to Virtue Ethics from Psychology." In *The Philosophy and Psychology of Character and Happiness*, edited by Nancy E. Snow and Franco V. Trivigno, 15–34. New York: Routledge.

Mischel, Walter. 1968. *Personality and Assessment*. New York: Wiley.

Mischel, Walter and Yuichi Shoda. 1995. "A Cognitive-Affective System Theory of Personality: Reconceptualizing Situations, Dispositions, Dynamics, and Invariance in Personality Structure." *Psychological Review* 102(2): 246–268. doi:10.1037/0033-295X.102. 2. 24doi:6

Moore, G. E. 1966. *Ethics*. London: Oxford University Press.

Nagel, Thomas. 1991. *Moral Questions*. Cambridge: Cambridge University Press.

Narvaez, Darcia and Daniel K. Lapsley. 2005. "The Psychological Foundations of Everyday Morality and Moral Expertise." In *Character Psychology and Character Education*, edited by Daniel K. Lapsley and F. Clark Power, 140–165. Notre Dame, IN: University of Notre Dame Press.

New Zealand Department of Conservation, The. 2016. "Powelliphanta Snail." Accessed January 25. www.doc.govt.nz/nature/native-animals/invertebrates/powelliphanta-snails/

Nielsen, Karen Margrethe. 2015. "Aristotle on Principles in Ethics: Political Science as the Science of the Human Good." In *Bridging the Gap between Aristotle's Science and Ethics*, edited by Devin Henry and Karen Margrethe Nielsen, 29–48. Cambridge: Cambridge University Press.

Nozick, Robert. 1974. *Anarchy, State, and Utopia*. New York: Basic Books.

Pellegrino, Edmund D. and David C. Thomasma. 1993. *The Virtues in Medical Practice*. New York: Oxford University Press.

PETA. 2016. "Why Sport Hunting Is Cruel and Unnecessary." Accessed January 26. www.peta.org/issues/wildlife/wildlife-factsheets/sport-hunting-cruel-unnecessary/

Pojman, Louis P., editor. 1998. *Ethical Theory: Classical and Contemporary Readings*. 3rd ed. Belmont, CA: Wadsworth.

Prinz, Jesse. 2009. "The Normative Challenge: Cultural Psychology Provides the Real Threat to Virtue Ethics." *The Journal of Ethics* 13(2–3): 117–144. doi:10.1007/s10892-009-9053-3

Rachels, James. 1975. "Active and Passive Euthanasia." *The New England Journal of Medicine* 292: 78–80.

Regan, Tom. 1983. *The Case for Animal Rights*. London: Routledge & Kegan Paul.

Ridge, Michael. 2000. "Modesty as a Virtue." *American Philosophical Quarterly* 37(3): 269–283.

Ridge, Michael and Sean McKeever. 2016. "Moral Particularism and Moral Generalism." In *The Stanford Encyclopedia of Philosophy.* https://plato.stanford.edu/archives/win2016/entries/moral-particularism-generalism/

Roberts, Robert C. 2015. "How Virtue Contributes to Flourishing." In *Current Controversies in Virtue Theory*, edited by Mark Alfano, 36–49. New York: Routledge.

Rolston III, Holmes. 2005. "Environmental Virtue Ethics: Half the Truth but Dangerous as a Whole." In *Environmental Virtue Ethics*, edited by Ronald L. Sandler and Philip Cafaro, 61–78. Lanham, MD: Rowman & Littlefield.

Ross, Lee and Richard E. Nisbett. 2011. *The Person and the Situation: Perspectives of Social Psychology.* London: Pinter & Martin.

Ross, W. D. 2002. *The Right and the Good.* Edited by Philip Stratton-Lake. Oxford: Oxford University Press.

Russell, Daniel C. 2009. *Practical Intelligence and the Virtues.* Oxford: Oxford University Press.

Russell, Daniel C. 2012. *Happiness for Humans.* Oxford: Oxford University Press.

Russell, Daniel C. 2013a. "Introduction: Virtue Ethics in Modern Moral Philosophy." In *The Cambridge Companion to Virtue Ethics*, edited by Daniel C. Russell, 1–6. Cambridge: Cambridge University Press.

Russell, Daniel C. 2013b. "Virtue Ethics, Happiness, and the Good Life." In *The Cambridge Companion to Virtue Ethics*, edited by Daniel C. Russell, 7–28. Cambridge: Cambridge University Press.

Sabini, John and Maury Silver. 2005. "Lack of Character? Situationism Critiqued." *Ethics* 115(3): 535–562. doi:10.1086/428459

Sandler, Ronald. 2005. "Introduction: Environmental Virtue Ethics." In *Environmental Virtue Ethics*, edited by Ronald L. Sandler and Philip Cafaro, 1–12. Lanham, MD: Rowman & Littlefield.

Sandler, Ronald. 2007. *Character and Environment: A Virtue-Oriented Approach to Environmental Virtue Ethics.* New York: Columbia University Press.

Schnall, Simone, Jonathan Haidt, Gerald L. Clore, and Alexander H. Jordan. 2008. "Disgust as Embodied Moral Judgment." *Personality and Social Psychology Bulletin* 34(8): 1096–1109. doi:10.1177/0146167208317771

Schultz, P. Wesley, Jessica M. Nolan, Robert B. Cialdini, Noah J. Goldstein, and Vladas Griskevicius. 2007. "The Constructive, Destructive, and Reconstructive Power of Social Norms." *Psychological Science* 18(5): 429–434. doi:10.1111/j.1467-9280.2007.01917.x

Sherman, Nancy. 1997. *Making a Necessity of Virtue: Aristotle and Kant on Virtue.* Cambridge: Cambridge University Press.

Sherman, Nancy. 1999. "Character Development and Aristotelian Virtue." In *Virtue Ethics and Moral Education*, edited by David Carr and Jan Steutel, 35–48. New York: Routledge.

Shoda, Yuichi, Walter Mischel, and Jack C. Wright. 1994. "Intraindividual Stability in the Organization and Patterning of Behavior: Incorporating Psychological Situations into the Idiographic Analysis of Personality." *Journal of Personality and Social Psychology* 67(4): 674–687. doi:10.1037/0022-3514.67.doi:4.674

Singer, Peter. 1972. "Famine, Affluence, and Morality." *Philosophy and Public Affairs* 1(3): 229–243.

Singer, Peter. 1990. *Animal Liberation*, 2nd ed. New York: New York Review of Books.

Slote, Michael. 2001. *Morals from Motives*. New York: Oxford University Press.

Slote, Michael. 2004. "Driver's Virtues." *Utilitas* 16(1): 22–32. doi:10.1017/S0953820803001031

Slote, Michael. 2010. *Moral Sentimentalism*. Oxford: Oxford University Press.

Slote, Michael. 2011. *The Impossibility of Perfection: Aristotle, Feminism, and the Complexities of Ethics*. New York: Oxford University Press.

Slote, Michael. 2014. "Virtue Ethics and Moral Sentimentalism." In *The Handbook of Virtue Ethics*, edited by Stan van Hooft, Nafsika Athanassoulis, Jason Kawall, Justin Oakley, Nicole Saunders, and Liezl van Zyl, 53–63. Abingdon and New York: Routledge.

Smith, Nicholas Ryan. 2014. "Constructing a Virtue Ethical Account of Right Action." Ph.D. thesis, University of Auckland.

Smith, Nicholas Ryan. 2017. "Right-Makers and the Targets of Virtue." *The Journal of Value Inquiry* 51(2): 311–326. doi:10.1007/s10790-016-9571-8

Snow, Nancy E. 2010. *Virtue as Social Intelligence: An Empirically Grounded Theory*. New York: Routledge.

Snow, Nancy E., editor. 2014. *Cultivating Virtue: Perspectives from Philosophy, Theology, and Psychology*. Oxford: Oxford University Press.

Snow, Nancy E. 2015. "Comments on *Intelligent Virtue*: Outsmarting Situationism." *Journal of Value Inquiry* 49(1/2): 297–306. doi:10.1007/s10790-014-9476-3

Solomon, Robert C. 1993. *Ethics and Excellence: Cooperation and Integrity in Business*. New York: Oxford University Press.

Spivey, Cashton B. and Steven Prentice-Dunn. 1990. "Assessing the Directionality of Deindividuated Behavior: Effects of Deindividuation, Modeling, and Private Self-Consciousness on Aggressive and Prosocial Responses." *Basic and Applied Social Psychology* 11(4): 387–403.

Sreenivasan, Gopal. 2002. "Errors about Errors: Virtue Theory and Trait Attribution." *Mind* 111(441): 47–68. doi:10.1093/mind/111.441.47

Sreenivasan, Gopal. 2013. "The Situationist Critique of Virtue Ethics." In *The Cambridge Companion to Virtue Ethics*, edited by Daniel C. Russell, 290–314. Cambridge: Cambridge University Press.

Stangl, Rebecca. 2008. "A Dilemma for Particularist Virtue Ethics." *The Philosophical Quarterly* 58(233): 665–678. doi:10.1111/j.1467-9213.2007.537.x

Stengel, Richard. 2010. *Mandela's Way: Lessons on Life*. London: Virgin Books.

Stocker, Michael. 1976. "The Schizophrenia of Modern Ethical Theories." *The Journal of Philosophy* 73(14): 453–466. doi:10.2307/2025782

Stocker, Michael and Elizabeth Hegeman. 1996. *Valuing Emotions*. Cambridge: Cambridge University Press.

Svensson, Frans. 2010. "Virtue Ethics and the Search for an Account of Right Action." *Ethical Theory and Moral Practice* 13(3): 255–271. doi:10.1007/s10677-009-9201-7

Swanton, Christine. 2001. "A Virtue Ethical Account of Right Action." *Ethics* 112(1): 32–52. doi:10.1086/322742

Swanton, Christine. 2003. *Virtue Ethics: A Pluralistic View*. Oxford: Oxford University Press.

Swanton, Christine. 2010. "Virtue Ethics and the Problem of Moral Disagreement." *Philosophical Topics* 38(2): 157–180. doi:10.5840/philtopics201038218

Swanton, Christine. 2011. "Virtue Ethics." In *The Continuum Companion to Ethics*, edited by Christian Miller, 190–214. London: Continuum International.

Swanton, Christine. 2013. "The Definition of Virtue Ethics." In *The Cambridge Companion to Virtue Ethics*, edited by Daniel C. Russell, 315–338. Cambridge: Cambridge University Press.

Swanton, Christine. 2015a. "Comments on *Intelligent Virtue*: Rightness and Exemplars of Virtue." *The Journal of Value Inquiry* 49(1): 307–314. doi:10.1007/s10790-014-9478-1

Swanton, Christine. 2015b. "A Particularist but Codifiable Virtue Ethics." In Vol. 5 of *Oxford Studies in Normative Ethics*, edited by Mark Timmons. Oxford: Oxford University Press.

Swanton, Christine. 2015c. "Pluralistic Virtue Ethics." In *The Routledge Companion to Virtue Ethics*, edited by Lorraine Besser-Jones and Michael Slote, 209–222. New York: Routledge.

Taylor, Paul W. 1981. "The Ethics of Respect for Nature." *Environmental Ethics* 3(3): 197–218. doi:10.5840/enviroethics19813321

Taylor, Paul W. 2011. *Respect for Nature: A Theory of Environmental Ethics*, 25th anniversary ed. Princeton, NJ: Princeton University Press.

Taylor, Richard. 2002. *Virtue Ethics: An Introduction*. Amherst, NY: Prometheus Books.

Tessman, Lisa. 2005. *Burdened Virtues: Virtue Ethics for Liberatory Struggles*. Oxford: Oxford University Press.

Tiberius, Valerie. 2006. "How to Think about Virtue and Right." *Philosophical Papers* 35(2): 247–265. doi:10.1080/05568640609485182

Tjiattas, Mary. 2007. "Against Moral Particularism." *Proceedings of the Twenty-First World Congress of Philosophy* 1: 19–24. doi:10.5840/wcp2120071270

Toner, Christopher. 2014. "The Full Unity of the Virtues." *The Journal of Ethics* 18(3): 207–227. doi:10.1007/s10892-014-9165-2

Van Hooft, Stan, Nafsika Athanassoulis, Jason Kawall, Justin Oakley, Nicole Saunders, and Liezl van Zyl. 2014. *The Handbook of Virtue Ethics*. Abingdon and New York: Routledge.

Van Zyl, Liezl. 2009. "Agent-Based Virtue Ethics and the Problem of Action Guidance." *Journal of Moral Philosophy* 6(1): 50–69. doi:10.1163/174552409X365928

Van Zyl, Liezl. 2011a. "Right Action and the Non-Virtuous Agent." *Journal of Applied Philosophy* 28(1): 80–92. doi:10.1111/j.1468-5930.2010.00514.x

Van Zyl, Liezl. 2011b. "Rightness and Goodness in Agent-Based Virtue Ethics." *Journal of Philosophical Research* 36: 103–114. doi:10.5840/jpr_2011_3

Van Zyl, Liezl. 2014. "Right Action and the Targets of Virtue." In *The Handbook of Virtue Ethics*, edited by Stan van Hooft, Nafsika Athanassoulis, Jason Kawall, Justin Oakley, Nicole Saunders, and Liezl van Zyl, 118–129. Abingdon and New York: Routledge.

Van Zyl, Liezl. 2015. "Eudaimonistic Virtue Ethics." In *The Routledge Companion to Virtue Ethics*, edited by Lorraine Besser-Jones and Michael Slote, 209–222. New York: Routledge.

Väyrynen, Pekka. 2008. "Usable Moral Principles." In *Challenging Moral Particularism*, edited by Mark Norris Lance, Matjaž Potrč, and Vojko Strahovnik, 75–106. New York: Routledge.

Veatch, Robert M. 2000. *The Basics of Bioethics*. Englewood Cliffs, NJ: Prentice Hall.

Vigani, Denise. 2016. "Construing Character: Virtue as a Cognitive-Affective Processing System." Ph.D. dissertation, University of New York.

Watson, Gary. 1984. "Virtues in Excess." *Philosophical Studies: An International Journal for Philosophy in the Analytic Tradition* 46(1): 57–74. doi:10.1007/BF00353491

Welchman, Jennifer. 1999. "The Virtues of Stewardship." *Environmental Ethics* 21(4): 411–423. doi:10.5840/enviroethics19992146

Williams, Bernard. 1973. "A Critique of Utilitarianism." In *Utilitarianism: For and Against*, by J. J. C. Smart and Bernard Williams, 77–150. Cambridge: Cambridge University Press.

Winter, Michael Jeffrey. 2012. "Does Moral Virtue Require Knowledge? A Response to Julia Driver." *Ethical Theory and Moral Practice* 15(4): 533–556. doi:10.1007/s10677-011-9310-y

Wood, Allen W. 2008. *Kantian Ethics.* Cambridge: Cambridge University Press.

Wood, Allen W. 2015. "Kant and Virtue Ethics." In *The Routledge Companion to Virtue Ethics*, edited by Lorraine Besser-Jones and Michael Slote, 307–320. New York: Routledge.

Index